7

AWAY FOR THE DAY

AWAY FOR THE DAY

The railway excursion in Britain, 1830 to the present day

Arthur & Elisabeth Jordan

Silver Link Publishing Ltd

First published in August 1991

British Library Cataloguing in Publication Data
Jordan, Arthur
Away for the day : the railway excursion in Britain, 1830 to the present day.
1. Great Britain. Railways, history
I. Title II. Jordan, Elisabeth
385.220941
ISBN 0 947971 63 7

Silver Link Publishing Ltd
The Trundle
Ringstead Road
Great Addington
Kettering
Northamptonshire NN14 4BW

Typeset by The TypeFoundry, Northampton
Printed in Great Britain byWoolnough Bookbinding Ltd, Irthlingborough, Northants
and bound by Butler and Tanner Ltd, Frome, Somerset

CONTENTS

Railways were all the rage! Marie Lloyd sang 'Oh Mr Porter' and 'naughty' young things danced to 'The Excursion Train Galop'.

INTRODUCTION
AND ACKNOWLEDGEMENTS

'Her first idea was that she had somehow fallen into the sea, "and in that case I can go back by railway", she said to herself. Alice had been to the seaside once in her life and had come to the general conclusion that wherever you go to on the English coast you find a number of bathing machines in the sea, some children digging in the sand with wooden spades, then a row of lodging houses, and behind that a railway station.' Lewis Carroll's little girl was quite right, and she might have added that the beach would be swarming with people who had arrived by excursion train, for the excursion has been as much a part of the British way of life as Monday washday or fish and chips eaten out of newspaper.

In setting out to write a history of the British railway excursion it is necessary to define 'excursion', since searching through newspaper advertisements, railway handbills, posters and other records of the past one finds: A Half-Day Excursion; A Day Excursion; Excursion Fares; Week-end Excursion Tickets; Mr Cook's Excursion; and so on. In many instances these refer to reduced fare facilities when travelling by ordinary scheduled trains, or to group travel at special fares arranged by tour organisers such as Thomas Cook, and possibly providing a courier, but travelling by scheduled trains. This history will, in the main, be confined to the excursion train, a trip, a special train at reduced fares, whether organised by the railway company itself or by a charterer, which includes works outings and trips by organisations such as Friendly Societies, choirs, Sunday Schools and the like.

Simply to list the venues of such excursions, even if including the events in connection with which they ran, would make tedious reading, therefore other aspects of excursion train history are considered, including the impact such traffic had on the resorts to which these trains ran, and prompting such poetical efforts as:

> I took the train to Brighton
> I walked beside the sea,
> And thirty thousand Londoners
> Were there along with me.

Years before the first excursion trains ran, whilst the nobility and gentry were spending their leisure hours at fashionable watering places, the 'lower orders' were going on outings to the sea or into the countryside. But the possible venues were very restricted by the limitations imposed by horse-power, whether applied to road vehicles or swept-out canal barges. Those living near river estuaries such as Boston on the River Witham, Bristol and Cardiff on the Severn and the towns along the Clyde, had enjoyed steamer trips from almost the beginning of the 19th century. Londoners had already invaded Southend, Margate and Ramsgate aboard the Thames steamers, with the piano thumping out its music-hall tunes and a right old 'knees-up' on the deck. The railways' unique contribution in this field of recreation, entertainment and travel was, firstly, that they made excursion facilities available to almost all who lived within a few miles of a railway station, and, secondly, that the speed and endurance of the steam locomotive made it possible to travel greater distances, and to return home within one day (or almost!).

In most 'select' resorts there was opposition to excursionists as expressed by one Scarborough resident in a letter to the local newspaper who had '. . .no wish for a great influx of vagrants and those with no money to spend'. But there were others, who usually concealed their pecuniary interest by expressing concern for the well-being of the toilers in the cities, and the tradesmen of Saltburn might be an example when they complained

> . . . Rumours have gained currency recently that the North Eastern Railway Company have resolved not to run any cheap excursion trains during the incoming summer . . . these trips have always been a great boon to our pent-up artisans and others in neighbouring towns.

Protesters on religious grounds warned that the Sunday excursion was a ticket to Hell, whilst others saw it as a means by which the working classes could escape for a few hours from the Hell-on-earth of the city slums and factories. These opposing attitudes are explored together with a picture of what it was like to travel on a cheap trip described by excursionists themselves. A day out for a family involved much more than buying a railway ticket, and an attempt is made to convey to the reader the weight of the responsibility and preparation which rested upon the 'mum' of a family going on a day trip. But the excursion train was only the means to an end, the transport to the seaside, or an exhibition, or a fair, and so to complete the picture the reader is taken out of the railway station to follow the crowd and find out how they enjoyed themselves.

Running scores, often hundreds, of special trains at Bank Holidays or in connection with a large race meeting or perhaps an air display, imposed tremendous demands upon the locomotive and rolling-stock resources of the railways so that the manner in which these demands were met and the operating problems overcome must surely form an essential ingredient of a history of the railway excursion.

Because the excursion train was an out-of-the-ordinary train, one not running every day, it sometimes caught railwaymen unawares, resulting in an accident. Some of these were terrible in their toll of lives and destruction of vehicles, and so a chapter is devoted to excursion train accidents.

No apology is made for quoting extensively from contemporary newspaper reports, petitions and the like, since doing so is to emphasise the news value of railway excursions, particularly in the early days. The often pompous style of these documents makes interesting, sometimes amusing, reading. This book is intended as a contribution towards recording in some detail the many aspects of the railway excursion, a somewhat neglected part of our social history.

The grouping of railways into the 'Big Four' companies in 1923 was not the end of railway excursions even though the motor 'charabanc' became an increasingly popular form of transport for an outing. Until recently British Rail ran its own day excursion trains marketed as 'Adex', 'Merrymaker' or 'Mystery Trips', but today it is mainly railway societies or private tour operators who charter special trains from British Rail.

When George Stephenson predicted the future electrification of railways it surely never entered his thoughts that the demise of steam would be followed by thousands of enthusiasts willingly paying to ride on excursion trains hauled by the out-dated steam locomotive. Yet today, trains are chartered to be hauled not only by steam but by obsolete classes of diesel locomotives or making use of withdrawn types of rolling-stock. These are included and, in so doing, the history of the railway excursion train is brought right up to date.

But the great changes that have overtaken our society during the past half century and more are reflected too in the changed character of the excursion train. Until recently, 'Chartex' trains were often filled with camera-toting, recorder-hoisting enthusiasts, the 'Footex' trains carried football supporters, whilst the 'Adex' provided a day out for families, for the under-privileged, for senior citizens and others who could not afford even one motor car. Before the craze for spending hours cooped up in a metal box, sweating it out in a 20-mile tail-back on a motorway, families travelled by the excursion train and there family met family, mum and dad talked to the other mums and dads, children played together and often long-lasting friendships developed. The modern car-cocooned family is insulated from all the other car-cocooned families. The community singing of the excursionists has been replaced by the transistorised voices of pop singers interspersed with the latest news of traffic jams, road repairs and pile-ups.

However, in the 1990s many travellers on business are parking and riding by train, preferring the speed, comfort and opportunity either to work or relax and so avoid the hassle and hazards of travel by car. If British Rail can provide the facilities, it is not unlikely that the 'Away for the Day' rail excursion will again become an enjoyable experience for families leaving their car in the garage or at the railway station.

Whatever its inadequacies this work could not have been produced without access to the vast store of information to be found in libraries, record offices and private archives around the country. We have been collecting material for ten or more years and our researches have taken us to many such repositories of information in the three kingdoms. At the risk of making omissions we list below those places from which we have obtained our material and, in doing so, we wish to express our appreciation for the courtesy and valuable assistance we have received from the librarians and archivists concerned.

We are fortunate in having acquired an extensive photographic collection of our own from which the illustrations are taken unless otherwise credited.

Libraries in Aberdare, Barnsley, Birmingham, Blackpool, Bournemouth, Bristol, Buckingham, Cardiff, Cleethorpes, Coventry, Doncaster, Edinburgh, Glasgow (The Mitchell Library), Grimsby, Hull, Kettering, Lancaster, Leicester, Lincoln, Liverpool, Manchester, Norwich, Nottingham, Preston, Reading, Scarborough, Scottish National Library, Sheffield, Stratford (Borough of Newham), Swansea, Royal Institution (Swansea), Swindon, Warwick, Weston-super-Mare, Wrexham.

British Library (National Newspaper Library), Lancashire Record Office, Liverpool Record Office, National Railway Museum, Northamptonshire Record Office, Public Record Office (Kew), Scottish Record Office, Shakespeare Birthplace Trust Record Office, City of Swansea Archives, Warwickshire Record Office.

The Boot's Co, C. & J. Clark Ltd, Coleman's Archives, Huntley & Palmer's Archives, Port Sunlight Heritage Centre, The Salvation Army Archives & Research Centre, The Shaftesbury Society Archives, Thomas Cook's Archives, John White Footwear Ltd.

NOTE All references to money are in the currency of the time, so that pre-1971 currency of pounds, shillings and pence is represented as £ s d.

Chapter 1
EARLY EXCURSIONS

*'We carried music with us, and music met us at the Loughborough station.
The people crowded the streets, filled windows, covered the house-tops, and
cheered us all along the line.'*

It is an undisputed fact that the first inter-city railway was the Liverpool & Manchester,
opened on 15 September 1830 – but to which railway company should go the credit for
the first excursion train? On the day following the official opening of the L&MR by the
Duke of Wellington, probably the first chartered train was run conveying 130 members of
the Society of Friends from Liverpool to Manchester for their quarterly meeting.[1]
However, they were charged the standard 1st class fare of 7s each way, therefore this
particular special was not an excursion train within the definition explained in the
Introduction. As a supplementary source of income, and as a further means of acquainting
the public with the railway, daily excursions were run (except on Sundays) from both
Liverpool and Manchester, to the Sankey Viaduct, midway along the line, and for which

Sankey Viaduct – not everyone's idea of a day out, but in 1830 the Liverpool & Manchester
Railway ran excursions to view it.

a return fare of 5s represented a reduction for 1st class passengers.[2]

Down in Kent, the Canterbury & Whitstable Railway opened almost 20 weeks before the L&MR, but it did not run its first excursion trains before 19 March 1832, when excursionists were conveyed from Canterbury to Whitstable at a reduced fare of 1s in covered and 6d in open carriages.[3] One railway historian credits the Leeds & Selby Railway with playing '. . .a pioneering part in promoting the idea of excursions by rail, one of the first cheap trips of this kind in Britain being run in August 1835 from Leeds to Selby from where coaches took passengers on to the York Festival.'[4]

British Railways, in 1966, marked the 130th anniversary of what was claimed to have been the first excursion train run in 1836 by the Bodmin & Wadebridge Railway when two trains of open wagons conveyed 800 passengers from Wadebridge to Wenford Bridge and back – 24 miles for one shilling.[5]

Railway historian Charles Grinling considered that

> one of the first excursion trains known in railway history was run on the Midland Railway (sic) from Nottingham to Leicester on August 24, 1840, to view the splendid alterations which have been made recently in the Leicester Exhibition.[6]

According to a contemporary account,

> . . . the enormous train of nearly seventy carriages passed majestically into view before the astonished spectators. It was indeed a wonderful scene. Grand, magnificent, sublime, were the terms which gave vent to the feelings as in countless succession the animated mass rushed into view. It was in truth a moving city, with banners, music, and accompaniments, and all the material of high excitement to enhance its efficiency.[7]

It was estimated that 2,400 passengers were conveyed in this single excursion train.

In 1939, *The Times* newspaper claimed 7 August as the centenary of the railway excursion, stating that in 1839 the organisers of a church bazaar at Grosmont, fearing a poor attendance, asked the Whitby & Pickering Railway to issue cheap tickets. The paper

A typical open carriage excursion train of the 1830s.

claimed that citizens of both Whitby and Pickering journeyed to Grosmont in horse-drawn trains at reduced fares, and that these were the forerunners of the army of holidaymakers who travel by cheap excursion train from London and other big cities to health and pleasure resorts.[8]

In Tomlinson's *North Eastern Railway*, the so-called excursion system is dated from May 1840 when reduced fares were introduced in connection with a Polytechnic Exhibition at Newcastle, but special trains do not appear to have been involved. However, shortly afterwards, in June 1840, and described as the first train of its kind, the same company, the Newcastle & Carlisle Railway, ran a Sunday excursion from Newcastle to Carlisle consisting of 15 carriages hauled by the *Wellington* engine and conveying some 320 employees of R. & W. Hawthorn.[9]

The Bolton & Leigh Railway contracted with a John Hargreaves of Bolton to provide locomotives and rolling-stock for their trains[10], and in due course the Liverpool & Manchester Railway granted Hargreaves running powers for his trains over their metals. Hargreaves is described as '. . . a pioneer of rail excursions'[11] for in 1841 he organised Sunday trips from Bolton to Liverpool for 2s 6d return, and in 1845 added Manchester.

But the name almost synonymous with 'excursion' is Thomas Cook, who devoted his life's energies to the promotion of cheap travel. He was the founder of the travel agency bearing his name and which today spans the world. It was on 5 July 1841 that Cook's first 'public excursion' left Leicester, and writing some years later Cook explained how

> . . . the thought flashed through my brain, what a glorious thing it would be if the newly-developed powers of railways and locomotion could be subservient to the promotion of temperance.

He was walking 15 miles from Market Harborough to Leicester for a temperance meeting and it was there that Cook's proposal for a special train to carry temperance folk from Leicester to Loughborough for a gathering was greeted by a roar of excitement.

> We carried music with us, and music met us at the Loughborough station. The people crowded the streets, filled windows, covered the house-tops, and cheered us all along the line, with the heartiest welcome. All went off in the best style and in perfect safety we returned to Leicester; and thus was struck the keynote of my excursions and the social idea grew upon me.[12]

This Midland Counties Railway train consisted of two of Bury's four-wheeled locomotives, 14 open 3rd class carriages and one 1st class carriage. The 570 abstainers paid one shilling for the return trip of 25 miles and Thomas Cook carried through the arrangements so satisfactorily that thereafter his services as an organiser of excursion trains were in ever-increasing demand.[13]

There is no doubt that the sea held a great attraction for city dwellers from the time that the railways made it possible to experience the vastness of the oceans and to breathe invigorating sea air. Reaching Southampton in 1839, the London & South Western Railway was organising combined rail and sea excursions in 1841 offering 220 miles of travel by land and water for only £1. Leaving the London Nine Elms station at 6.45 am, 300 passengers were conveyed in 20 carriages and joined by a further 100 passengers at Woking. The sea trip round the Isle of Wight was aboard the PS *Grand Turk*.[14]

Here is how the *Sheffield Mercury* described an excursion from Sheffield to Derby in 1841:

The Thomas Cook & Son premises in Gallowtree Gate, Leicester, although no longer in their occupation, and (above right) details of the frieze on the building.

On Tuesday the inhabitants of this town were generally on the 'qui vive' to witness the departure of the special train on the North Midland Railway from here to Derby. There were forty-seven North Midland and Sheffield & Rotherham carriages and five engines, containing about 2,000 persons, and about 100 were left behind, not having applied for tickets in time. There could not have been less than 20,000 spectators. The train started about half-

past nine, and arrived at Derby at a quarter-past twelve. It returned at 6.30, and reached Sheffield at 8.50 without any accident occuring, save a few hats being blown off and an individual falling out of a carriage when it arrived at Sheffield from getting up before it had stopped.[15]

Further north, it was the seaside which attracted the early excursionists, and by 1842 the Preston & Wyre Railway was pouring them into Fleetwood, from whence they made their way the short distance to Blackpool. A Bolton newspaper reported that 'The town literally swarms with human beings and every day fresh loads roll in covered with dust. . .'.

That same year an excursion train conveyed 2,364 Sunday School teachers and pupils in 27 coaches hauled by the P&WR's locomotive No 1, from Preston to Fleetwood, when 'the whole multitude' were engaged in singing hymns throughout the journey, which in those days of very long trains and weak couplings, was as good an insurance as any! There was a half-hour stop at Poulton where

> . . . the scene was truly inspiring, each carriage being studded with numerous colours bearing appropriate mottoes. Such a display was never before afforded to the inhabitants of Poulton, who mustered largely on the occasion, and were highly gratified in witnessing such an interesting and beautiful sight.[16]

It is no wonder that in August 1844 the *Preston Chronicle* proclaimed that 'Cheap trains and pleasure excursions are now all the go and fashion'. What is more, they were being run in a very big way for, on 12 September 1844, four excursion trains conveyed 6,600 passengers from Leeds to Hull using ten locomotives and 240 carriages[17], which works out at 60 coaches per engine and 37 human beings per small coach or wagon.

'Visit Extraordinary' is how the *Liverpool Albion*[18] described two excursion trains arriving at Lime Street station from Birmingham, by which the Grand Junction Railway conveyed 1,200 persons at '. . . a cheap rate providing an opportunity of visiting and viewing the great seaport of Liverpool and its lions.' The *Preston Pilot* too used the

Thomas Cook's grave in a Leicester cemetery.

adjective 'extraordinary' to describe the excursion train run by the Manchester &
Birmingham Railway in 1843 conveying charity school children to Alderley Edge at low
fares. Here is how the event was reported:

> . . . thousands took advantage of their [M&BR] liberality, and that delightful
> experience was quite 'alive' throughout the day. At eight o'clock in the
> evening the last return train consisting of 62 carriages containing above
> 3,000 persons, and extending about a quarter of a mile in length, left Alderley

16

for Manchester drawn by two engines. Although the evening was very unfavourable for those conveyed in open carriages, the spirits were not in any way damped as was evinced by their hearty cheers, which were answered by the assembled thousands along the line.[19]

Amazement might be expressed at the length of these early excursion trains, and perhaps horror at the number of people packed into each carriage, but such was the determination to travel that late-comers clung to the carriage sides. The *Paisley Advertiser* reported one such train:

> The special train, with the teetotalers of Glasgow on a trip to the land of Burns, amounted to thirty carriages, dragged by three engines. More accommodation being wanted, a couple of additional carriages were hooked on but even these were insufficient, and on some carriages passengers were clustering outside like bees.[20]

Answering the question 'How long is a train?', the pioneers of railway excursions would have replied 'As long as we wish', which was an over-optimistic or perhaps careless attitude having regard to the relatively fragile couplings and the absence of continuous automatic brakes. The Great North of England Railway, in 1844, conveyed 1,200 excursionists from Darlington to Leeds, a distance of 70 miles, in 3 hours 45 minutes at what was considered to be 'the lowest terms yet offered'. The train consisted of 37 carriages drawn by two locomotives.[21]

In the same year, the Manchester & Leeds Railway loaded 82 carriages drawn by three locomotives from Hebden Bridge and with two bands playing on board. At Normanton, the York & North Midland took over with only two engines as far as Selby, where the Hull & Selby Railway supplied the two engines which drew the train to its destination at Hull.

> ... The day was unusually fine, the trip was throughout characterized by great harmony, order and enjoyment terminated by the safe arrival of the whole party at Hebden Bridge at a late hour; not the slightest accident having occurred to mar the pleasure of the day.[22]

The first excursion train from London to Brighton on 8 April 1844 was so over-patronised as to delay the departure of the scheduled 8.30 am from London Bridge station for nearly half-an-hour. It at last started

> ... with forty-eight carriages and four engines; at New Cross it was joined by six more carriages and another engine; at Croydon by another six carriages and a sixth engine. The train not having arrived by 1 pm, the greatest apprehension prevailed at Brighton, so an engine with a director of the company went to look for it! [A not infrequent cause of early accidents.] At 1.30 the monster train at last steamed safely into the station.[23]

Over the Eastern Counties Railway, via Cambridge and Ely, the first excursion from Shoreditch station, London, arrived at Norwich with 800 passengers, taking 7 hours on the journey in June 1846. Shortly afterwards the first excursion train from Norwich to London left Trowse station with 1,500 passengers in 37 carriages, and by the time the train reached

London, passengers had increased to 2,000 and carriages to 52. Even with the Eastern Counties Railway's two most powerful locomotives the journey took 8½ hours.[24]

An experimental trip by the ECR, from London to Rotterdam in July 1846, was routed via Great Yarmouth. On the return journey the steamer crew got drunk, a storm blew up and the vessel got off course. The final disaster struck as the return train approached Ely, when the engine's boiler burst! These experimental excursionists faced a 1½-mile walk along the track to Ely station.[25]

Scotland was not far behind England in pioneering excursion trains. The Edinburgh & Glasgow Railway was opened throughout only in 1842, whilst the Glasgow, Paisley, Kilmarnock & Ayr Railway had reached Ayr by 1839. In 1846 the *Edinburgh Evening Courant* reported a special train by the E&GR to Ayr,

> . . . or as it is aptly termed, the Land of Burns, to afford an opportunity to the citizens of visiting those classic spots in that romantic neighbourhood, consecrated by the life and writings of our illustrious countryman.

The 88-mile journey was accomplished in 4¾ hours, including a half-hour stop in Glasgow.[26]

Robert Burns may have been Scotland's 'illustrious countryman', but Sir Walter Scott probably generated more tourism, and it was for the embellishment of the Scott Memorial in Edinburgh that the proceeds of the Waverley Ball were devoted in 1846. The E&GR ran a special train from Glasgow for the 'Accommodation of the Nobility and Gentry residing in the west', and wishing to attend the Ball. It was emphasised that only FIRST CLASS carriages would be used on this genteel excursion which left Glasgow at 8 pm and returned from Edinburgh at 5 am.

This being no ordinary jig, the Assembly Rooms were

> . . . magnificently decorated and arranged for the occasion. In the Music Hall the orchestra was beautifully fitted up for the representation of a series of tableaux vivants, which were exhibited in the course of the evening. A white panelling profusely sprinkled with gold and silver and coloured stars screened the whole of the orchestra from view, leaving . . . an open space in the centre through which the tableaux were seen as in a picture frame . . . The side rooms were thrown open, beautifully adorned with drapery and flowers; some of them were got up in the shape of tents, and looked particularly elegant . . . The staircases were all ornamented with evergreens . . . The whole arrangements and decorations . . . were very tasteful, and appeared to give general satisfaction . . . Mr McKenzie's excellent band attended in the large assembly room . . . while the band of the 92nd performed . . . in the Music Hall.
>
> . . . The tableaux . . . represented the following incidents:- 1.William of Deloraine taking the Book from Michael Scott's Tomb. 2.The Antiquary buying fish from Meg Mucklebacket. 3.The Fair Maid of Perth. 4.Montrose writing a Dispatch after the Battle of Inverlochy. 5.The Pirate cast Ashore. 6.The Templar carrying off Rebecca. 7.The White Maid of Avenel appearing in the Fountain. These were all very effectively represented, and drew forth much applause.[27]

By way of contrast, the Caledonian Railway's excursion to Lanark for the Falls of Clyde was advertised as 'FOR THE WORKING CLASSES' although 1st, 2nd and 3rd class fares were advertised.[28]

Edinburgh was connected by rail to Berwick-on-Tweed when the North British Railway line was opened in June 1846, and only one month later a 'Pleasure Excursion During the Holidays' was announced in the newspapers:

> The Railway communication now being completed between Glasgow and Berwick-on-Tweed, a distance of 104 miles, the Edinburgh & Glasgow Railway Company have advertised a Pleasure Excursion to the English border on Friday. As the rarest jaunt of the season, and one of the cheapest, the fares being from about a farthing to a halfpenny a mile, according to the description of carriage which the traveller chooses to patronise, we would recommend a trip by this route as one which is likely to afford the highest satisfaction. There is to be no change of carriages at Edinburgh, the party going right on to Berwick, through the most beautiful country and scenes imaginable. We have no doubt the public will avail themselves of the boon.[29]

From the report of this momentous excursion in the *Glasgow Argus* it appears that a sight of constructional achievements by the railway company was as much appreciated as were the ancient ruins and the natural beauties of the countryside.

> . . . it sped along the North British Railway through Edinburghshire and the rich agricultural country of Haddington, . . . and many other places of historical note, and arrived at Dunbar shortly after ten o'clock . . . (40 minutes stay – time to visit the castle). Leaving Dunbar, amongst the remarkable objects to be seen from the railway are Black Castle Hill, Fast Castle, the Siccar Point, Tower Dean, where there is the highest embankment which has yet been attempted in railway operations, Pease Bridge, one of the most singular structures of the kind in Europe, Dunglass Dean, Renton Houndwood, the river Eye, which the railway crosses, we think, seven times, and many delightful views of the German Sea. At quarter past twelve Glasgow time, the train reached the fine old town of Berwick-on-Tweed . . . [there follows a description of the town] . . . Nearly four hours having been allowed for dining and visiting the various objects of interest . . . the company were again collected by the whistle of the steam engine; and after being comfortably seated without the least confusion, bade adieu to Berwick a few minutes past four. Near Cockburns Path, the train stopped twenty minutes to allow the passengers an opportunity of seeing more distinctly than from the carriages the romantic Dunglass Dean, with the bridge and viaduct over it. After this there were no more stoppages, with the exception of a few minutes at Edinburgh and Falkirk, and the train arrived at Glasgow terminus at quarter past nine o'clock . . . the excursion seemed to give universal satisfaction.[30]

G. P. Neele, Chief Clerk of the South Staffordshire Railway in 1849, related that

> . . . the number of our carriages was small, and on the occasion of the Whitsuntide gathering at Lichfield, called 'Lichfield Blower' – a survival of a medieval pageant – we ventured on the very risky plan of using open wagons with planked seats, but the experiment was not repeated: cattle trucks were

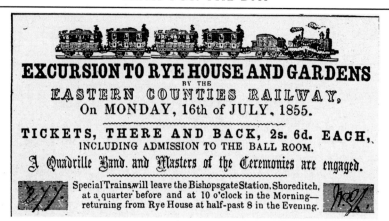

EXCURSION TO RYE HOUSE AND GARDENS
BY THE
EASTERN COUNTIES RAILWAY,
On MONDAY, 16th of JULY, 1855.

TICKETS, THERE AND BACK, 2s. 6d. EACH,
INCLUDING ADMISSION TO THE BALL ROOM.
A Quadrille Band and Masters of the Ceremonies are engaged.

Special Trains will leave the Bishopsgate Station, Shoreditch,
at a quarter before and at 10 o'clock in the Morning—
returning from Rye House at half-past 8 in the Evening.

This combined rail and dance ticket was found as packing in a piano in 1945.

next tried but as the rising generation took to 'mooing' at the passengers while the train was stationary, the dislike to using such vehicles, even at the low rate adopted, caused the plan to be withdrawn.[31]

Of course, to carry humans in cattle trucks was going a bit too far but, for one railway shareholder, what is today called 'customer care' had been overdone, for in 1858 he protested that excursionists enjoyed 'fifteen inch seats, stuffed cushions and backs to lean against'.[32] A newspaper notice of 1848 'respectfully' informed the public that 'A wagon train will leave Blackburn station at 12.30 pm on 14th, 15th, 16th June for Manchester races, returning shortly after the races are over.'[33] The fare was 2s 6d for standing in the trucks and apparently the corner standing places were the most sought after.

For an excursion from Cambridge to London in 1846, the *Cambridge Chronicle* advised

> . . . all those who intend to join in this excursion to provide themselves with a warm greatcoat for, of all the horrors of travelling, none are greater than the cutting draughts in those open carriages which the Eastern Counties Company say that the necessities of their position will compel them to use next Monday.[34]

An accompaniment of music was apparently a common feature of early excursion trains, for a railway enthusiast of the 1860s recorded in his notebook that

> . . . It was a common thing for bands to accompany excursion trains. On approaching a station the band used to begin playing and continue doing so until the train got away again. In fine weather the bandsmen were accommodated in a high-sided goods wagon.[35]

A frequent cause of injury, even death, was the attempt by passengers in open carriages to retrieve hats blown off by the wind, umbrellas and other personal possessions whilst the train was in motion. From complaints recorded at the time, women's clothes were particularly susceptible to scorching by hot cinders belched from the locomotives, whilst smuts in the eye provided many an amorous male with an excuse to get a little closer to

GREAT WESTERN RAILWAY.
EASTER HOLIDAYS.
EXCURSION TO LONDON AND BACK.

On *EASTER MONDAY, April the 13th,*

AN EXCURSION TRAIN will leave BANBURY STATION at 7.15, a.m., for LONDON, and will return from Paddington Station at 6.30, p.m., the same day.

FARES (THERE AND BACK):—

FIRST-CLASS, 8s.; COVERED CARRIAGES, 5s.

Tickets are not transferable, and are available only by the Trains above indicated.

Children, under Twelve years of age, Half-price.

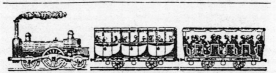

LONDON & NORTH WESTERN RAILWAY.
EASTER HOLIDAYS.
A CHEAP EXCURSION TRAIN

WILL LEAVE BANBURY FOR LONDON,

On *EASTER MONDAY, April 13.*

Leave BANBURY	7.30, a.m.
„ BRACKLEY	7.50 „
„ BUCKINGHAM	8. 5 „
„ WINSLOW	8 20 „
Arrive at LONDON	10.30 „

RETURNING from the Euston Square Station the same Evening, by Special Train, at Seven o'clock. Passengers desirous of proceeding to Fenchurch Street, for the City, can alight at the Camden Town Station, whence the North London Trains start every 15 minutes,

There will be no extra charge for continuing on to Fenchurch Street, but Passengers must join the Return Train at the Euston Square Station.

FARES FOR THE DOUBLE JOURNEY:—

	First Class.	Covered Carriages.
BANBURY	8s.	5s.
BRACKLEY ⎫ BUCKINGHAM ⎬	6s. 6d.	4s.

☞ Children, under Twelve years of age, Half-price.

Advertisements in the *Banbury Guardian* in 1857. Note the emphasis on covered carriages.

his heart's desire!

At least one railway company made a feature of its open carriages, for an advertisement in 1852 read:

SCENERY OF THE NEATH VALLEY

To Excursionists and Tourists: the Directors of the Vale of Neath Railway Company have provided FIRST CLASS and OPEN EXCURSION CARRIAGES especially adapted for viewing the justly celebrated scenery of this valley and its inhabitants.[36]

Was the special adaptation the removal of the roof on excursion carriages?

This new-found craze for making long trips to the seaside at low fares was all very well, but was it really worth the effort? The Editor of the *Poole Pilot* in 1868 was sceptical about the attractions of Burnham-on-Sea to which the Somerset & Dorset Railway took excursionists from Poole for 1s 6d return, and commented that 'If a long ride for little money is desired it is here available'.[37]

Rowsley was the destination of the first excursion run by the South Yorkshire and the Midland Railway companies on 4 July 1850, and was advertised in the *Doncaster Gazette* as including free admission to Chatsworth House at a fare of 7s 1st and 5s 2nd class with lunch available in a marquee for one shilling.[38] This was by no means a cheap trip and is a reminder that not all excursion fares were intended for the working classes.

Excursionists of the mid-19th century were a hardy lot who were neither deterred by exposure to the elements nor by early rising; the Grand Teetotalers Cheap Trip to Liverpool and Southport in 1855 began by their being led in procession by a drum and fife band to Heslington station at five o'clock in the morning.[39] An occasion when the excursionists were able to warm up by a spot of physical exercise was at Clifton Junction, Lancashire, when trains of two rival companies pulled up alongside each other. The railway officials became embroiled in altercations as to which train should be given priority through the junction, and the passengers joined in what became a pitched battle.[40]

Another opportunity for the trippers to generate a little body temperature occurred on the West Cornwall Railway in 1856 when the St Ives Teetotalers organised a picnic at St Erth for which 700 turned up at the station. Only 17 carriages were available, so 57 goods trucks were attached to the train. A start was made with three locomotives, two of which were in front and the other in the middle. On a slight incline near Polgrean the train was 'brought up', whereupon some 300 of the teetotallers alighted and assisted in getting the train 'over the bank'.[41] On the return journey this monster train was again 'brought up', this time near Bodriggy, and whilst halted there the delayed excursionists raided a lineside orchard which was denuded of its apples.

What was described as 'A New Feature in Railway Excursions' was organised by Thomas Cook in 1853 by which the Midland Railway would carry excursionists from Gloucester to Scotland. Cook stated:

> This being the first time I have had the honour of conducting a party of excursionists via Gretna Green, if any demand is made by Ladies and Gentlemen of the party for the services of Mr Linton or Mr Murray (the Gretna parsons) the special train shall be detained to enable them to terminate single blessedness.[42]

By long tradition, eloping couples could be legally married by the Gretna Green blacksmiths. Or, in railway parlance, 'Single out, return coupled'!

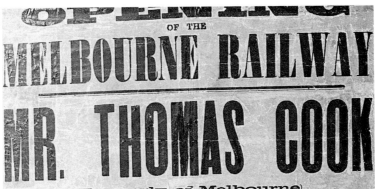

OPENING OF THE
MELBOURNE RAILWAY
MR. THOMAS COOK
(Formerly of Melbourne)

Respectfully intimates to his old Friends and Fellow Townspeople that, in connection with the visit of his

FIRST EXCURSION PARTY,
FROM LEICESTER,
ON THURSDAY, SEPTEMBER 10th, 1868,
To arrive at about 4·0 p.m.
HE WILL GIVE AN
ADDRESS
IN THE ATHENÆUM,
TO INHABITANTS & VISITORS,

Briefly recapitulating some of the events of his EXCURSION and TOURIST LIFE, since leaving Melbourne nearly 40 years ago; and anticipatory of his approaching Trips to

ITALY, EGYPT & PALESTINE.

FREE ADMISSION
AFTER TEA, AT HALF-PAST SEVEN O'CLOCK.

T. COOK, Printer, Granby Street, Leicester.

When the Midland Railway opened its line from Derby to Ashby-de-la-Zouch, Thomas Cook was quick to organise an excursion from Leicester. He had been arranging excursions for 27 years and was about to widen his scope to include foreign trips. *(Thomas Cook Archives)*

A scientific law states that every action results in a reaction, so the ever-increasing numbers of country-bred excursionists arriving in London encouraged a complimentary growth in the art of pocket-picking. Let *Herepath's Journal* tell of the reception prepared for Gloucestershire excursionists in 1841:

> On Monday last about 850 of the inhabitants of Gloucester, Cheltenham and Cirencester started by special train from Cirencester to view the sights of the modern Babylon . . . Fast as they had travelled, the news of their approach had reached London before them; and a few 'choice spirits' of the town were waiting to give the 850 Gloucestershire men a hearty welcome to the metropolis. One gentleman in deep mourning took his place in a bus filled with some of the jolly looking party, and after he had left the omnibus, being taken suddenly unwell, the company found they had lost – one a purse of £5, and another a pocket handkerchief, by the gentleman in the sombre suit.[43]

An early example of the 'generation gap' must have been an excursion on the Norfolk Railway to Great Yarmouth in June 1846, when adults were conveyed in trains for adults only at one shilling return, whilst their children travelled in separate trains at threepence return.[44] Some 6,000 people besieged the Norwich terminus station and one wonders how this small railway company found sufficient rolling-stock. It was an experiment in low fares which the NR directors did not repeat.

Open, 3rd class excursion carriages were too crowded for a 'knees-up', but the well-to-do could gavotte in the guard's van. The *Norwich Mercury* related the story of 'A Grand Railway Ball' which took place in 1843:

> On Wednesday last, a party of ladies and gentlemen, bent, as a quaint old author has it, on 'extracting the fangs of care with the forceps of pleasure', left the metropolis . . . for Colchester. Here they spent a pleasant hour in visiting the castle, the priory, and the other objects of interest. On returning to the train, they found a sumptuous luncheon spread out in the van, and as the train whistled off from the station the travellers sat down to the ample board. The health of the ladies of the party closed the feast; and they then passed on to the next van, where quadrilles and country dances were kept up with spirit – probably being the first railway ball on record – while their steed ran performing a 'gallopade' through the hills and by the villages of Essex.[45]

These well-heeled excursionists certainly 'fared well', more than 130 years before British Rail applied the name 'Travellers Fare' to its catering services.

Unlike Blackpool, Southend-on-Sea or Weston-super-Mare, Scarborough was already an established resort long before the railway's tentacles reached it, and its spa waters and sea bathing were the principal causes of its popularity. The advent of the railway was the most significant factor in the expansion of the town. There was controversy as to the likely benefits a railway could bring or the potential traffic to be generated. According to one observer, '. . .the inhabitants of the place were well pleased to see respectable people amongst them, having no wish for a greater influx of vagrants.'[46] Some even believed that in a few years the novelty of *not* having a railway would be one of the greatest recommendations of the town.[47] One resident was of the opinion that the railway robbed Scarborough of its genteel exclusiveness, and

... brought a new host of invaders who were the pale, emaciated inhabitants of murky and densely populated cities seeking to restore their sickly frames to health and vigour by frequent immersion in the sea.[48]

Robbed of its 'genteel exclusiveness', Scarborough's expansion knew no bounds, for the multitudes poured in by the railway, whether day excursionists or holidaymakers for a longer stay, and were not restrained by reverence for tradition.

The shattered castle on the hill had seen many things, but never anything like the marvellous new activity which it now witnessed. Promenade lengthening – palatial hotels rising on every side – valleys being bridged – cliffs strengthened. Scarborough had burst her medieval bonds and stood transfigured.[49]

A pre-railway population of 8,760 had increased to 12,915 by 1851, only six years, and it was not only large hotels and boarding houses which flourished. Cafes, shops, stalls and amusements catering for the day-trippers, as well as the long-stay visitors, proliferated. 'Coffee Foster's' son recalled how his father had owned two coffee stalls in Scarborough years before the advent of the numerous cafes and snack bars of the present day:

... His Adult School Coffee Cart used to stand in the station yard selling hot beverages and light refreshments much appreciated by the many trippers. His other cart usually stood on the South sands ...[50]

On the other side of the country, in 'Little England', as late as 1898 it was claimed that

... Tenby, like Newquay, has never catered for the rowdy 'half-a-crown there and back' picnickers, with their accompaniments of ginger-beer and sandwiches. Its clientele has always been of the respectable debonnaire class who, satisfied with their treatment and the very moderate tariff, return year after year ...[51]

Those present-day residents whose peace and quiet has been shattered by the holding of a pop festival, or who live on the approach to a football ground, will sympathise with those Victorian objectors to the railway excursion, but they should spare a thought too for the denizens of those 'murky and densely populated cities' who were making Britain the workshop of the world and creating the dividends on which their masters could enjoy the 'genteel exclusiveness' of their chosen resort.

The benefits of providing healthy leisure and recreation for poorer urban dwellers was recognised by many who otherwise were opposed to Sunday travel. As Dr Kay stated before a Select Committee in 1833:

At present the whole population of Manchester is without any season of recreation, and is ignorant of all amusements, except that very small proportion which frequents the theatre. Healthful exercise in the open air is seldom or never taken by the citizens of this town ... one reason of this state of the people is that all scenes of interest are remote from the town.[52]

Land enclosures in the 18th and early 19th centuries had deprived the city dwellers of their former access to open spaces, as a Sheffield cutler explained in 1843:

Thirty years ago it had numbers of places as common where youths and men could have taken exercise at cricket, quoits, football and other exercises . . . Scarce a foot of all these common wastes remain for the enjoyment of the industrial classes . . . To the want of proper places for healthful recreation may be attributed in measure, the great increase of crime in this town and neighbourhood.[53]

To some at least, the railway cheap trip provided a means of temporary escape from their dismal, squalid homes and dark, satanic workplaces:

The excursion train is one of our best possible instructors. It is also one of the cheapest . . . From all the great manufacturing and commercial towns excursion trains are constantly bearing the active and intelligent artisans with their families to some interesting locality, for a happy and rational holiday . . .[54]

Sex discrimination in 1864 worked against the 'gentlemen'!

The City of London Police Commissioner in 1853 observed that

> . . . at the railway termini you may see hundreds of families with their baskets of provisions, going to different distances in the country, and walking in the fields, and making the ground their table, who come home soberly and as healthful as you could desire to be.[55]

In fact the quest for health, as much as the attraction of entertainments, motivated the factory-working, city-dwelling excursionists to rush to the seaside whenever the opportunity arose and finances permitted. One early 19th-century observer wrote that

> . . . crowds of poor people from the manufacturing towns, who have a high opinion of the efficacy of bathing, maintaining that in the month of August there is physic in the sea – physic of the most comprehensive description, combining all the virtues of all the drugs in the doctor's shop and, of course, a cure for all varieties of disease.

After all, if sea water was so good for the 'better classes', as eminent doctors declared, then it had to be equally beneficial for the lower orders.

Sex discrimination today works to the disadvantage of women, but in early railway times they were sometimes 'wooed' with lower fares. In 1853, the Vicar of East Dereham, Norfolk, wrote in his diary: 'Went to spend the day at Lowestoft by the excursion train which politely, one day in the week, accommodates visitors and takes the ladies at half-price.'[56]

What must have been a 'close encounter' for the railway officials involved occurred at Mumps station near Oldham in 1848. The Lancashire & Yorkshire Railway issued day excursion tickets to Blackpool at a fare of 1s 6d for gentlemen and 1s for ladies, but the concession had to be withdrawn because it was suspected that men were masquerading as women to obtain the cheaper ticket. A Passenger Superintendent, together with four Inspectors, was sent to 'investigate', although the precise method employed in their attempt to differentiate between the sexes is not recorded. Whatever these officials were up to resulted in a rush by impatient passengers, overwhelming the Superintendent who had to be dragged to the safety of a waiting room by the Stationmaster.[57] Had the mini-skirt been introduced 120 years sooner, this 'ticklish' problem would have been obviated!

Chapter 2
TO HELL ON SUNDAY!

'At a recent mass meeting of the citizens, the Great Central Railway was fiercely denounced for running the cheap excursion trains to the place on Sundays.'

Excursion trains of any kind were opposed by those seeking to preserve their exclusiveness, but the strongest, the most virulent opposition, was directed against the Sunday excursion, and this mainly on religious grounds. Yet, for the majority of workers in factory, office, shop or on farms, Sunday was the only toil-free day in their lives. A weekly early-closing day for shop-workers was not introduced before 1911, whilst for factory workers the so-called half-day on Saturday meant a finish at 2 pm under the Factory Act of 1850. The Bank Holiday Act was not passed until 1871, and paid annual holidays for most workers were not achieved until between the two World Wars. So it was a case of a Sunday excursion or nothing, even though such outings for some called for a working day by others, and this the Sabbatarians Against Sunday Trains deplored:

> ... Some gentlemen are apt to imagine that they befriend the working classes when they promote a little Sunday work for them, and Sunday recreation. But this is a great mistake ... The railways and tea gardens cannot be kept open but by the labour of multitudes deprived of their recreation themselves.[1]

One of the earliest Sunday excursions from Newcastle to Carlisle, on 29 August 1841, aroused the wrath of, and extraordinary protest by, the Rev Burns of Kilsyth, who happened to be in Newcastle. By means of placards and handbills he denounced the trip thus:

A REWARD for SABBATH BREAKING.
People taken safely and swiftly to HELL!
Next Lord's Day, by the Carlisle Railway, for 7s.6d.
It is a PLEASURE TRIP![2]

Five years later, Peter Dixon, a director of the Newcastle & Carlisle Railway, resigned, stating in his letter to the Company's Chairman:

> ... Another reason which has induced me to resign from the Direction is the continuance and frequency of the Cheap Sunday Trains; a practice against which I have always protested, but which I see no hope will be speedily discontinued.[3]

Not all railway shareholders were in agreement regarding Sunday travel, excursion or otherwise, for some Liverpool & Manchester Railway proprietors felt it would be entirely wrong to receive compensation from the net profits gained from trains operated on the

Lord's Day, and so a special fund was set up into which the dividends, due in respect of Sunday travel to those objecting shareholders, were paid. This sum was used for grants to such charitable purposes as the Liverpool District Provident Society and the Stranger's Friend Society.[4]

Branded as sinners for running Sunday excursions, the Manchester, Sheffield & Lincolnshire Railway's directors appear to have ignored 'God's Command'. 'Sigma', writing to the *Barnsley Chronicle* in 1859, complained:

> Sir – I have been deeply pained during the last few weeks by observing from time to time large placards announcing cheap trips on the Sheffield & Lincolnshire Railway, from Barnsley to Grimsby, on Sunday. Have the directors forgotten that God has commanded that we remember the Sabbath day to keep it holy? Or do they wilfully disregard this command, and on a large scale tempt others to do so too, for the sake of paltry increases of dividends they may realise thereby? Shame upon them! . . .[5]

One Great Central Railway shareholder, John Tucker of London NW1, far from opposing Sunday use of the railway, advocated that more goods trains be run then to keep the lines clear for passengers on weekdays, and called for 'an increase in Sunday excursion trains' so that toilers may obtain country air and proper recreation at low cost.[6]

Anti-Sunday excursionists never gave up. Thirty years later the Society for Promoting the Due Observance of the Lord's Day published a 'Statement Touching Railway Traffic on the Lord's Day submitted to Directors and Managers and Shareholders in Railway Companies', and dated 15 May 1883. It read:

> The ordinary Sunday Traffic on English Railways is far in excess of any demand which can possibly be defended on the pleas of necessity or mercy. It causes many thousands of men in various grades of Railway employment to lose their Day of Rest . . . The provision of Special Facilities for travelling on the Lord's Day is a still more glaring offence against the mind of God . . . In addition to these facilities by ordinary trains, many Companies run Special Excursion Trains on the Lord's Day [and] several Companies grant Special Trains on the Lord's Day to various anti-Lord's Day Societies and Infidels Clubs by which not only does money profit result to the Shareholders but Societies are furnished with funds for evil purposes . . . some Companies grant Special facilities to gamblers, bookmakers, touts and other frequenters of Race Courses . . . As Boards, there may be no Judgement Day; but the individuals who comprise them will have to give account to the Lord of the Sabbath for the evil they have wrought, the souls they have hindered and the disobedience of the Law of God which they have exhibited.

Phew! All those board members have long since vacated their chairs, relinquished their shares and are presumably down-graded to 'Firing for the old bloke down below', as F. Skerrett would have it.[7] But did God, in allocating railway accidents, discriminate against those companies running Sunday trains? A shareholder in the Newcastle & Carlisle Railway wrote in the press in 1849 that

A Sunday excursion on the Clarence Railway.

... a return made to Parliament of the Accidents on Scottish Railways from January to June 1848, shows the comparative security of Sabbath Observing and Sabbath Breaking lines. The lines running Sabbath trains embraced 280 miles, the lines having no Sabbath trains embraced 240 miles. Upon the lines which ran Sabbath trains, 14 persons were killed and two wounded; on the lines that observed the Sabbath there were only two accidents, one person killed and one wounded. Without asserting that these facts show a miraculous Divine interposition, I would confidently affirm that the Providence of God concurs with the Law of God, and that when men have not the rest of Holy Sabbath they become jaded and over fatigued, and less equal both bodily and mentally for the discharge of their duties upon the other six days of the week.[8]

The Great Northern Railway was the target for attack by the Working Mens' Lord's Day Rest Association in 1896 which accused that company of allying itself with the National Sunday League (an organisation calling for more leisure facilities on the Sabbath). They chastised the GNR for

... its efforts to make the day of holy rest a day for excursions and holidaymaking with all the labour and toiling inflicted on many workers when such excursions take place.

But the sting of this protest was reserved for the tail, aiming to hit the railway company where it was calculated to hurt most – in the takings!

... Your concession of Sunday Excursions will ... injure you financially in the end, for not a few religious people who feel strongly on the subject will prefer travelling to the North by the London & North Western Railway as soon as they find that you are granting Sunday trips.

However, the LNWR shareholders too couldn't resist the additional revenue from Sunday excursions but, as if to placate God or the WMLDRA, or both, that company allowed its ladies' excursion waiting room at Llandudno to be the venue for meetings of the Railway Mission, but only during the winter months.[9]

There was, of course, profit to be had from Sunday excursions utilising coaching stock which would otherwise have been standing idle in sidings, and so these vehement religious protests were doomed to failure. Nevertheless, the anti-Sunday train campaign continued, and in 1872 a list of signatures more than 20 feet in length was appended to a petition from the Clergy, Ministers and inhabitants of Leamington Priors in Warwickshire, and which was submitted to the Directors of the Great Western Railway who were accused of being in union with the National Sunday League to arrange a Sunday excursion from London to Leamington.

It will be most inexpedient for the quiet and peace of the town ... to be thus destroyed by an inundation of persons whose presence of necessity produces noise and confusion, the overflowing of the Beer Shops and Public Houses, united with the immense increase of needless toil and labour to a large number of the Railway Officials as well as the Police.[10]

Were these Sunday excursionists as bad as they were made out to be? The National Sunday League, organisers of excursion trains, in an endeavour to refute the allegations made against their participants which the League considered '. . .reflected injuriously on the conduct and character of those who accompanied our Excursions to the Seaside . . .', addressed the following letter to the Chief Constables of the towns recently visited:

> Charges have been made against our Excursions, that they are characterised by drunkenness and rioting, and that infidel and blasphemous addresses are delivered and literature of the same kind distributed at the places to which we go . . . our Committee has resolved on asking the Chief Constables [concerned] for their official observations of the behaviour of our people . . .

Back came the replies; from Ryde in the Isle of Wight, '. . . never heard one single complaint'; from Portsmouth, 'the charges brought against your League . . . are wholly without foundation'; from Arundel, 'I and the Superintendent complimented the Secretary of the League (just before the train started) on the respectable and quiet way the Excursionists conducted themselves'; and similar replies came from Littlehampton, Maidstone and Hastings.[11]

Leisure Hour, a popular magazine of the 1800s, hit the nail on the head when it pontificated:

> . . . First and second-class passengers do not travel to any great extent upon Sunday. Third-class passengers who now travel about altogether much more than they did formerly, crowd the line. Public opinion, it is said, can influence the lower classes to remain at home upon the first day of the week, and thus by decreasing the number of Sunday trains, increase the opportunities of rest for railwaymen.[12]

In other words, those whose work prevents them from travelling on weekdays shall also be denied the joys of travel on Sundays.

Railway companies were not alone in deriving revenue from excursion trains. Many resorts were created by, or at least developed in response to, the excursion trade, and traders in such places were as vociferous in defence of the Sunday excursion as the Sabbatarians were against. A memorial of tradesmen and other householders of Saltburn, Co Durham, in 1873 pleaded:

> . . . It is currently reported that the North Eastern Railway Company do not contemplate running Excursion trains to Saltburn as in former years and that they have come to this decision through it being represented to them that the inhabitants were desirous they should be discontinued. At a Public Meeting of the inhabitants . . . it was Resolved without any dissentient that a Memorial signed by the householders be presented to the Railway Company to show that they attach great importance to the running of these trains to Saltburn. The experience of tradesmen and others proves that their interests are very greatly affected by these trains and if discontinued they will suffer a loss. There are those in Saltburn who have made their arrangements expressly to accommodate excursionists and should the policy . . . be reversed, to them it would be ruinous . . . The inhabitants feel that it is most desirable that the natural attractions and salubrious climate of Saltburn should be more widely known . . . there are some undertakings such as the Pier, and Hoist and Public Gardens which are entirely dependent upon the numbers which excursion trains bring to make them remunerative.[13]

(CORRECTED BILL.)

GREAT WESTERN RAILWAY
(SOUTH WALES DIVISION)

BUTE FESTIVITIES
AT
CARDIFF

Saturday, 12th, Monday, 14th, Tuesday, 15th, Wednesday, 16th, Thursday, 17th, & Friday, 18th SEPTEMBER, 1868,

SPECIAL TRAINS
AT
SUNDAY EXCURSION FARES
WILL RUN BETWEEN
NEWPORT & CARDIFF

As under, calling at MARSHFIELD.

		a.m.	p.m.
Newport	dep.	8.15	2. 0
Marshfield	,,	8.25	2.10

Returning from **CARDIFF** for **NEWPORT** at 8.30 p.m. and 11.45 p.m. each day.

Tickets not transferable, and available only on the day of issue, and by the above-named Trains.

CHILDREN UNDER 12 HALF-PRICE. NO LUGGAGE ALLOWED.

Superintendent's Office, Swansea, 1st Sept., 1868.

PEARSE & BROWN, MACHINE-PRINTERS, SWANSEA.

Weekday excursions at 'Sunday Excursion Fares' on the GWR, 1868.

Blackpool's Illuminations have been the destination of thousands of excursion trains over the years – and still they go! *(Lancashire Library)*

Those tradesmen need not have worried, for the General Manager of the NER replied, 'I am decidedly of the opinion that any policy like that of withdrawing facilities previously enjoyed in the North East district would be very unwise.'

Blackpool became, for many, the popular seaside resort without parallel and it was the railway, and excursion traffic in particular, which encouraged the transformation of a somewhat bleak, exposed but long stretch of 'golden sands' into a trippers' paradise, a town devoted entirely to the entertainment of holidaymakers and day excursionists, and with 'Five Miles of Lights.' In truth, Blackpool's development as a popular resort was almost an accident, a by-product of Sir Peter Hesketh-Fleetwood's ambition to create a seaport and fashionable watering-place on the estuary of the River Wyre. Although the port developed both for cargo shipping and passenger steamers, Fleetwood, as it was named, never achieved popularity as a 'fashionable' seaside resort. Perhaps that was because the railway day excursionists invaded it from the start!

To link Fleetwood with the expanding Lancashire rail network, the Preston & Wyre Railway was opened in July 1840 and, so long as the rail route from London to Scotland was to Fleetwood by train and then by steamer to Ardossan, the line prospered in a modest way. Alas, the completion of the West Coast Main Line throughout to Scotland, and the consequent withdrawal of the steamer service from Fleetwood, put the P&WR on the verge of financial collapse. According to the authors of *The Blackpool Story*, the salvation of the P&WR came about from a most unexpected source when, on a day in 1842, a group of Sunday School teachers from Preston arrived at the railway's Fleetwood office with a previously unheard-of request – namely to carry 250 of their pupils from Preston to Fleetwood at half the normal fare.[14] So, on 3 July 1842, the first cheap excursion on the P&WR took place, and soon that company was organising its own excursion trains in collaboration with other railways, and conveying passengers from the growing industrial towns of Lancashire to the Fylde coast. At that time Blackpool was reached by horse-bus, carriage or on foot from Fleetwood, and excursionists were quite prepared to undertake that journey, flocking to Blackpool in their thousands.

Within four years of the first Sunday School trip to Fleetwood, a single-line branch of the railway was constructed from Poulton, on the P&WR's main line, into Blackpool. Increasingly popular though it was becoming, Blackpool was not prepared for the great

LANCASHIRE & YORKSHIRE
RAILWAY.

SEA BATHING
FOR THE
WORKING CLASSES.

ON AND AFTER SUNDAY MORNING NEXT,
and on each succeeding Sunday until further notice, with a view of
affording the benefit of

SEA BATHING,

A Train will leave the following Stations for

FLEETWOOD AND BLACKPOOL.

FARES
THERE AND BACK THE SAME DAY.

	A.M.	Males	Females & Children
Leave Manchester at	6 0	3s. 0d.	1s. 6d.
„ Bolton at	6 40	2s. 6d.	1s. 3d.
„ Chorley at	7 10	2s. 0d.	1s. 0d.
„ Preston at	7 40	2s. 0d.	1s. 0d.

Arriving at Fleetwood at 9 a.m.

FROM SALFORD STATION.

MANCHESTER TO LIVERPOOL

FARES there and back same day.

	Males	Females and Children
At 7 a.m.	2s. 6d.	1s. 6d.

BURY TO LIVERPOOL, BLACKPOOL, AND FLEETWOOD.

FARES there and back same day.

	Males	Females and Children
At 6 20 a.m.	2s. 6d.	1s. 6d.

Parties availing themselves of these trains will be enabled to

BATHE & REFRESH THEMSELVES

In ample time to attend a Place of Worship.

These Trains will return punctually at 6 p.m., arriving at Manchester about 8 and 9 p.m.

The Tickets will take the Passengers to the above-named places for ONE FARE, but for the purpose of preventing any unnecessary confusion or BUSINESS ON THE SUNDAY, it is desirable that tickets be taken on SATURDAY EVENING.

Bradshaw and Blacklock, Printers, 47, Brown-street, Manchester.

The small print attempts to placate opponents of Sunday excursions: 'Parties availing themselves of these trains will be enabled to bathe and refresh themselves in ample time to attend a place of worship'.

influx of excursionists which the railways were to bring, but a portent of things to come occurred on 1 June 1849, when one of the biggest excursion trains ever seen brought more than 10,000 from all parts of Lancashire to the Fylde coast. One train started from Rochdale calling at Heywood and Bury, by which time it consisted of 55 carriages hauled by two locomotives. At Bolton this train was joined to a similar one from Ashton,

Stalybridge and Oldham. Two other separate trains from Manchester had 25 and 36 carriages, whilst a fifth from Bolton comprised 28 carriages, and from here this truly great excursion proceeded in convoy, each train following close upon the one in front. Thousands gathered at stations and on bridges along the route to witness this unique event, this exodus from the mill towns of Lancashire. The five trains, consisting of 198 vehicles, many of them open trucks, were too great for one station to handle, so they were split between both Blackpool and Fleetwood.[15]

Taking increasing advantage of this new opportunity for cheap travel, the mill and office workers of the industrial North West now poured to the seaside whenever they were permitted a day free from work and their pockets allowed. The 116,000 leaving Manchester for the Fylde coast during Whit Week 1848 had almost doubled to 202,543 by 1850.

The sheer weight of numbers of railway excursionists was to influence the social character of the resorts which they visited and, in the case of Blackpool, turn it into a pleasure paradise for the masses; but for the few, '. . . a town which respectable visitors frowned upon.'[16] Two years after that monster excursion of 1849 the *Preston Pilot* warned:

> . . . Unless immediate steps are taken, Blackpool as a resort for respectable visitors will be ruined . . . Unless the cheap trains are discontinued or some effective regulation made for the management of the thousands who visit the place, Blackpool property will be depreciated past recovery.[17]

That 'immediate steps' were not taken can be seen from the figures for day excursionists which, in 1885, numbered 30,000 per day, whilst by 1913 that figure had increased to 120,000 on several days during the season. The number of excursion trains arriving at Blackpool's two stations, Central and Talbot Road, over a four-year period was: 1909 – 1,784; 1910 – 1,699; 1911 – 1,576; and 1912 – 1,753.[18]

Excursion trains, and the crowds they conveyed, had a far-reaching impact upon every

SEASIDE BANK HOLIDAY ARRANGEMENTS

Beach Attendant from Prom: 'Yer'll have to move 'em all up a bit Stanley, 'eres *another* train in'.

aspect of life in, and the development of, resorts. Since it proved impossible to keep the day-trippers away, the alternative was to segregate the classes so far as this was possible. The mutual attraction for all classes of visitor was the sea, either to sit beside it or be immersed in it, but although it contains (or did) billions of gallons of sanifying salt-water, it was not acceptable that 'refined' bodies should immerse themselves in close proximity to bodies of the 'lower classes' who lived in terraced houses without bathrooms, in 'murky and insanitary' towns.

'By gow Bill, but Tha's mucky!'

'Aye, Tha see Ah missed t'cheap trip last year', being the conversation of two sea-bathing millworkers.

Where the beach, preferably sandy, stretched in a near straight line, unstipulated but nevertheless clearly defined sections were frequented by these incompatible classes of human beings. Brighton had its more select Hove; Scarborough was naturally favoured by two separated bays. Blackpool had the North Shore with the Norbeck and other majestic hotels, while from the famous Tower southwards to the South Shore fun-fair, bazaars, arcades and stalls lined the promenade and catered for quite a different class of visitor from those welcome at the Bispham end, or the nearby Lytham St Annes to the south.

Expansion of excursion travel was accompanied by the growth of facilities to cater for the excursionists; in 1895 the Town Clerk of Blackpool listed 316 standings on the foreshore, which included 62 sellers of fruit, 47 of sweets, 57 of toys and jewellery, 52 of ice-cream, 21 of oysters and prawns, plus 36 photographers and exhibitors of picture views. Performers included 24 ventriloquists, six quack-doctors, six musicians and five conjurors. One harmless form of entertainment was to watch a chiropodist cutting the corns on the feet of his customers.

But one visitor from Manchester complained that '. . . after all, there is nothing to do in Blackpool and the place swarms with trippers'. However, he appears to have enjoyed himself on the pier: 'The promenading up and down the pier was alarming to see – petticoats quite forgot their duties, and so our eyes were occasionally gladdened by a pretty foot and ankle . . .' This critic considered that the mill and factory hands of Manchester had never had it so good,

> . . . They get such enormous wages and are so very improvident, that a run down for a trip of some thirty or forty miles is quite a minor extravagance. Blackpool and Southport are the two most favoured spots . . . sleeping, eating, flirting and laziness are all promoted by sea air, and these are the real reasons of its popularity . . .[19]

Entertainment for the trippers developed from the beach performers and promenade booths to become big business requiring large-scale capital investment which earned huge profits for the moguls of the entertainment world. By the 1880s, most seaside resorts had a pier which served not only as a landing stage for the pleasure steamers but, more importantly, for the show-biz people, places of entertainment with theatres, bars, ballrooms, side-shows and rows of penny-in-the-slot machines. From the pennies surreptiously inserted by hen-pecked Victorian husbands to watch 'What the Butler Saw', and the price of a waltz on the dance-floor, large fortunes were made. Vast entertainment complexes became a feature of the larger resorts, such as Blackpool's Tower, which included a zoo, theatre, ballroom, organ, fun-fair, restaurants and cafes as well as the opportunity to ascend the 578-foot-high tower for a panoramic view, half of which is grey Irish Sea.

Southport, 'The Montpellier of England', once favoured by the fashionable folk of

Excursionists pouring from a Lancashire & Yorkshire train at Blackpool Central station. The engine carries the excursion train number on its smokebox. *(Lancashire Library)*

Lancashire as being a select resort, was not spared from the enterprise of the railway companies in attracting excursionists to travel to wherever their lines radiated, and on a journey which could be accomplished in a day, if often a very long one. Let the *Southport Visitor* describe Whitsun 1855:

> Never before within memory has the town witnessed so busy and bustling a scene as its streets presented during Whit week. The railways from the manufacturing districts poured in their thousands daily who flowed through the streets in one, vast living stream, and swarmed on the wide expanse of the shore like a newly-disturbed anthill. The order of the day seemed to be 'Merry and wise' . . . Good order and general sobriety prevailed . . . The donkeys and donkey carriages had a rare time of it and seemed to afford rare amusement to the excursionists . . . The Churchtown bus was crowded every journey from roof to steps, and every other species of conveyance was in continuous request.[20]

The East Lancashire Railway conveyed 22,120 and the Lancashire & Yorkshire 19,234 passengers to Southport during that week.

Crowds awaiting departure from Blackpool's Central station. There is a fine display of enamel advertising signs. *(Lancashire Library)*

Blackpool and Southport were but only a short distance by rail from the industrial towns of Lancashire and the bustling port of Liverpool, whereas in the far South West, the resorts were more protected from excursionists by their greater distances from industrial towns.

Bournemouth was completely bypassed by the London & South Western Railway's line from London through Southampton and on to Dorchester and Weymouth, a watering place of repute since its patronage by George III from 1789 onwards. Not until 1870, some 23 years after the line to Weymouth was opened, was Bournemouth connected to the main line by a spur, and a further 18 years elapsed before there was a direct main line from London.

The retired and invalid residents of Bournemouth set about defending their reserve from any threatened invasion by railway excursionists, and at a meeting to consider the aforementioned coming of the railway, a man jumped up and recited these lines:

> Tis well from far to hear the railway scream;
> And watch the curling, lingering clouds of steam;
> But let not Bournemouth – Health's approved abode,
> Court the near presence of the iron road.

Of course, the iron road, when once constructed, enabled the retired, ill or leisured so-called 'better classes' to reach Bournemouth at greater speed and in greater comfort than previously, a facility they wished to deny to those who created their wealth.

Disraeli's *Sybil, or The Two Nations* of 1845 had done nothing to change the outlook of the author of an *Illustrated Historical Guide to Poole and Bournemouth* published in 1885:

> We receive throngs of excursionists, who very gladly avail themselves of the advantages and liberal arrangements made by the various (very kindly) railway companies for giving them a day, which invariably means but 3 or 4 hours, the rest of the time being occupied by travelling, at the seaside. Thus one day we are surrounded by miners, the next with shoemakers, and indeed every class of manufacturer, each combining and coming to the place in their, and we may truthfully say it, thousands. This was at one time, and is even now, by the majority of tradesmen of the town, condemned and who dread this great influx of the masses into the place, and thereby as they assert, driving the better class of visitor (i.e. those who have more money) whose chief object is retirement and quiet, away. . .[21]

Miners, shoemakers and every class of manufacturer were not without their champions, though:

> . . . Seeing how many attempts are being made to debar the artisan and his wife or the local hard-working tradesman from getting their share of the mundane beauties. [sic] It is apparently the wish of the Bournemouthians to monopolise the pineland and to prevent those on Sunday outings from sniffing the sea air or inhaling the health-giving ozone, on the only day the working classes get the opportunity of breathing it.[22]

However, the arrival of a Sunday excursion in the summer of 1888 caused the Bourne-mouth Commissioners to muster, take up pens and let off a broadside with this memorial:

> Bournemouth numbers among its residents many invalids for whose welfare as well as the general welfare of the Town, the Board deemed it advisable that the excursions on Sunday should cease. The presence of large numbers of day excursionists in the town on Sunday would necessitate the opening of public houses and refreshment rooms and that, as this was likely to interfere with the quietness of the Sabbath, it would not be at all conducive to the best interests of the Town.[23]

Did those dreaded excursionists descend upon the town or not? The editor of *The Bournemouth Visitor's Directory* wrote:

> After a month's experience we are bound to admit that our fears have not been realised – simply because the excursions have not been largely patronised; instead of the hundreds which we feared might possibly flock hither, there have not been scores, the reason being according to Mr Scotter [LSWR General Manager], 'The fares are altogether too high to attract what may be called excursion traffic', and the ordinary Sunday excursionists are reluctant to pay these high fares when they can go to other watering places for less than half the amount.[24]

Why were the excursion fares to Bournemouth double those to other resorts? Did the LSWR connive at keeping Bournemouth exclusive? Did influential people live there?

'Bournemouthians' may have opposed excursions to their exclusive resort, but they themselves patronised excursion trains originating from Bournemouth. The local newspapers of the time regularly advertised excursions to such venues as Epsom for the race meetings, Winchester, for choral festivals, London, for Queen Victoria's Jubilee, the American Exhibition, the Boat Race, etc.

'A wet Bank Holiday is always a disappointment', was the observation of the *Bournemouth Observer* after Whitsun 1885. It was even more of a disappointment for two train loads of excursionists from Birmingham, of which one train was delayed for 3 hours by the derailment of a goods train, and the other stalled at Parkstone and had to await assistance from Bournemouth.

> . . . The people . . . must have had a very unpleasant time of it . . . Some, we understand, never left the Railway station from the time they arrived until they departed homeward . . .[25]

Nowhere was safe from these excursionists, for up in the Lake District, James Payne – a friend of Harriet Martineau, authoress of *A Guide to the Lakes* – wrote:

> . . . Our inns are filled to bursting point, our private houses broken into by parties desperate for lodgings . . . a great steam monster ploughs up our lake and disgorges multitudes upon the pier; the excursion trains bring thousands of curious, vulgar people . . . the donkeys in our streets increase and multiply a hundredfold, tottering under the weight of enormous females visiting our waterfalls from morn to eve . . .[26]

Brighton, 'Queen of Watering Places', achieved fame (or notoriety?) as a watering place due to the patronage of the then Prince of Wales, later George IV, who began his visits in 1783, and took up residence in the Pavilion four years later. The turnpiked road from London enabled the nobility and 'gentility', in their own equipages, to accomplish the journey in less than half a day, whilst the 18 daily stage coaches made it in 8 hours. One, the *Vivid*, covered the 57 miles in the amazing time of only $5^1/_4$ hours.[27] Such was the flow of the well-to-do between 'Town' and 'Prinny's Place' that the road became known as 'The Appian Way for the high nobility of England'. The arrival of the railway in 1841 brought Brighton within 2 hours of London and cut the coach fare by half, thus putting this resort within the reach and means of the rising middle class, as well as the day excursionists.

At Brighton, the problem of keeping the classes apart was solved in two ways; one, already mentioned, was to develop Hove and West Brighton as 'Belgravia-sur-Mer'[28]; the other, by having more than one season in the year. The fashionable season lasted from early October until after Christmas and began again at Easter. With perhaps a hint of racialism, G. Sala wrote, 'In July the more affluent members of the Hebrew community come down in vast numbers; in August and September there is the tradesmen's season.'[29]

By 1860 the London Brighton & South Coast Railway was running 36 excursion trains from London on a Sunday, offering 10 or 12 hours by the sea. The slogan 'To Brighton and back for 3s 6d' was a common expression in London during the 1870s, but it was considered that the influx of metropolitan holidaymakers who '. . .daily and weekly disgorge on The Steyne from the cancer-like arms of the rail-roads' brought little trade to the town other than to the gin-shops and public houses.

'To Brighton and back for 3s 6d.' A painting by Charles Rossiter.

In 1860 a correspondent to the local press was confident that the experiment (excursion trains) had proved so offensive to the people of Brighton that they would remonstrate with the railway company about the disgraceful scenes that took place. It was alleged that many excursionists got too drunk to make their way to the station in time and were left behind. Of course when 'people of fashion' got drunk, as indeed they did, they were driven home in their own equipages or by hansom cab.

Wherever excursionists turned up, inevitably voices were raised against them. At holiday times, and on Sundays, thousands took the trains out of Hull to the seaside and to inland stations from which they could explore the countryside. In 1904, a shareholder in the Hull & Barnsley Railway protested:

> It is a burning shame that we should have excursions at 6d to Little Weighton and South Cave, and that we should have the undesirables of Hull sent to our villages, bringing with them a stream of immorality – I am speaking from personal experience because I have been brought into immediate contact with it. I know some of our officials have been down, but it is alright for them taking a quiet walk, they do not see everything. I am satisfied if the same occurred in the neighbourhood of any Director's residence something would be done. No provison whatever is made for these people – in every lane you find men playing cards and gambling and polluting young life!

He was sure that the original directors of the railway would turn in their graves if they knew. The Chairman explained that it was desirable to run excursions from which the company derived benefit because '. . . it enabled hard-working men to enjoy a time in the country.'[30]

'Sunday Trippers' was the headline for an article in *The Globe* newspaper in 1906, championing the excursionists carried by the Great Central Railway to their Caergwrle Castle station in Denbighshire.

> Is the Sunday tripper a more objectionable person than the Saturday or Monday holiday-maker? That appears to be the opinion of the 'unco guid' at a Welsh town rejoicing in the name Caergwrle. At a recent mass meeting of the citizens, the Great Central Railway was fiercely denounced for running cheap excursion trains to the place on Sundays.
>
> The intruders on that day – apparently they are heartily welcome on weekdays for the money they spend – not only lower the 'moral tone' of the community, but drive away the best class of visitors, are thorns in the flesh to pious householders, and hinder the development of the superb local resources of virtuous Caergwrle. It is a terrible indictment, truly, but surely there ought to be set against the harm done by these searchers for fresh air and pretty scenery, the amount of benefit they themselves receive from mixing with the elect. It stands to reason that their own 'moral tone' must be raised by the force of example, while if superfine visitors refuse to rub skirts with the unrefined perhaps the railway company is hardly blameworthy for placing the two classes on an equal footing. It may further be suggested that, instead of Sunday excursions blighting the prospects of holiday resorts, they are the most powerful aids to quick commercial development.[31]

Opposition to Sunday trains was both prolonged and well organised by the Shareholders' Union for Reducing Sunday Labour on Railways, with a secretary in Brighton and pre-printed Memorials for signature by railway shareholders. Reproduced overleaf is an example of the protest against the increase in Sunday excursions in Scotland in 1909. Some railway shareholders did oppose Sunday excursion trains but most were too tempted by increased rail revenue and hence increased dividends. The interlocking of railway shareholdings is demonstrated in this memorial showing that the Bowdens had shares in the North British, Great Western, Midland and Hull & Barnsley railways, and that they were most definitely in favour of Sunday trains.[32]

A resort which encouraged Sunday trippers was Aberystwyth, which, in 1925, collaborated with the Great Western Railway to run Sunday excursion trains 'to enhance the town as a pleasure resort'. The Town Council also invited the Royal Navy's fleet to visit Aberystwyth which resulted in 12 special trains depositing some 8,000 trippers in the town. Catering facilities were absolutely inadequate, so much so that several shopkeepers opened their doors to the hungry and thirsty crowds.

Sixteen shopkeepers were summonsed for Sunday trading and their defending solicitor pleaded that if shopkeepers who took pity and supplied bare necessities were to be punished that would redound to the detriment of the town. The case against those selling food was dismissed, but those selling tobacco were fined 5 shillings.[33]

Two weeks later the *Birmingham Mail* carried a headline 'Opposition from Aberystwyth Tradesmen. Sequel to Birmingham Trip'. The report ran:

> Birmingham was mentioned during a discussion on Sunday excursions at the meeting of the Aberystwyth Chamber of Trade last evening . . . A crowd of excursionists had been reported by the beach inspector as being 'quite uncontrollable'. Colonel Lloyd deprecated the words used and said the crowd was quite orderly. One councillor said '. . .in view of the fact that they were

Sunday Traffic on the Clyde.

CALEDONIAN RAILWAY.

1909/10.

Dear Sir or Madam,

It is now a matter of common knowledge that the Directors, in agreement with the Board of the **GLASGOW & SOUTH WESTERN RAILWAY,** have increased their Sunday trains and through connections with certain of the Clyde Steamers on Sundays, during the season. This decision raised a considerable volume of adverse comment, and protests against the innovation, were heard from all quarters. "The Buteman," the leading newspaper in Buteshire—the part specially affected by the change, said, "It is not the mere running of one or two additional steamers, with the extra labour to local agents and others involved thereby, that disquietens the coast residents so much as the fact that this is looked upon as **merely the thin end of the wedge.** The inevitable result of the development of Sunday sailing, and the increasing crowds of trippers brought here, will be a demand for further facilities on land, such as Sunday cars and brakes, Sunday boating, the opening of restaurants and other shops, and a general extension of Sunday trading in one form or another."

The inference has been fully justified by experience, and in England, wherever Sunday Excursion trains have been run, the same demands have arisen, especially in all watering places affected, so that the quiet restfulness of "the Lord's Day commonly called Sunday," is in such places now a thing of the past.

We regret to find that in connection with the change **the railway man** appears to have been overlooked. Surely *he* is a factor in the case and should be considered. It is but yesterday that those of us who live south of the Tweed were thanking God for the dawn of a new hope for the many thousands of "Sabbathless toilers," whose pitiless labour rolls round with the year unstayed even for twenty-four hours. It now seems that the "almighty dollar" is seeking to assert its soul-less autocracy in the land so long regarded as the home of the "Puritan Sabbath"!

They would like to see a few more between say Oct. March

THIS FORM TO BE DETACHED

TEXT OF MEMORIAL.

"To the Chairman, Board of Directors, and Shareholders of the Caledonian Railway.

We, the undersigned Stock and Shareholders of the Company desiring the due and proper observance of the Christian Day of Rest which we believe to be in the best interests of the Company as well as their Employees, desire to enter our earnest protest against any departure from the policy of the Company in regard to the Sunday traffic which has been consistently followed for so many years.

We should be glad for your particular attention to be directed to this matter with a view to the abandonment of all increase in the Sunday trains and steamers, and the return to the *status quo ante*.

I give *no* authority to add my name to the above Memorial, *but shall support the Directors in providing all reasonable facilities for conveyance of the toilers into the country on the Lords day*

E. C. Bowden

Please give FULL NAME, style and address,

also Alfred Benjamin Bowden Shareholder in North British Great Western, Midland +

Note.—Where there are more Shareholders than one in a family, all such are invited to sign on the back of this form.

Should any of the Proprietors now addressed hold investments in other railways, it would be a favour if the Secretary were informed of the particulars, and authority given to add their names to any Memorial on Sunday Traffic, to such Companies.

This form to be returned after signature to the

Rev. Wm. Lawrence Tweedie,
19, Chesham Street,
Brighton.

The Memorial issued by the Shareholders' Union for Reducing Sunday Labour on Railways in 1909. The Bowdens obviously supported Sunday trains. (*Scottish Record Office*)

uncontrollable they were the very people we don't want.' The Town Council was urged to discourage the running of Sunday excurions to the town.[34]

The delightful town of Llangollen did not experience its first invasion of Sunday excursionists until July 1925, when the Great Western Railway ran a train from Birmingham. The *Birmingham Mail* reported that this excursion had taken place

> . . . notwithstanding vigorous protests from the inhabitants and Llangollen District councillors. The crowds however were very orderly, spending the afternoon on the hillsides and in wayside rambling. There was a complete absence of rowdy scenes and the police state that the visitors gave no trouble. There is still a strong feeling in Llangollen against this Sabbath invasion and further conferences are to be held to discuss the matter.[35]

In the 19th century the West Coast of Scotland was strictly Sabbatarian, so much so that they physically opposed the conveyance of fish traffic by the Highland Railway from Strome Pier on a Sunday; in what became known as the Battle of Strome Pier on Sunday 3 June 1879, a band of 150 protesters prevented the loading of fish into railway trucks. In August 1929, the LMSR arranged a Sunday excursion from Inverness to Kyle of Lochalsh, but not without some trepidation, for there were rumours that the Battle of Strome Pier would be repeated.

The motive power inspector accompanying the excursion later wrote:

> We had a good train – 250 passengers . . . the Wee Frees were vowing vengeance on us if we dared to come to Kyle on a Sunday so I did not want to let them think that I was afraid to come. However, everything was very quiet when we arrived. No one took any notice and we had a splendid day.

However, those excursionists intending to cross to the Isle of Skye were thwarted by the ferrymen who refused to carry them on the Sabbath.

Two years later a railwayman collapsed and died shortly after the departure of a Sunday excursion from Kyle of Lochalsh and this the locals interpreted as the wrath of the Lord taking vengeance for ignoring the Sabbath.[36]

An interesting connection between excursion trains and the crime rate was given by the LB&SCR's Chairman, Samuel Long, in 1854:

> . . . He would refer shortly to the excursion system, upon which the line depended so much for its prosperity. It was a bold experiment to take people from London to Brighton and back at 3s 6d a head. This experiment had, however, been completely successful, and the best evidence which could be afforded of its success was given by Sir Richard Mayne, the Chief Constable of the Metropolitan Police, who on being examined before the committee of the House of Commons which sat to investigate crime in the Metropolis said it was a positive fact that since the system of excursion trains had been carried out to such an extent crime had, to his own personal knowledge, very greatly diminished.[37]

A possible explanation not pursued is that the criminals purchased an excursion ticket and followed their prey to Brighton!

Chapter 3
BUNS, BAGPIPES AND BOVRIL

'They bring their dinners with them in baskets, in sheets of old newspapers, and in pocket handkerchiefs, and they dine in . . . a magnificent apartment under the cliff, having for its carpet the countless pebbles of the seashore . . .'

For early excursionists to be conveyed in open trucks, or even in purpose-built open carriages, appears to us, today, to have been an act of inhumanity by the railway companies, yet such facilities for the 'lower classes' were no worse than those which had existed before the railway era. The stage and mail coaches, rolling along the newly turnpiked roads of the 18th century, were responsible for a large increase in the number of people travelling, but it was a form of travel prohibitively expensive for working people. The nobility and aristocracy were borne along in their private equipages, so that it was mainly the rising class of industrialists and merchants who could afford to travel 'inside', together with perhaps the higher clergy, army officers, lawyers and others on 18th century expense accounts. At half the cost of riding 'inside', there rode on the top of the coaches the lower income groups from among those higher up the social ladder than the working classes; these included the lower clergy, dons and undergraduates, petty government officials and servant girls on their way to a new situation, their fare paid by the new mistress.

The majority of the population did not travel any further than their own legs could carry them, unless they could scrape together the few shillings needed to pay for a ride on a carrier's waggon, where passengers sat as best they could on, or amongst, the cargo, be it soft bales of wool or pungent piles of hides. Those rural trippers sometimes taken for a drive in a horse-drawn farm waggon or, if living near a river or a canal, for a cruise in a boat, did so in the open, unprotected from the weather.

So, all in all, the cheap railway excursion gave to more people than ever before, the working population and their families, opportunities for travel which had not previously existed and under conditions which were no worse than those which, hitherto, some sections of the better-off had enjoyed – or endured! The numbers carried on those 'monster' excursion trains of the 1840s are evidence enough of the appeal which this novel and cheap form of travel had for those who flocked to the new railway stations and squashed themselves into those overloaded trains. Often they were wind-swept, rain-soaked, smut-begrimed and very late arriving back home, but there they were again the next year or the next holiday, full of optimistic anticipation for 'a good day out with the missus and kids'.

Fortunately for human progress, the travelling public always demands still better

47

An 1850s artist's impression of trippers on the beach.

standards of comfort and service than those being provided. Covered carriages gave better protection from the elements than the 'opens', but the leather flaps which, in many vehicles, preceded glazed windows, prevented ventilation when down, or admitted too much wind and rain if raised. The closed excursion carriages, frequently unlit during the hours of darkness, provided one of the few opportunities for Victorian couples to kiss and cuddle protected from the admonishing frowns of their fellow passengers who had given up that sort of thing years ago. But, courting apart, it must have been unpleasant to travel for hours in a crowded, unlighted carriage, an experience not unknown to some unfortunate railway excursionists even today.

However, an inconvenience not imposed upon present-day trippers was the absence of a 'convenience' on these trains, nor indeed for any 3rd class passengers until quite late in railway history.

For many years the sheer volume of excursion traffic far exceeded the railway companies' facilities for handling it, and this was a major factor contributing to the unpunctuality of these trains whilst in the very early years the great length, and therefore weight, of excursion trains exceeded the pulling-power of the diminutive locomotives, so much so that the passengers were often required to get out and give the train a push up the gradient.

Enough of generalisations; let the records speak for themselves, for from them we can learn a great deal of what it was like to go on an excursion train, and the kind of things the trippers did when they reached journey's end.

Fleetwood was the venue for The Poor People's Annual Summer Excursion from Preston, *circa* 1848. This was an occasion when the Lancashire & Yorkshire Railway conveyed some 2,000 of the Preston poor at the reduced fare of 6d per head; an additional 2d was allocated by the organising committee to 'provide each person with a bun and as

During a period of economic depression, the South Wales Miners' Union leader, William Abraham, whose Bardic title was Mabon, agreed with the colliery owners that there should be no work on one day each week. This became known as Mabon's Day. In this picture locomotive *Dyfatty* hauls coal wagons filled with miners on a Mabon's Day excursion to the seaside at Burry Port in 1895, on the Burry Port & Gwendraeth Railway. *(Glyn Davies)*

much milk as they wished'. The Excursion Committee's booklet pontificated:

> . . . The toiling poor, the aged and infirm, look to the time with pleasing anticipations, and always speak of it afterwards with pleasure. In thus treating the poor, a benevolent feeling is cultivated, and an additional step taken for supplanting, debasing and degrading habits by innocent and healthful recreation.[1]

Advice to those poor and elderly excursionists was to be at the station a quarter-of-an-hour before departure time and to take their seats without delay. A band was to accompany the train and the signal for starting was to be the band's striking up the tune 'Over the Hills and Far Away'. Amusements available at Fleetwood included a steamer trip round the lighthouse at a charge of 2d per person, '. . . commencing at 2 pm, you will hear the bell ring'. The buns and milk were to be given out at 1 pm in the Market House. Comforting for those who could contain themselves long enough was the knowledge that 'The Booths at the North Euston Hotel will be open at 2 o'clock, one for males and the other for females, FREE'. Dancing on the Lawn (weather permitting) was to take place around the Charity Banner, and bathing could commence before High Water.

In those early days of train excursions the participants frequently paraded in the streets of the resorts they visited, as did the employees of G. W. Cotton of Bristol when they went to Weston-super-Mare in June 1846. The local newspaper considered the visit to have been '. . . one of the gayest and most enlivening scenes we ever recollect witnessing in

Weston-super-Mare'.[2] Upon arrival, the 1,700 excursionists formed up for a procession headed by the band of 'The Star in the West Lodge of Oddfellows', and perambulated the town amid a display of flags and banners bearing several appropriate mottoes and inscriptions, such as:

Kindness from Employers
Ensures Gratitude from
The Employees

Prosperity to the Proprietors
Mr G. W. Cotton's Factory

All Our Recreation Should
Be Accompanied by
Virtue and Innocence

Groups of '. . . both sexes engaged in the merry dance to the very heart-stirring airs played by the visiting band', and it would seem that the local population turned out in great numbers to witness this novel event. In fact, the locals appear to have taken the visitors to heart for the *Weston-super-Mare Gazette* described the departure of the excursionists in these words:

> . . . As time drew nigh for leave-taking between 8 and 9 o'clock, the assembly of spectators in Regent Street and Locking Road must have numbered 2,000, and as the whistle announced the starting of the monster train from our station, the mutual greetings that followed the waving of handkerchiefs and

'Now for the sea' (or the Severn estuary!). Crowds pour off excursion trains at Weston-super-Mare's Locking Road station. (*West Air Photography*)

hearty cheers emanating from all parties gave termination to the proceedings of a day, a true gala day, that will long be remembered by Westonians and their welcome visitors from Bristol.

Present-day travellers, who complain of British Rail's failure to keep them informed when delays occur, should take consolation from the knowledge that it was just the same 130 and more years ago. A correspondent to *The Times* in 1851 complained against the London & South Western Railway, concerning an excursion from Farnham to Waterloo which had been punctual on the outward journey but '. . . on our return we were kept waiting half-an-hour beyond the stated time and could get no information from any of the porters'. He went on to claim that 'I think I could get nearly half the population of this town to bear testimony, who have been fellow sufferers with me'. When these delayed travellers arrived at Guildford there was no engine to take them forward to Farnham, and they were stranded there for another hour awaiting an engine.

Next follows a complaint about another occasion when a special excursion train conveying nearly 1,000 passengers, among whom were many children, went from Farnham having been advertised as providing closed carriages but, the writer complained, the company

> . . . kept them waiting in the same manner as on Monday last and sent them down, not only in open carriages but in sheep pens and luggage waggons, with less accommodation and comfort than the animals would have had ... the passengers (the children especially) were not prepared with such extra clothing as was necessary for them to be exposed to the night air in open carriages . . . Now Sir, I am assured that you will agree with me, that such gross misconduct on the part of the railway company ought not to be tolerated . . .[3]

Some years earlier the Midland Railway is reported to have displayed a more humane attitude to its excursionists travelling in open trucks during pouring rain on a 6-hour journey returning from London to Oakham in 1848.[4] They were allowed to transfer to covered 3rd class carriages. Perhaps it was the passengers' good fortune that the excursion was not well patronised.

For the opening of the Zoological Garden in Hull in 1861 excursion trains were run from Leicester, Derby, Nottingham, Boston, Grantham, Sleaford, Grimsby, Newark, Louth, Halifax, Bradford and other places, being an example of the eagerness of the public to patronise the many new places of entertainment which Victorian enterprise was creating, and for which the expanding railway system, and cheap excursion trains in particular, provided the means of attracting attendances sufficient to make the project viable. What a racket it must have been on that occasion! Some 3,000 people arrived by train for what was described as the novelty of the day, ' . . a musical, military, sham fight':

> . . . The sham fight consisted in the whole of the bands stationed in different parts of the gardens playing different pieces simultaneously, and the abilities of each band could only be appreciated by the throngs who patronised the respective stands . . . the artillery platoon pounded forth volley after volley, whilst the bands were playing. The crowds were so scattered that none could possibly tell when the affair was over, or even what it meant . . .[5]

As if those attending had not already been deafened by the procceedings of the afternoon, there was a firework display in the evening.

One of the attractions at Brighton was Volk's Electric Railway from the Pier to Rottingdean, opened in 1896. Carriages 23 feet above the rails, which were laid on the sea bed, were propelled electrically.

Crowds of excursionists passed through Brighton's Mocca-designed railway station, and whilst one observer discounted any benefit they might bring to the town, he did paint a very vivid description of their picnic arrangements:

> They are not in the habit of resorting to the York or the Bedford, or even to hostelries of a humbler order. They bring their dinners with them in baskets, in sheets of old newspapers, and in pocket handkerchiefs, and they dine in company at the 'London Ordinary', a magnificent apartment under the cliff, having for its carpets the countless pebbles of the seashore, and for its roof the vaulted sky. The carte here is substantial, if not recherche. It comprises pork chops cold; brisket of beef, ditto, cut with a hammy knife; bacon fried; knuckle of ham; and bread and cheese and onions. The liquors, chiefly ale and porter, are brought to the festive scene in stone bottles, which when emptied of their contents, being made cockshies of, turn up in sea-worn fragments after many years, to attract the eye of amateur collectors of curiosities, and find a place in some domestic museum of the treasures of the deep. The native inhabitants look down with supreme contempt upon these economical festivities; for all the delicacies of the season, even including the beer and the 'drop of something short' are brought from London and Brighton reaps no benefit save from the extra pint that may be consumed as a supplementary treat in one of the numerous inferior houses of entertainment in which the town abounds.[6]

When the London, Tilbury & Southend Railway reached Southend-on-Sea in 1856, what had been a 'select' resort was soon to be transformed into 'East London's seaside'. The Great Eastern Railway's line reached Southend in 1889, adding to the excursion facilities, so that at weekends and on Bank Holidays thousands of trippers left Fenchurch Street and Liverpool Street stations for 'Sarfend'. Here is one description of the exodus from Poplar:

> Bank Holiday was enjoyed by many Poplar people, some families went on cheap day trips to the countryside to Hainault, Epping Forest, Abridge and other beauty spots. Many used to line up at Bromley-by-Bow Station with the family, to get a day return ticket on the LT&S line, at the price of half-a-crown. When the train for Southend came into the station, it was already packed, every seat taken on its journey from Fenchurch Street and it was a battle to get aboard the train, standing room only. Thousands travelled this way. When many families arrived in Southend they went straight to the house or shop hiring out babies' prams, which saved the parents the job of carrying the offspring about. Some went for the trip on the pier train, or the sailing boats, or a trip in the 'Kursaal', for all the fun of the fair. They never went home without rock and cockles.[7]

Vanbrugh's Castle Howard, in Yorkshire, was the venue for a singularly unsuccessful excursion by the Young People's Christian & Literary Association from Hull in 1861. Some 900 excited young people filled 31 carriages, which comprised this excursion train, for a $2\frac{1}{2}$-hour journey which, according to the local newspaper, went '. . . without any incident worthy of note occurring on the road, if we may except the cutting in two of a dog which attempted to cross the rails at Beverley'. (Obviously not well trained!) On arrival at Castle Howard station, these intrepid excursionists faced a 3-mile walk to the castle, and it seems that membership of the YPCLA did not inhibit some from being

> . . . drawn aside by the signs of 'The Cow' and the 'Crown and Cushion', and tempted to partake of good things to be had within! No one indulged more than a minute or two . . .[8]

At 3 pm, big rain drops heralded a continuous downpour, and it was now that this intended enjoyable occasion turned into a most disappointing and unpleasant experience for which the weather was only partly to blame. Of the whole party, 350 had booked for tea at the Castle Hotel where it transpired that there was only accommodation for some 50 or 60 persons. Many decided to forego the 1s 3d tea rather than wait outside the tearoom in pouring rain. All faced a 3-mile wet trek back to the railway station, where, soaked to the skin, they faced another $2\frac{1}{2}$-hour rail journey, but this time in wet clothes. The reporter commented:

> . . . To make matters worse, some of the carriages were anything but watertight, and to many, the ride to Hull was almost as wet as the walk from the Castle. We can see no reason why a 2nd or 3rd class carriage should not be made to keep out the wet as well as a 1st class . . . not a few will have cause to remember with sorrow their trip to Castle Howard.

The opening of the Neath & Brecon Railway in 1866 appears to have been a joyous experience for the 700 or so excursionists from the Neath and Swansea area who travelled

CAERPHILLY CASTLE

THE HOME OF KING HENRY III

PLEASURE FOR ALL

AN

EXCURSION

TRAIN

Will Leave PONTYPRIDD STATION

On MONDAY, SEPTEMBER 2nd, 1889,

At 11.55 a.m., returning from Caerphilly at 7.44 p.m.

EXPLORE THE RUINS

Tea will be provided in the Castle at " p.m.   Ticket's, Tea and Railway Fare,
Adults, 1s. 6d. each; Children under 12, 1s.

PENTYRCH BRASS BAND

Will be in attendance, assisted by several Artistes to entertain. Admission to the Castle 3d. each,
Children half-price. Tickets to be obtained of David Gibbon, Esq., Great Western Colliery, Chairman of Committee ; J. Tracy Thomas, Vice-Chairman ; J. Manuel Rees, Esq., Treasurer ; J. Thomas, P.O., Hafod Sec.

No Tickets will be issued at the Railway Station on the morning of Excursion.

TICKETS SOLD HERE.

Davies Brothers, Printers, "Chronicle" Offices, Mill-Street, Pontypridd.

A 'castle' excursion on the Rhymney Railway, hopefully more successful than that to Castle
Howard!

up to Brecon for the occasion; that is, until they commenced their return journey.
Apparently the new company had adopted as its motto the words 'The Direct Road', but
that can have been of little consolation to its unfortunate passengers who did not reach
their home stations until the early morning of the following day, over a distance of some
45 miles!

But allow *The Cambrian* to relate the miserable tale:

> We are sorry to be compelled to state, that the arrangements for the return
> journey entirely marred the whole pleasure of the day, and were of the most
> discreditable nature. From the best information we can obtain, it appears that
> . . . [all] . . . thought they would be able to get back at a reasonable hour in the
> evening. But they were sadly and even cruelly doomed to disappointment. For
> some unaccountable reason, the return was not fixed to start until half-past
> eight. Absurdly late as this was, it was half-past ten before a move was
> effected, and then only some few yards were traversed before the train came
> to a dead stop, where it remained for about another hour. Another few yards

were then got over – then another stop, and thus continued for the whole of the night! We record the fact in the history of railway enterprise and speed, thirty-three miles of rail were actually traversed in seven hours – or at the rate of about four-and-a-half miles per hour. Add to this the fact the passengers were crowded together in carriages without a gleam of light of any quality or description – that it rained in torrents the whole night, and that rumours of accidents were exceedingly rife, and our readers have some faint idea of the exceedingly unpleasant position of the Neath & Brecon excursionists.

On arrival at Neath, connections with other trains were lost and, at 6 o'clock in the morning, no shops were yet open. The lamentable tale continues:

> . . . a cup of tea or coffee could not be obtained for love or money. Nor did our miseries end here. We had to wait for at least four hours before the next train started for Swansea . . . we do not know upon whom rests the responsibility of this unhappy denouement. We merely state the facts, leaving all the officials of the line to help themselves to as much of the blame as their consciences (doubtless very elastic) will tell them they are entitled to.[9]

'Oh Lord lighten our darkness!' might well have been the prayer offered up by the Rev Francis Kilvert on an excursion in 1870, but instead he and his fellow travellers used their own initiative and in his diary he wrote:

> Went down to the Bath Flower Show in Sydney College Gardens. Found the first train going down was an Excursion train and took a ticket for it. The carriage was nearly full. In the Box Tunnel, as there is no lamp, the people began to strike foul brimstone matches and hand them to each other all down the carriage. All the time we were in the tunnel these lighted matches were travelling from hand to hand in the darkness. Each match lasted the length of the carriage and the red ember was thrown out of the opposite window, by which time another lighted match was seen travelling down the carriage. The carriage was chock full of brimstone fumes, the windows both nearly shut, and by the time we got out of the tunnel I was almost suffocated.[10]

An excursion train that didn't go anywhere but remained stationary to allow the attractions to roll by, is how one might describe the Swansea & Mumbles Railway's enterprise in lining-up its coaches along the track parallel to the road to be traversed by the Prince of Wales and his party after the opening of the new dock at Swansea in 1881. An advertisement in *The Cambrian* read:

> Seats to view the Royal Party returning to Singleton on the 18th October. The Carriages of the Swansea & Mumbles Railway Company will be stationed between St Helens Junction and Gorse Lane. Tickets for Saloon carriages 2s 6d; 2nd class carriages 1s; inclusive of Railway fares from Swansea or Mumbles 3s 6d and 1s 6d may be obtained at Rutland Street station or St Helens Junction Booking Office.[11]

This same ceremony was the occasion for the S&MR to provide 'Upper class' excursion facilities enabling fortunate ladies and gentlemen to travel to the Ball taking place at The Grange, and for them to be conveyed home by special trains at 2, 3 and 4 o'clock in the morning. What is more, the company promised that 'A temporary platform will be laid down opposite the entrance and a dry crossing over the road provided'. The fare for this special service was 2 shillings and, unlike those lesser beings so frequently herded into open trucks, for this Ball excursion the number of tickets issued was limited to the capacity of the carriages.

In fact, the S&MR probably carried more passengers per mile of track than any other railway in the world, a claim put forward by the author of Rock and Roll to Paradise[12], and, since the only reason for travelling from Swansea to Oystermouth was to enjoy oneself, most of these passengers were excursionists disgorged into Swansea by the main-line railway companies. This is amply confirmed by local newspaper reports such as this for August Bank Holiday, 1897:

> It is estimated that 80,000 people visited Swansea, Mumbles and Gower, on pleasure bent, on Bank Holiday . . . the streets were crowded from early hours with excursionists from the Rhondda, Brecon, Carmarthen etc, the great majority of which, in the course of the day, visited the Mumbles . . . Thousands were carried over the Mumbles Railway, and the fact that not a single accident occurred reflects credit upon the management capabilities of Mr Hemmens, and the watchfulness of the general staff . . .[13]

Travelling on the S&MR, particularly at holiday times, must have been quite a unique experience, if not a test of endurance. Steam locomotives were introduced from 1877 and hauled trains of double-decked tramcars, similar to the horse trams operating in several towns and cities at that time. The upper decks were open but the lower decks were of both enclosed and open type. Contemporary photographs show trains of up to 15 or more cars loaded with holidaymakers, seated, standing and clinging to the sides.

If the supply of tramcars was insufficient to meet demand, the company brought into use long, open trucks fitted with wooden seats along the sides and down the middle, and with slatted sides. Passengers in these excursion vehicles were permitted to stand, or more likely had no option. Not surprisingly these open cars were known to the public as cattle trucks. When these vehicles were not added to an already overfilled train, they frequently comprised a whole train of 12 to 15 cars, but either way those who rode in (or should it be on?) them were almost certain to arrive at the Mumbles with black faces and smut-begrimed hats and clothes.

One spin-off from the Mumbles excursions was the pocket money which small boys earned by performing cartwheels, somersaults and acrobatics alongside the track as they called out 'Ha'penny oh, penny oh!' in response to which copper coins showered upon them from the entertained excursionists.[14]

It was said of the Whitsun Bank Holiday at Mumbles in 1900 that:

> Monday was a day of radiation. Many people aver that there never was such a spring holiday before; that never had Swansea been so empty or desolate, the country-bound trains more crowded, the Mumbles more thickly thronged, or the open spaces, parks, sands etc scenes of livelier merriment . . . Upwards of 30,000 people visited the Mumbles; over 25,000 of that number were carried by the Mumbles Railway Company . . .[15]

When the Cambrian Railways' branch from Llanymynach to Llanfyllin was ready for traffic in July 1863, the opening was marked by an excursion from Llanfyllin to Borth, on the coast of Cardigan Bay, and for which 23 carriages were required. Many of these

'Ha'penny oh, penny oh!' Urchins perform their tricks alongside a Swansea & Mumbles Railway train.

excursionists had never before seen the sea and some of the ladies intending to bathe were embarassed when surrounded by 'gentlemen' in anchored boats! There must have been some other attraction causing a good many people to miss the return train, which is reported as having 'started punctually', which no doubt came as a surprise, as it had been very unpunctual on the outward journey.[16]

Not all excursion trains ran to the seaside and one may, today, be somewhat surprised by the venues advertised and the pleasures arranged for excursionists. The Royal Border Bridge at Berwick was nearing completion in 1849 when the North British Railway ran an excursion from Edinburgh to view 'the stupendous works in progress for carrying the York & Newcastle Railway across the Tweed'.[17]

In August 1867, the GWR advertised 'The People's Excursion of the Season' from Swansea at 7 am, heading for Pontypool, with an opportunity to view the Crumlin Viaduct.[18] A few years previously several hundred excursionists from Neath and Aberdare rounded off their day in Swansea with a musical evening at the Ebenezer Chapel.

'From the four corners of the earth they come to kiss this Shrine,' wrote Shakespeare, not knowing that his own birthplace would one day become a shrine for tourists. However, one corner the Stratford-on-Avon local paper did not want them from was Birmingham and the Black Country:

> We think that after the disgraceful scenes witnessed in our streets on Tuesday last something ought to be done to put a stop to the cheap trips from Birmingham and the Black Country which run to our town frequently in the summer months. They do not benefit us one iota, and we are quite sure that the class of people that generally 'honour' us with their company on those occasions know as much about Shakespeare and his writings as a donkey does about the Eastern Question. Tuesday last brought in a contingent from our 'Midland Metropolis' who principally amused themselves with getting in a beastly state of intoxication (we are sorry to say that this was not confined to the male sex) and fighting one another, and placing the town in a state of riot

and confusion for several hours together – in fact, the excursionists on that day were a disgrace to civilisation and to the town from which they came. We think it quite time the Town Council petitioned the Railway Company not to run excursions, or if they wish to do so, let them charge such a fare as none but those who care to conduct themselves properly will take advantage of them; and let the Railway Company bear in mind that Stratford-on-Avon does not aspire to the honour of being classed with the Tea Garden type of public showplaces, but a town to be reverently and decently approached as the birthplace, home, and grave of that great man who

'Outstripped time, exhausted worlds,
'And then imagined new.'[19]

It must have been more fun at Skegness where, it was said,

... The habits of some of the excursionists were reckoned to be rather primitive – both sexes bathing together in hundreds and floundering about in the waves with apparently an utter unconsciousness of impropriety.[20]

It was further complained that occasionally the excursionists dropped down upon the place in numbers so overwhelming as to leave the town as bare of nutriment as was Egypt after the visitation of locusts. No wonder that such an influx of visitors was '. . . looked upon with a feeling somewhat akin to dread by some of the quiet people of Skegness.'[21]

In 1878 there were 220,000 excursionists arriving in the town over the single line of railway, but getting them away again proved too much for the Great Northern Railway, with the last train not leaving until 2.30 am and '. . . many hundreds spending the night in waiting rooms or in the streets.'[22] Four years later, arrangements could not have improved greatly when the Chairman of the GNR took a philosophical view as he observed that

. . . Although we got the people to Skegness all right, we could not get them away like clockwork. Some people were rather later getting to bed than usual but it was a beautiful day and no doubt they all enjoyed themselves very much.[23]

After all, 'Skegness is so Bracing'.

The first time the now famous 'Jolly Fisherman' poster appeared was to advertise an excursion from King's Cross, London, to Skegness on Good Friday 1908, when the return fare was 3 shillings in corridor coaches and with a non-stop run of 162 miles.

Seventy-five years later, this event was marked by British Rail running an excursion from King's Cross to Skegness for only 15p, being the equivalent of the original 3 shilling fare. Passengers wearing period costume included a bunch of Edwardian girls in the charge of a nanny, and bathers in knee-length bathing suits.[24]

It would be interesting to trace the development of numerous resorts following the arrival of the railway, but that would be subject enough for an entire book. Some resorts were developed by the railway companies themselves who invested in hotels and other facilities, and Cleethorpes is an example of this.

The East Lincolnshire Railway reached Grimsby in 1848, and the Manchester, Sheffield & Lincolnshire Railway in 1852. Both brought thousands of excursionists who made their way from Grimsby station to Cleethorpes by horse-bus or on foot. On 19 June 1850, for example, 5,000 people were on the sands, in the pleasure grounds or disporting themselves in the sea. By 1852 there were 32 bathing machines and Claude Duvali performed on an elevated rope from the highest point of the cliff to a pole fixed in the mud. There were also Ellis's Splendid Bazaar and Fancy Goods, Canty's Royal Bazaar and The Very Noah's Ark of a Toy Shop, 'selling off daily at a reduction of 20%'.

In 1863 the MS&LR extended a single line of railway from Grimsby to Cleethorpes with the immediate effect of multiplying the number of trippers ten-fold on the first August Bank Holiday. Every Victorian seaside resort was expected to have a pier, and Cleethorpes got one in 1872, to which 37,000 visitors were admitted in the first five weeks.

The MS&LR doubled its line in 1874, so increasing the pressure on the resort's amenities. A shortage of bathing vans in 1881 caused the local Board concern for 'both sexes were bathing together, not by the dozen, but by the hundred, bathing entirely without gowns or covering'. This was considered to be offensive to people walking along the beach.[25]

In 1881 the MS&LR purchased 17 acres of foreshore for £1,670 and spent £33,000 on sea defences. The pier was leased from the Cleethorpes Pier Company in 1884 and bought outright in 1903. £10,000 was spent on a swimming pool, a colonade, a restaurant, gardens, lighting, a photographic studio, refreshment rooms and stalls for hire. A new pavilion was erected on the pier, and in 1892 the railway bought the remaining 33 acres of foreshore.

Edwardian crowds leaving an excursion train at Cleethorpes. Great Central Railway six-wheeled coaches are much in evidence, and the Class '9' 0-6-0, built in 1899, still has a well-filled tender at the end of its journey.

The 'prom', pier and sand were only a step from the Great Central Railway's Cleethorpes station.

Altogether the MS&LR Company invested over £100,000 in Cleethorpes, and this proved to be one of its few profitable investments. Cleethorpes's population increased by 50% between 1851 and 1861; 40%, 1861-1870; 60%, 1871-1880; and 50%, 1881-1890.

The *Grimsby Observer* observed, regarding the improvements made by the company,

> . . . a smiling garden artistically laid out with due regard to the natural undulation of the ground, and planted with shrubs and flowers . . . The jagged and dangerous edge of the cliff has given place to grassy slopes with rustic and picturesque paths down to the lower grounds and promenade.

'Surpassing Blackpool' was the *Grimsby News*'s opinion:

> . . . A sea wall and promenade like that at Cleethorpes set down at Blackpool would set the Lancashire people half wild with delight.

Blackpool nonetheless must have continued to set 'Brummagem' people wild with delight, for they performed great feats of endurance to reach that Mecca of entertainment. August Bank Holiday 1925, at Birmingham's New Street station, took railway officials by surprise as thousands thronged the station from midnight onwards, desperate to join the overcrowded excursion trains:

> . . . The train had to be sent on as it came in. Fortunately there was a relief

An Edwardian holiday crowd on the beach at Blackpool. On August Bank Holiday 1910, the two main stations handled 207 incoming and 216 outgoing trains. Some 195,000 passengers passed through the ticket barriers. (*Lancashire Library*)

but Birmingham people having been seated or standed [sic] – for there were not seats for all – then there came the problem of providing for those waiting to join further on at the Black Country stations . . . A further fresh train was added for those beyond . . . One man who had crushed in was perturbed at finding a portion of his lounge coat caught in the door. His signal of distress brought a railway official to the rescue but when the door was opened great difficulty was occasioned in closing it again as there were 17 or 18 people in the compartment . . . so bent were some trippers on not being left behind that, failing to enter the crowded compartments through the doors, they clambered in through the open windows adding further to the discomfort of the passengers in the already packed carriages.[26]

Getting to Blackpool sounds a bit of an ordeal, but the return journey prompted this complaint:

Arrived [Blackpool] Central station 3.45. Good going. Inspector shouts 'All return 1 o'clock Talbot Road station.' Now for a good time. Had a good time. Blackpool at its best. Arrived Talbot Road station 12.30 in good time for a seat. Stood in queue till 2.30 waiting for the 1 o'clock train to arrive. Fed up. Hooray! Here she comes . . . Train travelling at awful speed. Arrive at Crewe at 7.15. Porter says 'Stopping 10 minutes'. I think his watch had stopped . . . here we are at New Street again at 10.18 Sunday morning, a record run, 7 hours 23 minutes. GM.[27]

Things didn't get any better:

In view of the advertisement displayed inviting people to see the illumina- tions at Blackpool . . . last Saturday night's scenes were a disgrace to a civilised country . . . Our train was due out at 12.35 am so we formed up behind a queue in Queen Street about 11.30 pm . . . We stayed in the queue until 2.30 am before being allowed to enter the station. There were women and children standing three and four hours in the pouring rain, in a dismal street, soaked to the skin, and when the gates were opened there was an ugly rush to enter . . . ADSUM[28]

The LNER was no better than the LMSR in exercising customer care for the excursionists, as this complaint shows:

In June 1937 I travelled to Liverpool and back on a day excursion from Lincoln, advertised by 'Pullman' carriages. The train consisted of about ten coaches of old NER six-wheel non-corridor stock, with a toilet compartment at one end and a luggage space at the other. A table ran the length down the centre. The two seats were lengthwise, backs to the windows; they were of wooden slatted construction without cushions . . . The outward journey was bad enough, but the return in the dark! We departed Liverpool Central at 10.30 pm and arrived Lincoln 5.30 am . . . Lighting comprised gas lamps of such low illumination it was impossible to read . . .[29]

A chapter on what it was like to go out for the day on a railway excursion cannot be concluded without sparing a thought for the 'mums' who had the task of organising the

'Shall we get a seat?' These Blackpool excursionists look far from happy! Perhaps they have queued for several hours before getting on to the platform and now – there's no train. *(Lancashire Record Office)*

commissariat for the whole family's survival on the trip. Those bulging bags and heavily laden baskets represented many hours of preparation, but that was not the end of her responsibility for, throughout the day, 'mum' would remain in charge of the refreshments. Although not the age of convenience foods, excursionists were not overlooked by the manufacturers of Bovril, the beef extract recommended for sandwich fillings, with advertisements on station hoardings advising:

NO SUMMER EXCURSIONS WITHOUT BOVRIL

THE DAY TRIPS ALONG MERRILY ON BOVRIL SANDWICHES

Chapter 4
THE RAILWAY CHILDREN

'The children were already marshalled on the platform and every grimy face was bubbling over with excitement and fullest expectation of a good time to come . . .'

In the lives of many Victorian, Edwardian and even Georgian children their most memorable day was the annual trip to the seaside or the country. With widespread poverty among both the unemployed and the employed, there was ample scope for office holders and office seekers, Parliamentary Members and candidates, to solicit support by providing an annual treat for the children of their low-paid and ill-housed constituents. Then there were the philanthropically minded, whose motives might be questioned, but whose efforts undoubtedly gave some enjoyment, at least on one day of the year, to thousands of children whose lives were very hard and dreary.

Ten thousand people assembled at Norwich Thorpe station on 30 June 1846 to witness the return of 6,000 excursionists conveyed in two special trains to Great Yarmouth and back. Hundreds of Nonconformist Sunday School children were carried at 3d each return, whilst adults paid 1 shilling.[1]

The Deeside Railway provided the link to Ballater, the station for Queen Victoria's Balmoral Castle. Victoria ruled over the greatest empire the world had ever known, yet only a few miles down the line were children dependent upon charity, not only for a yearly picnic, but for their very existence. In July 1860, the railway company agreed to the request of the 'Superintendent of the City Poor's house' for a gratis trip from Aberdeen to Aboyne and back in favour of the children attending the school.[2]

Many of the children of the Scottish capital were also dependent upon the benevolence of the railway companies for a very short annual trip. In September 1849 the children of the Cannongate Charity Workhouse were

> . . . through the liberality of Eagle Henderson Esq and the other Directors of the North British Railway Company, conveyed along the line to Dalhousie Station (9 miles) free of charge. Also, through the liberality of a gentleman connected with the Cannongate, they were plentifully regaled with an excellent dinner, of which they partook within an enclosure in the neighbourhood of Newbattle Abbey.[3]

In the same year that the North British Railway reached Berwick, a train of ten 3rd class and two 1st class carriages took 180 boys together with their teachers from Heriot's Hospital, Edinburgh, on a 'Pleasure Excursion' to Berwick. The train

> . . . reached Dunbar a few minutes past 10. The boys marched down the High

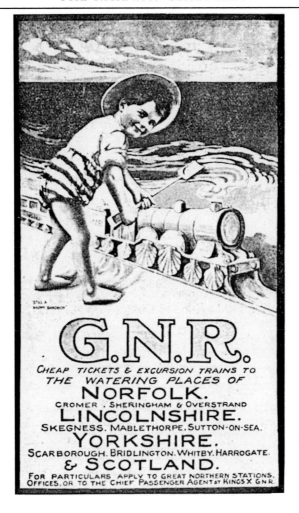

For children, a day excursion promised the seaside, sand castles and paddling.

Street and round the remarkable harbour of Dunbar; and the number and fine appearance of the boys excited much attention among the townsfolk. On returning to the station the party found that a less powerful engine had been substituted for that which had taken them thus far, and with it they could not proceed beyond Cockburnspath. Whilst waiting there for about an hour for the arrival of an engine sufficiently strong to proceed up the high ground, the boys were regaled with bread and beer ... The party arrived at Berwick about two, and proceeded to view the town and its ancient walls. The visitors excited a great sensation among the inhabitants and were everywhere followed by a large and admiring crowd. They marched round the walls and across the beautiful bridge to Tweedmouth, where, being firmly on English ground, the boys gave three such cheers as brought the whole population of the village to their doors and windows, and all along the way to Spittal great crowds followed and cheered the interesting procession. The two small ferry steamers carried the party over the river from Spittal to Berwick, where they all dined together upon the grass in a small park ... and after some songs in full chorus from the boys, the party returned to the station, and set out for Edinburgh a little before 8. Not the slightest accident occurred to mar the pleasurable effect of the excursion, and the weather was beautiful throughout.[4]

For sheer scale of operations, the Pearson Fresh Air Fund (FAF) must take the prize. Sir Arthur Pearson, a newspaper proprietor, published *Pearson's Weekly*, a one penny magazine offering mainly puzzles and educational features, but with an immense circulation. In 1892 the FAF was launched, appealing to individuals, groups, societies, offices and firms to raise and donate to a fund to be used to provide at least a day in the country or at the seaside for the poor children of the industrial towns and ports. For a lucky few, a two-week holiday was arranged.

Such was the public response that in the first year 20,000 children were given a day in the fresh air of the country. The Nimrod Cycle Company offered a cycle as a prize to the person collecting the highest sum for the FAF; concerts, football matches and art shows all helped to swell the fund. One novel idea for raising money from the skaters at the Denmark Hill rink was to have two gigantic FAF collecting boxes on skates. 'The motive power of these boxes will be charming young ladies who have kindly undertaken this role'.[5] London's 20,000 was doubled to 40,230 in 1893, and in 1894 the scheme was extended to other cities including Birmingham, Liverpool, Manchester, Glasgow and Hull. Another organisation, the Ragged School Union, became involved in the organisation of the FAF's mammoth excursions in several towns.

With our end-of-the-20th-century values, the sums required to provide a day out for a child a hundred years ago seem incredible:

> ... twopence halfpenny will supply each child with a substantial meat pie and threepence halfpenny more will pay for a sufficiency of bread, jam, cake and

Collection sheet for the Ragged Schools Children's Outing Fund. (*The Shaftesbury Society*)

milk ... Each child's railway fare costs 3d. Ninepence pays for a day's happiness for a child; £8.2s pays for a complete party of 200.[6]

Let the *Pearson's Weekly* reporter describe the scene at Burdett Road station (London) when 400 children were conveyed from the Whitechapel area to Epping Forest in 1892:

> ... The children were already marshalled on the platform and every grimy face was bubbling over with excitement and fullest expectation of a good time to come ... They cheered the long suffering railway officials, they cheered the passing trains, they chaffed their fellow passengers. I was surprised at the comparatively large number of children who were provided with hats and boots – sole-less and heel-less may be, certainly for the most part, but still boots.
>
> 'Surely,' I said to Mr Varney of the Ragged School Union who was in charge of the merry crew, 'surely these are not such very poor children after all?'
>
> 'Indeed they are,' he answered smiling, 'but the clothes that you see on them . . . are for the most part borrowed . . . the whole neighbourhood has been ransacked for boots and hats and dresses . . . All the inhabitants of the surrounding streets have lent what they could . . . some will even take an old hat or an old coat out of pawn ... to lend to a neighbour's child.'
>
> At this point a cheer broke out from the eager ranks of the little ones as the special train hove in sight. They literally threw themselves upon the carriage doors . . . they vaulted over the seats or scrambled underneath them and of their own free will, parked themselves like sardines in a box, instead of distributing themselves more evenly over the length of the train. Those who could not find room for their heads outside the window made up for the loss by singing the most extraordinary collection of street ditties, music hall songs and hymns it has ever been my lot to hear. Half way down a big crow was espied sitting on a telegraph post – some said it was a chicken, others were equally sure it was a blackbird or a big starling.
>
> At twelve o'clock dinner was ready and the hungry little mortals were ranged at long wooden tables in the shelter . . . and the kind donors could want no better thanks than to watch how speedily the huge meat pies and other good things were demolished ...
>
> It was late in the evening and not until an ample tea had been disposed of and many a slice of bread and butter stowed away for future reference or for some starving friend at home that the note of the whistle warned the little ones that it was time to be getting back . . . [7]

The Pearson's FAF outing to the Clyne Valley conveyed 2,000 children over the Swansea & Mumbles Railway:

> As was expected there was no difficulty in getting the children to the Rutland Street [Mumbles Railway] Station by 9.50 when they were supposed to start. There was no fear of any of the invited oversleeping on Wednesday morning and it would not be far wrong in stating that seldom do they show any anxiety to get up so early as they did. They were down at the Mumbles Railway Station in Rutland Street, hundreds of them, fully an hour before the time of starting. As many as five hundred boarded the 9.10 train – forty minutes

The Pearson's Fresh Air Fund outing on the Swansea & Mumbles Railway. Note the 'cattle trucks' and the lad on the front of the engine to warn the driver of danger on the line. (*Swansea City Council*)

before their proper time – and to try and persuade them to wait was clean out of the question. That was how the first lot went! Shortly after half past nine there were 1,000 more at the terminus in charge of the officials and helpers and the road was rendered well nigh impassable. The little ones were buzzing all over with excitement. Many came there without tickets and were told by the committee men that all the tickets had gone, they even approached the press men and asked if they had any to spare.

Quarter to ten saw the Mumbles train coming in, and attached to it ten long open carriages. As soon as these were espied there was a tremendous rush. The boys and girls jumped over seats in an excited fashion, irrespective of the proper footways, in order to be at the side of the carriage! ... a long piece of linen with the words 'Pearson's Fresh Air Outing' in big black type was nailed to one of the carriages, the guard's whistle was sounded and to the accompaniment of the children's loud cheering the train steamed slowly away.

Once in the Clyne Valley they were delighted, and still more were they at 12 o'clock when the bugle was sounded for them to assemble under the respective numbers for dinner. This was perhaps the most important item with a good many of those who had not seen anything perhaps that morning. Ten minutes later there was another bugle call and this meant COMMENCE GIVING OUT PIES AND DRINK. This was the special dinner of the day! There is no need to comment on the appetites of the little ones.

A windowful of fun on Reckitt's 'Sunshine Outing' in 1926.

After lunch the helpers of each section received a parcel of toys, etc for distribution among the children in races, cake walks, etc. Tea was served at 4 o'clock, followed by a distribution of cake and sweets.[8]

Many bankers and industrialists were Quakers (Society of Friends) or non-conformists, such as the Cadburys, Rowntrees, Frys, Colmans and Reckitts, and in furtherance of their philanthropic ideals, arranged outings for poor children. At Hull, Reckitt's 'Sunshine Outing' each year took children by train to the countryside a few miles distant. In 1921 1,400 children and 110 adults were taken by train from Southcoates station to Beverley, and to ensure prompt departure they were lined up under the letters A to X, after which they were checked off by two railway officials and one of Reckitt's. As the children passed through the station gate at Beverley each was handed a small envelope containing 3d in copper.[9]

The Sunday School outing was, for most children, their only outing of the year; eagerly awaited, long remembered. It was the railways which opened up new horizons for the organisers, whilst for the children a ride on a train was an occasion for great excitement, as was their first encounter with the sea and sand, which the railways made possible for many land-locked city-dwellers. Whether such traffic was profitable for the railway companies is debatable, but perhaps Sunday School excursions were regarded as 'loss leaders', keeping in mind the fact that many a prominent non-conformist was equally influential as millowner or manufacturer and thus potential railway customer.

In 1900, the Rhondda & Swansea Bay Railway conveyed 500 Llantwit Lower School Board children to the sea at Jersey Marine, and *The Cambrian* emphasised that 'Mr Law bore the whole cost of the transit . . . also of the very excellent tea . . . for which there was (sic) no less than ten distinct varieties of cake.' No wonder the 'little ones' raised 'thrilling cheers for Mr and Mrs Law'.[10]

Twenty-seven years after the railway first reached Bournemouth, opposition to excursion trains had withered and that select town was itself the starting point for many excursion trains, including Sunday School trips. In 1897 the *Bournemouth Visitor's Directory*[11] reported that the children of the McGill Memorial Sunday School had marched from the hall to the East Station where they were joined by the St Andrews Presbyterian School and conveyed by special train to Brockenhurst. Cricket, tea and racing, 'for which most received a prize', made their day, whilst the Richmond Hill Congregational Sunday School outing by train to Brockenhurst took the children on to Balmer Lawn where they participated in 'whistling and singing contests'. St Stephens Church Choir outing, no doubt with more funds available, travelled as far as Glastonbury and Wells, which must have been a delightful journey along the Somerset & Dorset Railway, passing pretty country stations with fascinating names such as Shillingstone, Sturminster Newton and Evercreech Junction.

Those Preston Sunday School teachers of 1842 were certainly quick off the mark in requesting a special train and reduced fare for their children (see Chapter 2), but the Penwortham, Lancs, teachers managed to arrange an excursion even before the new West Lancashire Railway was officially opened.

> The Teachers' Trip employed, this year, the first railway train that ever took up passengers in the Township of Penwortham. Through the kindness of the contractors, Messrs Braddock & Matthews, and of the West Lancashire Railway Company, the train was brought up to Back Lane, and there and at New Longton embarked rather more than 162 passengers, that being the number of tickets issued – many of which, however, admitted 2 children. The day was very fine, and greatly enjoyed, and both the Company and the Contractors did everything possible for the convenience and safety of the travellers.[12]

St Pauls Sunday School, Peterborough, organised an excursion for 500 to Edenham in 1870[13], and this was the only Great Northern Railway train ever recorded as traversing this line, privately owned by Lord Willoughby de Eresby, to connect his village with the main line at Bytham.

Crewe was a railway town created by the London & North Western Railway which provided the houses, the schools, the hospital, the churches, the water supply, the sewer, and eventually, a park. Church leaders prayed not to God but to the directors of the LNWR when they wished to organise a rail trip for the children. This petition of 1861 leaves no doubt but that all denominations were humbled in the same degree before the all-powerful railway gods of Euston Square:

Girls from Muller's orphanage, Bristol, at Ashley Down station, GWR, ready for an excursion to Weston-super-Mare, *circa* 1912. (*H. Bowden*)

To the Chairman and Honourable Board of
Directors of the London and North Western
Railway Company

> The Memorial of Ministers of Various
> Churches and Superintendants of Schools
> established in Crewe

Sheweth that your Memorialists bear in grateful rememberance past favours received from the Honourable Board of Directors by granting the annual trip to the Children and Teachers of these Schools.

That your Memorialists pray that the Honourable Board of Directors will be pleased again to shew their favour to these Schools by granting to the Children and Teachers a trip for the present Season.

That as a fitting time of the year is of much importance for the Children's recreation and enjoyment your Memorialists beg to intimate that they consider the most suitable time would be on the <u>earliest day convenient after midsummer.</u>

Signed by the Ministers and Priests of
> Coppenhall Parochial School
> Weslyan School
> Presbyterian School
> Congregational School
> Primitive Methodist School
> Baptist School
> Free Church School
> Catholic School

Total Children 1,377   Total Teachers 191

When it came to non-railway owned towns and their churches, the boot was on the other foot, for the LNWR wooed Sunday Schools with a glossy 32-page booklet containing photographs of desirable destinations in Hertfordshire and Buckinghamshire.[14] This included a list of caterers and sample menus, such as that of Grays of Bricket Wood offering:

Children's Tea
Bread & Butter, Currant & Seed Cake,
Watercress & Good Tea   6d

Children's Dinner
Meat, Bread, Custard Pudding, Lemonade   6d

Pie or Sandwich, Jam Tart, Lemonade   3d

Bath Bun & Lemonade   2d

Meat Teas
Ham & Beef, Milk Rolls, Preserves, Best Genoa,
Madeira, Cherry & Seed Cake, Watercress or Lettuce,
Bread & Butter, Tea   1s 3d

Mothers Meeting Tea
One Plate of Meat, Bread & Butter, Cake,
Tea, Watercress   1s 0d

In 1901 the Blackburn Road Sunday School left Bolton by special train for a visit to Port Sunlight, a journey taking 2 hours. On arrival at Bebington station, a procession was formed which wound its way to the Gladstone Hall where Mr Lever, owner of the soapworks, welcomed his visitors as they enjoyed the refreshments provided. After a tour of the works there was a cricket match between the visitors and a Port Sunlight Sunday

The Sunday School outing from Tollesbury to Walton-on-the-Naze in 1934 was conveyed in ex-GER six-wheeled coaches.

An excursion train for the children from the Woking Orphanage of the London & South Western Railway in the 1920s.

School team. Tea followed, and then a procession back to the station. Several of the visitors were so favourably impressed by Port Sunlight village that they 'never wished to leave it again, looking upon it as a foretaste of Paradise.'[15]

In 1857, the Great Western Railway held its annual fete at Nuneham Park, near Oxford, for the benefit of the Widows' and Orphans' Fund. A special train ran from Paddington to Culham, the nearest station for Nuneham Park, picking up at Slough, Taplow, Reading and Didcot. Horse-drawn omnibuses ran from Culham station to the Park at a fare of threepence.

Some 20,000 people attended this fete and the special train from London was described as a 'monster train containing much of the beauty and elegance of the metropolis'.[16] An example of sex discrimination was the charging of lower fares for the ladies:

Inclusive ticket for Fete and travel

Ladies	1st	3s 6d	2nd	2s 6d
Gentlemen	1st	5s 0d	2nd	4s 0d[17]

Thankfully, although over 5,000 people crowded on to Culham station for the return train, the *Reading Mercury* reported that 'not the slightest accident occurred'.

Railwaymen are usually ignored by the media, unless they are involved in an industrial dispute, but their trade unions have a long tradition of caring for railway orphans. For many years passengers on trains from Waterloo to Bournemouth passed, at Woking, an imposing brick building bearing the inscription 'THE SOUTHERN RAILWAY SERVANTS HOME SUPPORTED BY VOLUNTARY CONTRIBUTIONS'. Railway excursions have been one of the means, in addition to railwaymen's contributions, by which this home has been supported since it was opened in 1909 by the Duchess of Woking. 1886 was the year in which the first railway excursion was organised to raise funds to maintain premises situated in Clapham[18], when the committee member organising the event reported a loss of 3s 6d. Undaunted, further excursions were organised until 1895, when three trains were required, and a profit of £440 was made.

The drastically reduced number of railwaymen has had an adverse effect on the contributions to maintain this home, but the will to provide outings for the children continues, a typical example being an outing organised by the London Orphan Fund Committee of the National Union of Railwaymen to Weston-super-Mare. Each of the 216 children received £1 5s spending money and the 101 widows £1 each. Breakfast on the train was served by 40 volunteer staff and at Weston the party was met by the Mayor and Mayoress, an NUR reception committee, TV and press. A rosette worn by these excursionists gave them open sesame to many facilities in the town and on the return journey a four-course dinner was served.[19]

A great excursion for London school children, and a marvellous feat of organisation by the railway companies concerned, was the occasion when King George V entertained 100,000 at the Crystal Palace as part of the Coronation festivities in 1911, and for which 96 special trains were utilised, coming from all parts of London, and all handled within 4 hours.

This gathering called for an elaborate plan which involved the suspension or alteration of hundreds of scheduled trains and the closing of 21 stations to ordinary passengers. In this, as in the case of many similar events to which special trains are run, the problem for the railway officials is not only the arrangements for the passage, arrival and departure of the specials, but what to do with them while the excursionists are enjoying themselves. In this instance the main running lines for several miles were utilised for stabling coaches.

Crystal Palace was a terminus station, therefore each train, having disgorged its passengers, had to be reversed out before the next could be admitted, so expeditious

A day at the seaside was an annual event for London's East End children. In this picture hundreds of returning children form into groups at Liverpool Street station.

movement of the children off the platforms and into the Palace was critical. The average time for this exercise was 4-5 minutes, and a similar time for the departure of the return trains, when the importance of boarding the children on the correct train was paramount. This was facilitated by the boys wearing caps corresponding in colour to badges on the train by which they were to travel, whilst the girls' hats were draped with coloured scarves for the same purpose. All this colour 'gave the railway station and the Palace grounds the effect of a living flower garden.'[20]

After the suspension of excursion facilities for the duration of the First World War and its aftermath, Sunday Schools were eager to take advantage of the restored excursions in 1920. One of the first to do so was Carrow Sunday School, associated with the Colman company of Norwich. It was decided 'to mark the first real year of peace by having the summer party at Lowestoft . . . and very good arrangements were made by the Great Eastern Railway'. About 250 scholars travelled accompanied by Miss Colman and tea was served in the United Methodist Free Church.[21]

When a motor coach firm failed to turn up for the Retford Baptist Sunday School Outing in 1931, the organisers appealed to the Retford Stationmaster and, within 20 minutes, they were offered a rail trip to any LNER station. Leverton, the next station, was chosen, and extra carriages attached to the next scheduled train. The Stationmaster's enterprise turned threatened disappointment into a day of pleasure for the 100 children and 50 adults concerned.[22]

South Wales valleys, a stronghold of chapel folk, were the starting point for many a Sunday School outing, but one from Cwmaman in 1932 achieved a double first – the first uniting all the religions of the town and the first through passenger train from Cwmaman to Porthcawl since the line opened 60 years earlier.

Via the Viaducts
A Red Letter Day at Cwmaman

Dreams and visions of long ago were realised on Saturday last when the first through passenger train ran from Cwmaman Colliery Halt Terminus direct to its destination – Porthcawl. Scenes of 'unparalleled excitement' were witnessed.

It is interesting to note that the railway line was laid over 60 years ago by the Great Western Railway Company and was utilised for mineral and goods traffic only . . .

Recently the local Sunday School Union conceived the idea of a united seaside trip and steps were taken to resusitate the idea of a through passenger train from Cwmaman to Porthcawl. Undoubtedly the idea commended itself to the GWR authorities and after negotiations it became a realised fact. So great was the interest taken in the proposed excursion that it assumed unexpected proportions which necessitated two trains. The first left Cwmaman about 7.20 am and picked up various contingents at the Crossing and Cwmneol Halts and then ran direct through to Porthcawl. The second train left about 8.30 am and picked up passengers at all the halts including Tonllwyd where a strong quota of the Hebron Sunday School joined . . . At each vantage point en route hundreds of sightseers cheered the trains. This was particularly so at the viaducts where a number of cameras were busy and at Trecynon. Both journeys were accomplished without any mishap of any kind. The scenes upon the return of the trains were memorable and the excitement was intense. It is hoped that this is only the forerunner of many similar events, and that Cwmaman will find its place on the railway map again.[23]

Some of a large party of children excursionists on an educational visit to Hull docks in 1934.

No doubt C. J. Allen, the renowned author of railway books, appreciated the value of impressing the sons of the influential for which the London & North Eastern Railway were prepared to pull out all the stops in 1938. Members of the Crusaders' Union, of which Allen was a supporter, numbering 670 from public and private schools, were conveyed by special train from Sleaford, Lincs, to King's Cross, after a visit to RAF Cranwell. Here, they saw a Hurricane plane flying at 350 mph, but it was on their return journey that the LNER officials performed 'a remarkable feat of exact timing'. Not only was the Class 'A4' locomotive, *Sir Nigel Gresley*, rostered to haul the boys' special, but their train was slowed on the Barkston curve to act as a mobile grandstand from which the Crusaders could watch the 'Coronation' train speed by at 90 mph, 'the fastest train in the British Empire'.[24]

Educational visits became a feature of railway excursions in the inter-war years, the GWR alone carrying over 20,000 passengers on these trains in 1928, whilst the Southern Railway, in 1935, took 20,000 children in 45 special trains for a tour of Southampton docks and inspection of an ocean liner, followed by tea served on the return journey.

The GWR's Swindon Works was the destination for many educational excursions, and highly organised they were, with apprentice engineers acting as guides and the visitors' route through the works marked by white arrows on the floor.

> By far the most amusing of visitors are school-children, who, in huge parties, come from all parts of the country. Every conceivable combination of school colours and all manner of badges have been seen at Swindon works, sported on caps and hat-bands of these children. 'Where d'ye come from?' comes the kindly enquiry from the workmen, and their little trebles will pipe up with

eagerness to advertise their particular town or shire. The school children always have their satchels, not for books, but to carry the day's fuel for their sturdy young frames. It is thirst, however, which seems to assail them more than hunger, for just inside the gates at Shepherd Street is a water-tap, and this they surround like flies, drinking to capacity and then filling the bottles which they produce from their satchels.[25]

Not really an excursion, nevertheless an enjoyable experience for children visiting Maggs' Store, Bristol, at Christmas 1938, was a realistic reproduction of a GWR engine cab in which they stood before the glowing firebox as the scenery rushed past the cab side! At Morley's Stores, Brixton, there was a full-size GWR coach converted into a cinema in which 2,000 children daily went on a journey either to the North Pole or to 'Cornwall – the Western Land'.[26] Before the next year was out Britain was at war, and many of those children would be travelling on real trains, not to the North Pole but on evacuation trains to the safety of the rural areas, some in 'the Western Land'.

War ended in 1945 but not the austerity, which continued for several more years, although the GWR attempted to give children a glimpse of the brighter future to come by organising 'The Kiddies Express'. The GWR Magazine told its readers:

> Laughter, music and cheering echoed under the vaulted roof of Paddington station on a sunny mid-August morning, telling of something memorable afoot. Clowns were cavorting among a crowd of dancing, singing, excited children; the air was filled with merriment and tense with glorious anticipation. No wonder; this half-hour was the prelude to an eagerly awaited day of marvels and a journey full of mysterious promise; this was the Kiddies Express.
>
> Sparing time from the more serious aspects of running a railway, the Great Western had decided, with the restoration of cheap day fares, to run the first post-war excursion from London for the benefit of the younger generation. Pleasure has been severely rationed for children during the last few years. Here was a chance to give them a preview of the delights to come as the world recovers its equilibrium again. The Great Western took that chance with both hands. With the enthusiastic co-operation of the Weston-super-Mare authorities, plans were laid for a day at that resort that would live in the memories of the young ones for many a month – perhaps for always . . .
>
> Great Western men and women in workshops and offices had worked hard for weeks on the many preparations necessary to ensure the success of the trip. The train – eleven vehicles plus a generator van – was agleam from its grooming, and most artistically decorated. The leading and rear vans had been transformed into charming miniature theatres, complete with raised and lighted stages. A buffet car was provided to serve ices, minerals, sandwiches and other good things to delight the children's eyes and tummies. Puzzles were handed around to the older children – although how they found time to solve these, with all the counter attractions, was in itself a puzzle . . .
>
> A covey of ardent young engine fans had to be dragged away from their adoring inspection of the massive 'County of Somerset', as she stood waiting to haul her youthful cargo to her own home county. Doors slammed, a few latecomers made thrilling sprints to join their friends, the whistle shrilled again, and the Kiddies Express glided out into the open sunshine.
>
> It was difficult to decide just what to do next, and which show to see – the

musical clowns in the front of the train, or the magician and accordianist at the rear? A glance at the programme brought a solution; there would be three performances before arriving at Weston-super-Mare, and therefore time to see both shows. In the front coach the clowns had already persuaded their audience to sing – and how they sang! Those who couldn't remember all the words tra-la-la'd with gusto . . .

[On arrival] came fresh excitement. Standing in the sunshine, a band of girl pipers skirled a welcome to Weston. A donkey carriage fashioned to resemble a locomotive drew alongside the real engine. As the kiddies scrambled out of the train, they found, instead of a taxi rank, a fleet of donkey carts to parade them through the holiday town.[27]

Railway excursionists in the past, particularly in the early days, may have broken endurance records but never speed records! Yet the Variety Club of Great Britain's children's charity trip to Brighton did just that in 1983, when it ran from London Bridge in 41 minutes 33 seconds at an average speed of 73.6 mph and touching 92 mph at times.[28]

Matthew Honicombe, living in the village of St Cleer, near Liskeard, Cornwall, in the 17th century, would have been astonished if told that 300 years later a special railway train (a what?) would convey 160 of his children's children's children, and so on, from Paddington to his village on the occasion of one of his descendent's 48th birthday. After 20 years' research, Gordon Honeycombe, broadcaster and author, had traced 350 of Matthew's descendents scattered around the world. The 'Honeycombe Special' was his idea of enabling his relatives to explore their Cornish roots. Grown-up children they may have been, but still Matthew's children![29]

An Excursion Agent for the South Staffordshire Railway, in 1849, outlined the attractions for a children's trip to Lichfield and promised that 'After viewing the Cathedral, the children will be taken to Barrow Cope Hill where tradition asserts the three Kings were slain for refreshment and amusement.'[30]

Moreton Hall School, Oswestry, organised a trip to York for 650 pupils and teachers from local schools on 28 June 1983. A group poses on Gobowen station as the Class '47'-hauled train arrives.

Chapter 5
OFF TO THE RACES

'Every six minutes between the hour of 7 am and 11 am on Friday March 28th, a special train left some point on the LMSR for Aintree and the Grand National.'

Until the spread of the rail network, horse-racing, if not solely the Sport of Kings, had been largely the sport of those wealthy enough to own horses and to race them. Both James I and Charles II are credited with helping to start horse racing at Newmarket.[1] Racecourses, usually on common land, were unenclosed, and entries both of horses and spectators were, by later standards, comparatively local. Railways transformed racing into a spectator event of national proportions, a gold-mine for horse-breeders, trainers, bookmakers and caterers, as well as a lucrative source of traffic for the railways themselves. Special vehicles, horseboxes, were constructed to convey the entries from stable to course, and from course to course. Even special racecourse stations, used only for meetings, were provided, but most important for the turnstile takings were the race specials conveying thousands of racegoers, 1st class for the well-to-do, 3rd class for the rest, including tipsters, tick-tack men and card sharpers. The working classes could find neither the time nor the money to travel far to meetings.

The elitist racing fraternity did not always welcome the intrusion of their inferiors made possible by the railways, so much so that the Jockey Club sought to thwart the excursionists to Newmarket by running different races at widely separated venues, thus ensuring that only those spectators on horseback could move from race to race.[2]

Nevertheless local meetings became national events, the railways transported the horses and delivered the daily newspapers upon which the punters relied for their betting intelligence. Newspapers and sporting papers from the mid-19th century onwards carried half a column and more of advertisements for race special trains. 'On the slightest provocation railway companies placard half London with lists of cheap trains to any country place where races are to be held,' it was said.[3]

This mushrooming spectator and betting interest in racing stimulated the profit-making instincts of the race meeting organisers, so up went the railings around the courses and in went the turnstiles – the first enclosed park course was Sandown in 1875. Between the mid-1870s and mid-1890s, £1.5 million was invested in courses and grandstands. This transforming of horse-racing from a local to a national sport resulted in a reduction in the number of courses from 130 in 1874 to only 65 in 1884, and these were all served by one or more railways, often with a special racecourse platform as at Cheltenham, Goodwood, Aintree, etc.

Undoubtedly the first railway race special was run by the Liverpool & Manchester Railway to Newton-le-Willows for Newton races on 1-3 June 1831, and for which 26 cotton wagons were fitted for temporary use as 2nd class carriages.[4] Anticipating trouble, the company requested extra constables to assist the railway police at Sankey Viaduct, but this was refused by the Mayor. These first race excursions must have been well patronised because more were run in connection with Liverpool Race Week in the following July.

In 1838 the London & Southampton Railway advertised in *The Times* trains from Nine Elms station, London, to Kingston for the Derby. To the astonishment of the station officials, 5,000 intending passengers descended on the station in the early morning, but although several trains were got away, the crowd increased in size faster than the trains could carry them. The booking office doors were broken down by the crowd, who took possession of a private party special train, causing the police to be summoned. All trains after midday were cancelled.[5]

Returning from Ascot races in 1839, an excursion train stopped in Slough station and, the train being full, waiting passengers climbed on to the carriage roofs, refusing to come down. A railway official, in turn, refused to start the train until the roof-top passengers came down, so causing a half-hour's delay. The railway official was commended by the Secretary of the Great Western Railway.[6]

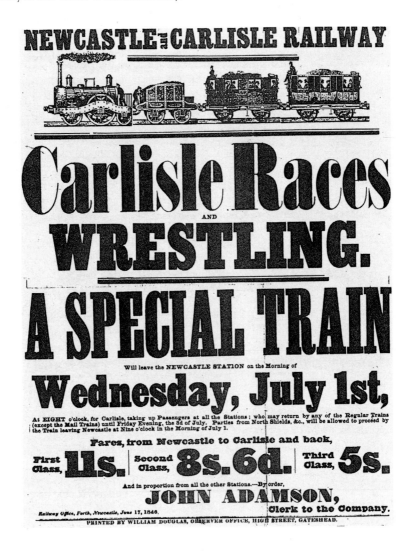

Advertisements in Scottish newspapers are evidence that early race specials were not run for the lower classes:

GRAND STEEPLECHASES AT KILMARNOCK
THURSDAY 12th MARCH 1846

The Glasgow and Ayrshire Railway will send an EXPRESS train of 1st and 2nd Class carriages from Glasgow to Kilmarnock at a quarter past nine, morning, returning from Kilmarnock at a quarter past ten the same Evening.

Calling only at Paisley and Beith stations. To ensure ample accommodation for horses going down, early indication should be given to the Agent at Glasgow Station.[7]

A special train from Newcastle to Carlisle for the Races in 1846 would not have conveyed many, if any, working people at a 3rd class fare of 5 shillings. In addition to the Newcastle & Carlisle, the Maryport & Carlisle and the Lancaster & Carlisle railways poured in excursionists.

. . . We never saw the race course so densely crowded as on Thursday; it presented a thick mass of people, who had availed themselves of the facilities of travelling afforded by the railways to pass a few hours of recreation in our merrie city . . . The wrestling, which is generally the most attractive sport at our races, drawing together immense numbers of visitors and a rich field of competitors, was this year brought out with much spirit.[8]

There is no record of when country gentry and farmers took up racing their horses around the church steeples of surrounding villages but there has been racing at Epsom for over 300 years. Queen Anne (1702-14) decreed that there should be horse-racing in the Royal Park at Ascot, whilst the Racing Register dates from 1709.[9] Aintree's course was not laid out until 1820 by the second Earl of Sefton in collaboration with a hotel keeper, William Lynn, and the first Grand National took place in 1837.[10]

In Victorian and Edwardian times, more people could have told you the date of the Grand National Steeplechase at Aintree, Liverpool, than that of Empire Day or the Monarch's birthday, whilst those who normally didn't bet on horses would have a sixpence each way flutter on one of the 'certs'. The vast majority of these punters never got within 100 miles of Aintree, but thousands did, probably a quarter of a million at the turn of the century, and most of them by train, even over the short run from Liverpool and its suburbs.

Aintree's first station opened in 1849 on the East Lancashire Railway's line to Preston, ten years later to become the Lancashire & Yorkshire Railway and, in 1922, part of the London & North Western Railway. Twenty years elapsed before the second Aintree station was opened at the end of the Cheshire Lines Committee's extension from Hunt's Cross, but both these stations were some distance from the course, and with limited facilities for handling the ever-increasing volume of race traffic, both horses and racegoers. Because of this an Aintree Racecourse station was opened on a normally goods-only line connecting the north Liverpool rail complex with the L&YR's main line to Manchester.

Over the years, and from all over the kingdom, special trains have poured their crowds into Aintree, and the figures for 1913 tell the story most vividly. Between 11 am and 2 pm, a train arriving and disgorging its passengers every 2 minutes, 91 trains plus the shuttle service of electric trains on the Liverpool Overhead Railway altogether poured

A Lancashire & Yorkshire Railway electric train to Maghull deposits racegoers at Aintree, Sefton Arms, in 1922.

34,000 people on to the racecourse. Race specials arrived from Manchester, Chester, Stockport, Cleethorpes, Sheffield, Leeds, Barnsley, Derby, Burton, Birmingham, Bristol, Leicester, Nottingham and, of course, London.[11] Some trains conveyed ardent racegoers directly from the meeting at Lincoln to the Grand National, but obviously they were not from the classes who would be worried about getting time off from work.

Most of these race specials catered for all classes, from the top crust Members of the National Hunt with their all-Pullman special from London given priority along the line, to the local 'Scousers' arriving by the 'Dockers' Umbrella', the Liverpool Overhead Railway.

As Shakespeare wrote, 'They have their exits and their entrances'[12], and from the Aintree racecourse platform 1st and 3rd class passengers were directed to separate exits, and for departure the trains drew up with 1st and 3rd class carriages opposite the appropriate entrances.

Grand National day saw locomotives and trains from several railway companies at the Cheshire Lines Committee and Lancashire & Yorkshire stations, including the London & North Western, Midland and Great Central. Even the Great Western Railway conned racegoers into believing they were being taken to Liverpool when in fact they were deposited at Birkenhead, on the wrong side of the Mersey.

Just before war put a stop to it all in 1914, the railways were utilising all the coaching stock they could find for the Aintree specials, and that included not only the old six-wheeled coaches sandwiched between two electric motor cars on the L&YR local services, but 1st class saloons and dining cars on the main-line trains. Of the 77 specials over the CLC, 11 had dining cars, and the trains were so heavy that two engines were required. A LNWR 1st class special from Euston included six 12-wheeled dining cars and kitchen cars from which luncheon, tea and dinner were served to 1st class racegoers at 64 shillings a head, including the rail fare. For those on 3rd class trains, the combined fare,

GRAND NATIONAL
SATURDAY, 26th, MARCH, 1955.
TRAVEL BY
OVERHEAD RAILWAY
WITHOUT CHANGING
DIRECT TO AINTREE RACECOURSE

		a.m.	a.m.	p.m.	p.m.	p.m.	p.m.	p.m.	p.m.	p.m.
DINGLE	dep.	11 25	11 40	12 25	12 35	1 5	1 14	1 23	1 37	1 54
JAMES STREET	"	11 35	11 50	12 35	12 45	1 15	1 24	1 33	1 47	2 4
PIER HEAD	"	11 37	11 52	12 37	12 47	1 17	1 26	1 35	1 49	2 6
SEAFORTH SANDS	"	11 53	12 8	12 53	1 3	1 33	1 42	1 53	2 9	2 23
AINTREE (No. 3 Platform)	arr.	12 2	12 16	1 1	1 13	1 41	1 52	2 3	2 18	2 32

		p.m.	p.m.	p.m.	p.m.	p.m.	p.m.	p.m.
AINTREE	dep.	3 50	4 7	4 24	4 42	4 51	5 1	5 31
SEAFORTH SANDS	"	4 4	4 19	4 34	4 51	5 4	5 12	5 41
PIER HEAD	"	4 18	4 33	4 48	5 5	5 18	5 26	5 55
JAMES STREET	"	4 19	4 34	4 49	5 6	5 19	5 27	5 56
DINGLE	arr.	4 28	4 43	4 53	5 15	5 28	5 36	6 5

FARES from	Single	Return
DINGLE, HERCULANEUM, TOXTETH, BRUNSWICK, WAPPING and CANNING	1/-	2/-
JAMES STREET, PIER HEAD, CLARENCE, NELSON HUSKISSON, CANADA, BROCKLEBANK, and ALEXANDRA	9D	1/6
GLADSTONE, SEAFORTH SANDS	6D	1/-

The issuing of Through Tickets is subject to the conditions and regulations referred to in the Time Tables, Bills, and Notices of the respective Companies on whose Railways, Coaches or Steamboats they are available, and the holder, by accepting a Through Ticket agrees that the respective Companies are not to be liable for any loss or damage, injury, delay or detention caused or arising off their respective Railways Coaches or Steamboats. The Contract and liability of each Company are limited to its own Railway, Coaches or Steamboats.

Hargreaves Building,
5, Chapel Street, Liverpool, 3.
March, 1955.

H. MAXWELL ROSTRON,
General Manager & Engineer

including breakfast and dinner, was 21 shillings, or 16 shillings fare only. With skilled wages at around 40 shillings per week for the 'aristocracy of labour', comprising about 15 per cent, and with 50 per cent of the working class paid between 20 shillings and 25 shillings per week[13], they could not afford even the 3rd class fare and certainly not to lose a day's pay.

For thousands of folk on Merseyside, their participation in the Grand National was restricted to walking around the course on Jump Sunday before the meeting, and for this the trains of the Overhead Railway and the street tramcars were crowded.

That the railways transformed racing is confirmed by the following extract from *The World* in 1888, recording Doncaster Races:

Whatever may be the advantages of the 'special train' system, it has one decided drawback. It has altered the character of the assemblage at the morning sales in the paddock . . . The Fitzwilliam 'Yellow' enlivened the road; and the Earl . . . sat on the box seat of his well known omnibus, with a very white hat as usual tilted well over his eyes . . . there was a prodigious variety of vans and breaks (sic), mostly with four horses . . .[14]

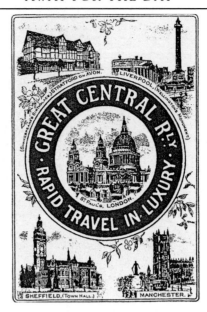

Racegoers by Great Central Railway excursions could purchase GCR playing cards, but it is doubtful if the places of interest pictured on the cards would appeal to them. *(C. Atkins)*

A few years afterwards the Doncaster meeting was described as

> . . . a Carnival of the Rail, because of the vast numbers of people who visit this most popular of North Country meetings at least five-sixths – not to put the figure too high – reach their destination by train. On Ledger Day, when the biggest crowds assembled on the Town Moor, between 50,000 and 60,000 excursionists are brought into Doncaster by rail and carried away again at night.[15]

Before Doncaster had a railway station, racegoers were reaching the races by alighting at Swinton station, some 10 miles distant, on the North Midland Railway opened in 1840, and from there the journey was completed by canal boat or road coach.[16] The St Ledger, named after its sponsor Colonel Anthony St Ledger in 1776, was placed on the railway map when the Great Northern Railway opened its Doncaster station in August 1848, and on St Ledger day, 3 September, six race specials comprising 243 carriages disgorged 8,000 passengers between 11 am and 1 pm.[17]

Two years later, the Great Northern Railway's main line was opened throughout to London, and a special express for the St Ledger was run from London, departing from the Great Eastern Railway's Bishopsgate station at 5.45 am and arriving at Doncaster at noon, after a 15-minute breakfast stop at Peterborough.[18] A pilot engine attached here had a 'green fire' resulting in serious loss of time to Boston, where the train's engines were replaced by two others considered not fit to work an express. At Lincoln, the station pilot engine scheduled to replace one of the failing engines had been sent away for shunting duties.[19]

An example of the ugly face of competition occurred in 1849 when the GNR

The Great Northern Railway's Doncaster station on St Ledger Day, 1849. (*Illustrated London News*)

attempted to run its race specials from Leeds over the metals of the Midland Railway as previously agreed. The latter company pulled up the rails at Methley Junction to prevent the passage of GNR trains.[20] The GNR's locomotives were designed for flat-racing, not steeplechasing, but eventually common sense prevailed and the rails were restored.

The *Illustrated London News* depicted the scene at Doncaster station with well-heeled racegoers on the platform and an accompanying column which read:

> . . . From far and near, as early as the dawn, groups of pleasure seekers – destined to find in profusion that which they sought – thronged the thoroughfares of Doncaster. London having breakfasted at home, was there by noon – reading its matutinal papers by the way. The town was astir with wholesome excitement . . . Thousands of holiday folk, bent on seeing 'T'Ledger' run, arrived by train after train with marvellous safety and despatch, until the human flood that poured into the town from all quarters was swelled into an immense extent. By 2 o'clock the principal points of the view on the course were densely occupied; and the stands and enclosures were crowded . . .[21]

So too, no doubt, were the beer tents, although it may come as a surprise to learn that a local shop sold 14 tons of butterscotch during the four days of racing.[22]

By 1867 the volume of race traffic was such as to compel the GNR to borrow coaches from several other companies, and a total of 70 excursion trains reached Doncaster, mostly GNR but including those of the North Eastern, Manchester, Sheffield & Lincolnshire, Lancashire & Yorkshire and Midland railways. This is how the *Doncaster Gazette* described the scene at Doncaster station:

No station was ever more unlike that of Mugby Junction. There is no dull, sleepy silence here. All day long huge trains come thundering in, with terrific clatter, snort and crash, belching forth fire and smoke, as if so many monsters had been let loose to carry fell destruction in their path instead of thousands of persons who are to be made gladsome or wretched by the result of a few minutes' race; and thousands of others who come for mere pleasure and to enjoy the great annual 'outing' in the company of their friends. Cabs dash at headlong speed in all directions.[23]

Unlike Aintree and Epsom, with three railway stations each, Doncaster had only one, and no racecourse platforms were ever installed, although the South Yorkshire Railway erected a platform in its goods sidings at Cherry Tree Lane for use by race specials. In the Great Northern sidings there were no platforms:

> ... sporting men have to scramble down from their carriages on to the naked track and they have also the task of finding their way back to these out of the way and improvised platforms at night.[24]

Here is a description of how this traffic was dealt with in 1887:

> In all directions round the station are immense sidings for coal and goods traffic; adjoining the locomotive shops there are miles of line filled as a rule

Race specials at Doncaster on St Ledger Day, 1911. Passengers rejoined these trains in the sidings. *(National Railway Museum, York)*

86

with engines and carriages waiting their turn for repair. But when the St Ledger is on, goods, and minerals, and repairs all alike must give way to the race traffic. As a warning of what is coming, a few days beforehand the company's staff receive a 'special additional working timetable'. Last year [1887] its arrangements were comprised in 47 folio pages. The stock in the loco sidings is swept away, the shops are closed for the week. Coal and minerals are sent off to their destination, while no new trains except for a few hours at night, are allowed to come in. Extra signal boxes are erected on either side of the station so as to cut the block sections into half their usual lengths. A special breakdown gang to repair the telegraphs should anything go wrong with them, is drafted into the station . . . At the busiest time of the day the trains push each other in and out of the platform for every train almost is running in two portions and there are relief trains, and private specials, and horse trains to and from every point of the compass . . . On the Ledger day of 1887, when I visited the place, there were 82 train loads of them from every part of the country, not only from London and Birmingham and Liverpool, but from Barrow, Carlisle, Newcastle, Chester, Bristol and King's Lynn. In the locomotive sidings alone there were 34 trains drawn up side by side. Each train in the morning runs into the place whence it will depart at night, and each passenger on his arrival is handed a printed notice giving the number of the train (a number corresponding with that on a huge placard affixed to the train itself), its situation, with directions how to reach it, and finally the hour at which it is timed to start on its return journey. And start they did . . . one about every minute and a quarter from 5.45 pm to 7.30 pm.[25]

War, from 1914 to 1918, saw much reduced race traffic, but by 1920 attendance on Ledger day was put at half a million and, despite the growth of motor coach, car and air traffic to the races, the railways still carried 100,000 to the four days' racing at Doncaster in 1929.[26]

A race meeting at which the horses couldn't get round the course for spectators was held on The Meadows at Reading in 1857, when the South Eastern Railway's train brought in 1,000, followed by the London & South Western's special adding a further 900, but the 'Leviathan train was that on the Great Western line . . . adding as many as 1,200 visitors to the already thronged course.'[27]

It seems that those racegoers arriving on the Great Western's train shunned the proper exits from the station and, instead, swarmed down the railway embankment on to the course just as the bell rang for the jockeys to saddle their horses. The local special constables, reinforced by 'two or three London police', were powerless to prevent the crowds standing on the course until '. . . the horses were close upon them, and one or two races were completely spoilt by reason of this . . .'.

There were many smaller race meetings to which the railways ran special trains, but the arrangements made were not always up to the passengers' expectations, as this letter to the Cambrian made clear:

Sir – On Monday last I, with hundreds more, wended my way to the Victoria station for the purpose of availing myself of the opportunity of going by the excursion train to Llandilo. Arriving at the station about 10 o'clock, the first thing was to secure your ticket, which was by no means an easy task, for there was crushing for one's dear life, and being carried off my feet and rendered quite powerless. I, however, succeeded at last in procuring my ticket, and got out of the crush with no greater harm than being besmeared with a few drops of blood which fell from the nose of a person who was not quite so fortunate as myself. A crush for a seat was the next event, which after a little difficulty was secured, and we arrived at Llandilo about one o'clock. The homeward train was announced to leave Llandilo at 7.30 pm. We managed, however, to get off a little after eight, and at first we found a very comfortable seat and were congratulating ourselves upon being so fortunate as to pop into a first class carriage, when the door was opened by the guard and two persons were ushered in where there was room for only one. At this we did not complain, but in about another minute two more persons were pushed into our compartment which necessitated some sitting on the others knees. But, Mr Editor, what I complain of most sadly is that we had to travel the whole of the way from Llandilo in total darkness, being scarcely able to see one's hand before your eyes. Who knows what may happen or what crimes may be committed during two and a half hours total darkness; and no one knew anything about being obliged to travel in this darkness until it was too late. As to getting any attention from the guard was quite out of the question. Fortunately all went on well, each individual keeping his seat, almost afraid to move hand or foot, knowing not what they may be charged with, for the following words were often heard to fall from the lips of a rather masculine woman, who apparently knew almost everybody and everything – 'Shame on them not to give us lights – a good job we are among a respectable lot of men who know how to behave themselves, and not among some of those old blokes who don't care what they do, – it is not right, mind you.' When we arrived at the Mumbles Road station a young woman, who lives at Blackpill, particularly wished to get out there, the guard was called at the top of one's voice to open the door, but all to no purpose. You may sing and shout as much as you like, but not the slightest notice is taken. On went the train until we came to another stoppage for the collection of tickets (which occupied about 20 minutes). Off we go once more and arrived in the Victoria Station about half past ten, after which time the said young woman had to walk all the way back to Blackpill where her friends would be anxiously waiting her return. Trusting you will give insertion to the above few lines in your valuable and widely circulated journal, and hoping it will be the means of the powers that be seeing that at their next excursion they will at least get their carriages lighted and that a certain amount of attention will be paid to the passengers, and also that they will be as careful to stop and put down passengers at the various stations as contracted for. Yours very truly, An Excursionist.[28]

A crush of returning racegoers at Towcester station on the Northampton & Banbury Junction Railway caused an accident in 1886, following which a local newspaper reported:

> . . . The excursionists were waiting for the train about 7.20, and as soon as it came into the railway station there was a rush for the handles of the carriages. Two men, one of whom was Billing, made for the same compartment, but were hustled so much by the crowd behind that both of them lost their grip and fell between the carriage and the platform . . . Billing got under the wheel and his body was torn open from abdomen to chin. The spectacle presented was of a sickening character and a painful sensation was created. It is not

surprising to hear that several members of the fair sex were overcome . . .[29]

Newmarket provides a good example of changing attitudes brought about by recognition of the fact that swollen takings at the turnstiles could only be achieved by encouraging attendance by the lower orders. At Newmarket:

> For many years the Jockey Club has endeavoured to retain for Newmarket its prestige as the 'Mecca of the plutocrat', and on this account the Great Eastern Railway has been prevailed on for many years to arrange no excursions from London saving only the days on which the Two Thousand Guineas, the Cesarewitch and the Cambridgeshire Stakes have been run. Signs are not wanting now, however, that the famous and exclusive course is to be democratised, and the Jockey Club for the first time approached the railway company ... with a view to an excursion being run from London every day of each meeting.[30]

Instead of building a race traffic station at Newmarket, the company built a new main-line station in 1902 to handle all passengers, whilst the original terminus station was set apart for horse traffic only, and a third station, Warren Hill, handled race specials.

It was not only the horses, jockeys and racegoers that had to be transported but, before the widespread use of motor vehicles, all the catering equipment, marquees, tables, chairs, food and drink, as well as catering staff.

A chapter on race meeting excursions would not be complete without mention of the Derby, for many as much a carnival as a sporting event. There has been horse-racing on

Derby Day at Epsom Downs station, on the London, Brighton & South Coast Railway, in 1878.

Epsom Downs for over 300 years[31] whilst, until recent times, a gigantic fairground plus Sangers Circus spread between Tattenham Corner and the winning-post, attracting thousands to stroll among the sideshows, fortune-tellers, tipsters and pick-pockets.

From that first London & Southampton Railway excursion to the Derby in 1838, the number of racegoers' tickets collected at Epsom's three stations climbed to 85,000 in 1937.[32] The Downs and the races attracted railways like a magnet, first the London & South Western at Epsom in 1859, next the London, Brighton & South Coast at Epsom Downs in 1865, whilst the South Eastern & Chatham opened a station at Tattenham Corner in 1901 and reaped an immediate reward with 15,000 excursionists conveyed in 50 special trains for the next meeting.

Below and right **First, Second and Third Class on the Railway. Epsom Races 1847. *(Illustrated London News)***

First Class

Second Class

Third Class

Prospects of carrying crowds of excursionists to the races and the Downs, as well as developing a service for the then increasing popularity among city types of 'commuting' from what would one day be the 'stockbroker belt', lay behind the promotion of an atmospheric railway from Croydon through Carshalton to Epsom in 1845.[33] The atmospheric system, dispensing with steam locomotives, was not successful and so, for the next 83 years, Epsom racegoers' trains were hauled by a variety of steam engines which added their quota of smoke and soot to that of the showmen's engines powering the galloping horses and gondola cars on the fairground.

Not least of the problems facing the railways in handling race traffic was that of fare evasion and swindling of booking clerks. Station manning was usually strengthened to provide additional ticket collectors but, with thousands of racegoers funnelled through the station exits, it was almost impossible to check every ticket. Many a wily, ticketless racegoer leapt from the carriage into the 'six foot' between the tracks and over the fence to the course.

In the 'twenties, many travelled to race meetings in cars or coaches, and some by air; even so, in 1930 the London Midland & Scottish Railway could claim that

> Every six minutes between the hour of 7.0 am and 11.0 am on Friday March 28th, a special train left some point on the LMSR for Aintree and the Grand National. There were forty-three trains in all . . . and the catering department made arrangements to serve 15,500 meals on Grand National specials. The stocks they laid in included: 2,500 lbs of fish; 1,700 lbs of rashers; 8,300 eggs; 5,400 lbs of meat; 750 grapefruit; 125 hams and 6,500 bottles of beer.[34]

One racegoer recorded his experience at the 1938 National when he wrote:[35]

> As our train draws in, the LNER Pullman from King's Cross is disgorging its passengers; on yet another platform a local train from Southport is pouring its hundreds into the swelling throng. Outside the station we get into the thick of things. On the road to the course we struggle desperately through a barrage of women race-card vendors, who, incidently, on our return will have metamorphosed into rock-sellers . . .

South Eastern & Chatham Railway Derby Day specials unloading at Tattenham Corner station in 1922.

After being taken in by tricksters and hood-winked by an escapologist, this race-goer puts his shirt on 'Springheel Jack', but

> . . . Curiously enough, each occupant of our compartment on the homeward journey had backed the same luckless horse. 'Springheel Jack,' snorted one racegoer indignantly, as he snuggled down into well-sprung comfort. 'Don't talk to me about that devitalised donkey. Next time that paralysed perisher faces the jumps he should have one of these seats fastened to each hoof.'

Punters, disgruntled at the tipsters' 'certs', might have taken the hint from the Great Western Railway, which claimed to have 'TRAINED' the winner of the 1937 Grand National, adding that the Derby winner was also a 'Western' horse![36]

In 1929, a new system of betting was introduced, the 'Totalisator', or 'Tote' as it became known, and for this a staff of some 250 or more had to be transported from meeting to meeting by special train, often overnight to be ready for the next day's racing.

The Southern Railway's extensive electrification programme reached Epsom and Tattenham Corner in 1928. Perhaps surprisingly, for the 1st class racegoers in 1935, steam-hauled two-race specials from Victoria to Epsom Downs consisting of Pullman cars 'Cleopatra', 'Myrtle', 'Princess Helen', 'Vivienne' and 'Bessborough' were hauled by 0-4-4 tank No 1517 and 4-4-2 tank No 2021.[37]

Resumption of racing in 1946, following the Second World War, once again saw race crowds flocking to the Southern Railway's London termini, with 18 specials from Charing Cross, five from Cannon Street and 11 from London Bridge to Tattenham Corner, and 26 trains from Victoria to Epsom Downs for the Derby.[38]

Although petrol rationing and difficulty in obtaining new cars lasted until 1953, rail-borne race traffic never again reached pre-war proportions. In 1950, only six specials ran to Aintree[39], but other meetings generated rail traffic causing some lines, closed long ago to regular passenger traffic, to be used once or twice a year for race specials. One example was Towcester, closed in 1952 but still handling race crowds until 1964; another was Haddenham, on the ex-Great Eastern line from St Ives to Ely, which lost its regular service in 1931 but race specials still ran to meetings at Hunstanton and Great Yarmouth until 1970[40]. Ashton-in-Makerfield, on the Manchester to St Helens line, was re-opened for Haydock Park race traffic in 1975.

Surely, for enterprise and customer care, the palm must go to the Eastern Counties Railway for the facilities it provided for a steeplechase at Romford in 1842. The 'elite of the sporting world' were not only conveyed to the meeting but their train was used as a moving grandstand. The course was close to, and parallel with, the line, so the train started simultaneously with the horses, 'thus affording an opportunity never before presented of witnessing a steeplechase throughout'.[41] Nor since!

Chapter 6
FOOTBALL, FLYING AND OTHER 'SPORTS'

'It is hardly claiming too much to regard the work of the railway in serving Wembley on Saturday April 28th 1923, on the occasion of the English "Cup Final", as one of the greatest transport feats ever achieved . . .'

Football today is associated with violence, and it was with violence that it was originally 'played', but this was characteristic of popular 'sports' of the 18th and early 19th centuries such as

> . . . bullbaiting, badger baiting, dog fighting and eating dishfuls of scalding porridge with bare hands, and often the most disgusting exhibition of eating a pound of tallow and stripping the wicks through the teeth for wagers.[1]

Land enclosure and the growth of industrial towns denied the working classes open spaces for their traditional pastimes and football became the game of the universities and gentlemen's clubs. Working men were denied not only the space but also the time in which to participate in open-air recreation. As late as 1878, W. S. Jevons could write:

> If old amusements are by degrees to be suppressed, and no new ones originated, England must indeed be a dull England. Such it has in fact been for a length of time. Taking it on the average, England is as devoid of amusement as a country of such wealth can be. The people seem actually to have forgotten how to amuse themselves, so that when they do escape, by an excursion train from their depressing alleys, there is no provision of music, no harmless games, no other occupation for the vacant time . . . Now I believe that this want of culture greatly arises from the fact that the amusements of the masses instead of being cultivated and multiplied and refined have been frowned upon and condemned, and been eventually suppressed by a dominant aristocracy . . . Accordingly villages and towns have grown up in the more populous parts of the Kingdom absolutely devoid of any provision whatever for recreation. It seems that the end of life is accomplished if there be bread and beef to eat, beer to drink, beds to sleep in and chapels and churches to attend on Sundays. The idea that the mass of the people might have their refined and yet popular amusements is only just dawning.[2]

In the late 19th century the newly formed municipal authorities began to provide recreation grounds and parks where football could be played and this, together with the advent of the Saturday half-holiday for factory workers in 1850, led to the formation of football teams in which working men played and which their workmates would support.

A significant factor in transforming football into big business, by the collection of vast sums of gate money from spectators, was the development of a rail network making it possible for teams to travel away to matches and, by excursion fares, for their supporters to follow them. The whole superstructure of football, fixtures and results in newspapers, and the multi-million pound 'pools' system, was made possible by the railways' ability to distribute newspapers nationwide overnight.

> . . . So by about 1900, football had been transformed from a haphazard collection of scratch amateur teams playing games whenever they could into a highly complex network of about 200 mutually dependant business operations, supported by thousands of smaller amateur clubs, much as it is today.[3]

Railway companies were quick to appreciate the potential for business in this fast-growing sport, making increasing use of newspaper advertising to attract passengers to their excursions. However, the London & North Western Railway was an early victim of

football hooliganism by Oxford University students returning from a match at Cambridge when they 'damaged internal fittings of two or three carriages and several of the party grossly misconducted themselves'.[4] At least the Company received an apology from the President of the College and a cheque for £57 14s 2d, being £5 for damage to property, 4s 2d for 'refreshments at Bletchley' and a donation of 50 guineas to the Railway Benevolent Fund.

An audacious piece of partisan advertising for a football match occured in 1904 when the Great Central Railway displayed a large poster on its Manchester station forecasting that Billy Meredith would score the winning goal for Manchester City against Bolton Wanderers at the Crystal Palace – AND HE DID![5] The General Manager of the Great Central had his salary increased to £3,500 the following June.[6]

Before the Wembley Stadium opened in 1923, International football matches were staged at the Crystal Palace in South London, and in 1897 the Scottish newspaper *The Bailie* considered the International to be 'the greatest event of all in the football year'. For this the Glasgow & South Western Railway provided the special train which took the Committee, players and supporters to London over the Midland's Settle and Carlisle route. It was estimated that 1,000 persons travelled from Scotland to see the match, which Scotland won.

> . . . To the great majority of the visitors, the wonderful extent of the enclosure, the vastness of the Palace, and the admirable behaviour of the crowd were at once striking and instructive . . .[7]

The most audacious railway poster of all time? It confidently predicted a win for Manchester City over Bolton Wanderers – and they did!

The first test of the railway's ability to handle Wembley crowds came in 1923, a year before the British Empire Exhibition opened, when the FA Cup Final between Bolton Wanderers and West Ham was held in the newly completed stadium.

> It is hardly claiming too much to regard the work of the railways in serving Wembley on Saturday April 28th 1923, on the occasion of the English 'Cup Final', as one of the greatest transport feats ever achieved . . . The railways had provided services which, it was anticipated, would meet all requirements, avoid congestion, and reduce overcrowding and discomfort to a minimum. In practice, they carried about double the numbers of passengers expected, commenced return services before the outward pressure had ceased, improvised train services practically on the spur of the moment, and called upon their staffs to give up rest and 'breathing space' periods, a call which was willingly and fully answered.[8]

A new six-platform station, with staircases giving covered access to the stadium, was built by the Metropolitan Railway. Preparations were made for trains conveying football crowds to arrive every 1$\frac{1}{2}$ minutes, enabling 30,000 passengers to be handled in an hour.[9]

Cup Final crowds leaving their train at Wembley Park station in 1934.

The London & North Eastern Railway installed a circular loop line to a new Exhibition platform and this, together with the use for the first time in Britain of three-aspect colour light signalling, was planned to enable trains to arrive and depart every 3 minutes.

Over the LMSR lines, 49 specials ran to Euston and 20 to St Pancras; over the LNER, 20 to King's Cross, 19 to Marylebone and four to Liverpool Street; over the GWR, 24 to Paddington; and over the Southern, four to Victoria and one each to Waterloo and Charing Cross. Even the Metropolitan ran three football specials. Altogether some 270,000 passengers were conveyed to London by rail.

All was going well until about 2 pm when the stadium gates were closed against thousands of disappointed fans who failed to gain admission. What happened next had not been anticipated by the railways, for thousands forced to return home early came face to face with thousands still arriving![10]

For the 1931 International at Hampden Park, Glasgow, 218 football specials were run from various parts of England, Wales and Scotland, including Wick, the farthest north station in the British Isles. For the return traffic, 20 trains were placed on the Inner Circle line, buffer to buffer, and as one was filled and pulled away the next followed into the platform. With an attendance of over 130,000 it is not surprising that

> . . . at one period the crowd became rather lively and the pressure at the head
> of the stairway became acute. The police endeavoured to hold them back, but

An example of artistic ability and enterprise by a Rutherglen signalman in connection with the 1932 Football International at Wembley.

had ultimately to get the assistance of two mounted police, whose well-trained horses, nosing into the crowd, soon recalled them to order.[11]

In 1936, for the International match at Wembley, the LMSR provided over 500 coaches to convey 22,000 Scots in 41 trains to Euston from as far north as Inverness, and from the west coast of Scotland. In that same month of April, the same company had also to provide 36 excursion trains for the Rugby League Cup Final and 50 for the FA Cup Final, both also at Wembley.

In the 1950s the railway was still carrying the majority of football supporters to Cup Finals, but in 1953, with two Lancashire teams competing, Blackpool and Bolton Wanderers, loadings were particularly heavy, requiring 21 specials. Four years later, 20 trains were required to carry Peterborough supporters to their Fourth Round Cup Tie with Huddersfield – a record for a non-league club?[12] However, symptomatic of British Rail's declining share of football traffic was the closing of the Wembley Stadium loop and station in 1969.[13]

Tackling the man as well as, or instead of, the ball, a feature excluded by the eventual rules of the Football Association, was continued in Rugby football, a sport attracting smaller crowds than 'soccer', but still requiring railway special trains for international matches. It was for a 'Springboks' visit to Twickenham in 1932 that the Southern Railway, for the first time, used 'loud speakers' at Waterloo Station, '. . . an experiment by the Marconiphone Company to assist in controlling the crowds . . . the experiment was quite successful'.[14] With 30,000 passengers to handle and 43 trains to dispatch from Twickenham station, a 'loud speaker' there would also have been useful.

Football fans arriving at Mount Florida station for the International match at Hampden Park, Glasgow, in 1931, for which 218 special trains were run.

International matches could create language problems for railway staff – and not just bad language. For the Scotland versus Wales Rugby match at Edinburgh in 1934, the LMSR transported some of its Welsh staff from Swansea to the Scottish capital to ensure that supporters disgorged from 31 special trains from Wales would find their way to the ground. As an observer commented,

> . . . As the Welsh team beat the Scottish by two goals and a try to a penalty goal and a try it is perhaps as well that the departing Welsh could not understand the language of the Scots.[15]

A 'Kick-Off Disco' coach, a cinema-saloon with four television screens showing video programmes, and two carriages equipped with headphones giving each passenger a choice of three music channels, were included in a 12-coach, 1st class train provided by British Railways for the exclusive use of the Football League in 1973.[16]

However, a correspondent to *The Railway Magazine* did not agree with BR's provision of the 'Kick-Off Disco' train:

> During the last few years vandals and wreckers have cost British Railways tens of thousands of pounds in damage to special trains run for football fans. Now we learn that these people are to be rewarded by being provided with a new train composed entirely of first class accommodation, and equipped with four television sets, piped music, and a 'disco', all at a cost of £250,000, yet law-abiding and civilized travellers are refused a new 'Brighton Belle' on the grounds of expense . . . [17]

"IN LEAGUE"

Civic launching of the season's first Football Special!

A fictional football excursion was featured in Will Hay's film *Oh, Mr Porter!* in 1937. As William Porter, Will Hay is posted to the remote Buggleskelly station in Ireland as Stationmaster in charge of a staff of two – an aged Jeremiah Harbottle and an overweight youth, Albert. No passengers have used the station for years; the staff have not been paid, but they do quite well with their sidelines. The new Stationmaster hits on the idea of running an excursion to improve his receipts. Surprisingly, a one-eyed character purchases all the tickets, ostensibly for his football team. There are numerous adventures, such as the excursion meeting an express train head-on, but that is nothing compared with what follows William Porter's discovery that the 'football team' comprises cross-Border gun-runners. The baddies chase the 'not much betters' who take refuge high in the air on the sails of a windmill. The gun-runners are captured, but at the ceremony when the Superintendent of the Line congratulates Porter, the aged, decrepit excursion train engine, *Gladstone*, explodes.[18]

Cricket does not seem to have stimulated as much excursion traffic as did football, but as early as 1862 the Manchester South Junction & Altrincham line named a station Old Trafford Cricket Ground. This station derived from a temporary platform opened for the Manchester Art Treasures Exhibition in 1857.[19] For the Royal Jubilee Exhibition in 1887, extra platforms were laid in, after which as many as 16 special trains in 45 minutes were dispatched following an important cricket match, and these in addition to the regular service.

Horse-racing and football, with their mass spectator following, not surprisingly attracted the enterprise of the railways in running special trains, but what about the less popular sports? Scottish curling is played by teams of four players sliding heavy granite stones across the ice to rules similar to those of bowls. The first requirement is for the ice to be $5^{1}/_{2}$ inches thick; as a result, advance publicity for a 'Bonspiel' was impossible, so if the railways were to run excursion trains then the arrangements had to be at short notice. In 1935, at Carsebreck Loch, 13 miles north of Stirling, on Christmas Eve, a Grand Match organised by the Royal Caledonian Curling Club was held. Now in football the spectators far outnumber the players, but for this 'Bonspiel' there were 3,000 competitors and only 2,000 spectators.

There being no habitation around the Loch, there was no railway station, but a wooden platform beside the line stood ever ready for such an occasion as this when the London Midland & Scottish Railway ran four specials from Aberdeen, Moffat, Glasgow and Stirling, whilst the London & North Eastern Railway ran one each from Dunfermline and Edinburgh. In addition, seven ordinary trains made an additional stop at the 'Bonspiel' platform. With each team of four players bringing its own 40 lb curling stone, it was necessary to provide extra luggage vans on the trains.

> A visit to the ice but confirmed my thoughts as to the earnestness of these people in their game. The shouts of the skip mingled with the 'roar' of the stones as they hurtled across the ice, while the praise and applause accorded a good shot urged the players to greater efforts.
>
> Each player carries a broom or a brush, and on feverish instructions from the skip urges the stone forwards to its goal by sweeping away any loose impediment before it. Shouts of 'Yes! Yes!' mean sweep and sweep hard, indicating that the stone has hardly enough impetus in itself to carry it forward, while shouts of 'No! No!' mean leave it alone with the hope that it will stop at the desired spot. The very earnestness of the players infuses in the spectators a spirit of keen anticipation to see a good shot come slowly along

A North v South Scottish Curling 'Bonspiel' in progress. A special train waits in the distance.

the ice and terminate its journey just where it was so desired.

At the railway platform a temporary Telegraph Office had been installed in a platelayers' hut adjoining, and here a clerk was kept busy transmitting press and railway telegrams to all parts of the country.

Right on the stroke of 2.30 pm another shot told of the termination of the match.

Almost immediately thereafter the competitors commenced their journey to the railway platform, where we had the return trains ready to receive them. The six return specials and four ordinary trains left, each with its respective quota, on time, accompanied by much good humoured banter from the occupants.[20]

Although prize-fighting had been made illegal, railway companies connived with the fight organisers to convey large crowds to the 'secret' venues. In 1845 the London & Birmingham Railway brought crowds by excursion trains from Liverpool, Manchester, Sheffield, Leicester and Nottingham to Wolverton station to attend a fight between two famous pugilists of their day, Caunt and Bendigo. After 93 rounds Bendigo was declared the winner! Minute books of the South Eastern Railway for 1850 confirm receipt of letters protesting about the running of excursion trains to prize fights, but undeterred, an excursion conveying over 2,000 spectators ran from London's Cannon Street station to Headcorn, Kent, for a fight in a field. After only three rounds the police arrived and broke up the gathering. Despite a rebuke from the Home Secretary, yet another excursion took spectators to a fight held on an island in the Medway in 1861.

Bare-knuckle fighting was illegal, but railways ran excursion trains to remote venues nonetheless.

In that same year, the London, Chatham & Dover Railway ran an excursion to a fight at Meopham, Kent, but, following a tip-off, police arrived, whereupon the spectators climbed back aboard their train which took them and the contestants further down the line to complete the contest beyond the jurisdiction of the local police.[21]

Ancient forms of football, bear-baiting and bare-knuckle fighting were evidence of the spectators' love of violence, so it comes as no surprise that hangings also attracted large crowds. With an eye ever open for additional revenue, the railways were only too keen to run excursion trains to such macabre events.

In addition to running excursion trains to the local Assizes, one of the oldest railways in the land, the Bodmin & Wadebridge, ran three special trains to Bodmin

> . . . so that Wadebridge people might see the hanging of William and James Lightfoot, convicted of the murder of a Mr Norway, one of their townspeople. No fewer than 1,100 people travelled on this occasion, almost exactly half the population of the town! As the jail adjoined the railway depot at Bodmin, passengers were able to see the spectacle in comfort from their carriages.[22]

Executions were crowd-pullers in the early years of railways as, for example, the execution of Samuel Yarham for the murder of Harriet Chandler in 1844. On Tombland Fair Day, 11 April 1845, 30,000 spectators gathered on Castle Hill, Norwich, and all business for the day was suspended.

> . . . Eight hundred persons came from Wymondham in one train; it was found necessary to use bullock-trucks to convey the people, there not being a sufficient number of regular carriages . . . After the execution, gongs, drums and other instruments commenced their uproar, mountebanks and clowns

their antics, the vendors of wares and exhibitors of prodigies their cries, while the whirligigs and ups-and-downs were soon in full swing. The public houses round the Hill were crowded and hundreds finished the day in riot and intoxication.[23]

To Liverpool, the London & North Western Railway arranged excursion trains for a public hanging in 1849, attracting custom with notices which read 'To enable the public to witness the last moments of an expected victim'. The *Liverpool Courier* described this spectator event in detail.

> EXECUTION OF JOHN GLEESON WILSON AT KIRKDALE GAOL
> . . . On Saturday, so early as 6 o'clock, numbers of persons had taken up positions opposite the gallows, determined at any personal sacrifice not to be disappointed in their desire to witness the end of one who had so outraged humanity by the horrible crime he had committed. By 7 o'clock the roads leading to the gaol became thronged with people, and the numbers continued to increase every hour until the time fixed for the execution approached. Various estimates have been made of the numbers present, some computing them at 100,000, and many placing them as low as 40,000 to 50,000. The railway turned the occasion to a business purpose by running cheap trains, all of which were densely packed. The multitude was such as was never congregated together in this neighbourhood under any circumstance whatever. The spectators displayed the usual levity exhibited on such occasions, though generally speaking, good order was maintained. There were, however, none of those disgusting and brutal manifestations which so frequently prevail at public executions . . . A slight cheer was the only expression of feeling on behalf of the immense multitude . . . A great number of respectably dressed females were present on the ground, and several cars were requisitioned to convey them to and from the scene ... A representative from Madame Tussaud was in attendance to possess himself of the murderer's clothes for exhibition in London.[24]

Seven years later, even greater crowds arrived in Stafford by train for the execution of William Palmer, a poisoner. This time the local newspaper reported that

> . . . intense anxiety to witness the execution has already manifested itself by the numbers pouring into Stafford from every direction; yesterday the trains from all parts being crowded, even during the early portion of the day, and the number of passengers constantly augmenting by each successive train.[25]

Great efforts were made to provide a view of the gallows for as many as possible in Stafford's narrow streets. In County Road, slates were removed from a roof to enable spectators to obtain a view, and the public houses stayed open throughout the night. The *Advertiser* concluded its account of this spectacle thus: 'The railway authorities made all necessary arrangements to meet the increased demands upon them by the public . . . [the trains] kept admirable time and nothing like confusion prevailed.'

   This source of railway revenue was terminated after public executions were stopped in 1868.

Monsieur Salmet's Air Display on Doncaster Racecourse in 1913, for which railway excursions were run.

When a Flying Week was arranged at Doncaster in 1909 the crowds attracted resembled those of the St Leger race meeting. Some 50,000 people were estimated to have been present on the first day, and most of these had arrived by excursion trains, with the Great Central Railway running a service of special trains from Sheffield and Grimsby.[26]

A 50 guinea silver cup was presented by the Great Northern Railway to be competed for during the week's flying trials and so earned the congratulations of *The Railway Magazine* for its

> . . . readiness in realising that aviation, so far from proving a serious competitor to railway locomotion, bids fair to become a profitable promoter of railway travel on the part of large numbers of people who wish to view the contests between rival flying men.[27]

Airship races at Blackpool that same year generated even more excursion trains than usual to that popular resort.

Lanark's Aviation Meeting in the following year was marred by the non-arrival of Mr Colemore's Short biplane which went missing on the railway. Two planes dispatched from Blackpool by the London & North Western Railway caught fire at Lancaster and were completely destroyed.[28]

Fortunately, no mishap occurred to the dozens of excursion trains carrying visitors to Lanark's Racecourse Station on the Caledonian Railway, and how these were handled is explained in another chapter. The railway played an unexpected role in the recovery of a lost aviator. Two monoplanes and a biplane set off on a cross-country flight, gradually disappearing into the distance. Drexel, one of the aviators, drifted away to the north until he could no longer be distinguished without glasses, and gradually disappeared from view at about 7.30, heading east by south. Time passed and, as there was no news of him, a feeling of alarm set in at 8.30 when the officials were still without information. Shortly

A special platform erected adjacent to RAF Finningley on the former GN&GE joint line to cater for spectators to the annual air show on 19 September 1981, with a Lancaster bomber overhead and a DMU from Doncaster.

before 9 o'clock, the following telegram was received from Drexel: 'Have landed near farm house at Wester Mossat near Cobbinshaw Station. Please send mechanic to station.'

Drexel had borrowed a bicycle to ride to Cobbinshaw Station at which he arrived numbed with cold and starving with hunger. The Stationmaster took him into his house and tea was prepared for the aviator, who 'expressed himself as not having enjoyed a meal so well for a long time'. The news of his presence spread, and in a short time the station was besieged by a cheering throng. Crowds returning from the aerodrome in special trains joined in the enthusiasm.[29]

An early example of the advantages of rail travel over road occurred when the German airship *Graf Zeppelin* visited Hanworth in 1931. The Southern Railway, at short notice, ran special trains to Feltham station conveying some 5,000 passengers. However, such was the congestion on the roads that an additional 1,000 descended on the station for the return journey.[30]

'Croydon Flier' was the unofficial name of the LNER excursion train which conveyed members of the Hull Technical College Old Boys Association over the metals of the LNER, GWR and SR to reach Croydon in 1933. The 'Flier' derived from the flight the party made in Imperial Airways planes over London. Rail coaches were named after airliners such as 'Hadrian' and 'Hercules', and the train included a cinema coach. The organiser of this excursion was so appreciative of the arrangements made by the LNER that he sent a telegram to the passenger manager at Hull which concluded with a suggested slogan:

> The LNER proclaim
> Their untiring aim
> To serve the public well and true;
> Just see what they can do for you.[31]

The Daily Express Air Pageant at Gatwick Airport in 1938 attracted 30,000 excursionists for which the Southern Railway provided 17 special trains from Victoria, London Bridge,

Brighton, Portsmouth and other stations. In addition, 12 scheduled trains were strengthened and stopped specially.[32]

In 1981 the Royal Air Force's Battle of Britain At Home Day was staged at RAF Finningley, South Yorkshire. For this, British Rail erected a temporary platform, Finningley station having been closed since 1961. South Yorkshire Passenger Transport Executive chartered two trains starting from Barnsley and Chesterfield to Finningley.[33]

A special train from Manchester to London to enable the excursionists to see *What the Butler Saw* sounds unlikely. This was not a seaside pier peep-show but a theatrical performance at the Savoy Theatre. The Great Central Railway's 4-4-2 locomotive No 267 covered the 206 miles with ten coaches at an average speed of 55.25 mph. The theatregoers were conveyed between Marylebone station and the theatre by motor cars and, on the up journey to London, accommodation was provided for dressing before taking dinner in the restaurant car.[34]

> On the morning of June 29th [1927] will take place a celestial phenomenon which has not been seen in this country since May 22nd 1724 and will not be seen again until August 11th 1999 . . .

So began an article on the Solar Eclipse in the *Great Western Railway Magazine*.[35] It explained,

> . . . coming up from the South West over St George's Channel and entirely missing Ireland and Pembrokeshire, the thirty-mile-wide umbra will strike North Wales at 5.23 am GMT and travelling at about 100 miles per minute in a North East direction, reach the North Sea at the Durham and North Yorkshire coast at 5.25 am.

So the Great Western, London Midland & Scottish, and London & North Eastern Railway companies all had stations on the line of 'totality', and all made extensive preparations to convey large crowds to the best vantage points.

A LNER poster read 'Eclipse of the Sun 29 June 1927 – TOTALITY VIEWPOINTS', and displayed a map of suitable LNER stations at the foot of which was a final reminder, 'Your Last Chance Until 1999'. In addition there was a booklet 'Eclipse of the Sun. See the sunrise and the Event of the Century', the astronomical information being supplied by the British Astronomical Association. Excursions were advertised from King's Cross to Grimsby and Leyburn, Colchester to Leyburn, and King's Cross to Richmond; travel agents Dean and Dawson ran an excursion from Peterborough to Richmond for boys and a separate train for girls; and Oundle School, Northamptonshire, had a special to Croft Spa. For those excursionists travelling to Richmond, Yorkshire, to observe the eclipse, the railway handed out a folder containing a plan of Richmond racecourse and the advice,

> . . . Buses will meet all trains at Richmond station and convey passengers direct to the racecourse where the town authorities have arranged for music by a military band and other entertainments to while away the time prior to the eclipse.

Each rail ticket carried a letter between A and H, indicating where each train would be drawn up to serve breakfast. Thirty-six special trains were run by the LNER alone, which conveyed by special and ordinary trains a total of 50,000 passengers to various viewpoints.

After all that preparation what, was the eclipse like? 'At Richmond we saw nothing'[36], but here is what things were like at Criccieth on the North Wales coast:

Criccieth, the 'home station' on the GWR of the Solar Eclipse on June 29th and the official HQ for Wales of a huge party of observers under the leadership of Mr A. Taylor of Penarth presented an animated appearance from 3 am, the hour when the lengthy excursions began to arrive in quick succession from Ruabon, London, Wrexham, Cheltenham, Oswestry and elsewhere. It was most unfortunate that on a day of such exceptional history regarding things celestial, nature should greet the thousands of all-night travellers with so displeasing a frown. Rain came down in torrents for hours. Scores of people never left the coaches until noon whilst every conceivable corner of the station was commandeered by the storm-drenched passengers. The clerk in the large shed on the platform used as a cloakroom was practically evicted and even the booking clerks had to struggle hard for elbow room to 'carry on' so abnormal was the rush for shelter from the raging elements.

As the time of 6.24 am (BST) drew near the platforms and coaches were packed and all eyes directed towards St Trudwells Island of which the station premises afforded a splendid view. As the moon's shadow swept gracefully across Cardigan bay the crowd became motionless; shunting ceased, engine whistles were silenced and escaping steam was stilled. The gloom deepened and every voice was hushed. The old 12th Century castle close by was blotted out for a while but the lights of the GWR carriages pierced through the darkness, in bright relief to the sombre scene. Beautiful and awe-inspiring as the 'shadow' was the 'substance' which the thousands had anxiously looked

Crowds awaiting return trains from Leyburn after the total eclipse of the sun in 1927. (R. M. Casserley)

forward to beholding was hidden from view by low, heavily-laden clouds. The Prodigal Sun was not in a mood to sup at the festive board prepared in his honour and the assembled guests had no alternative but sadly to disperse to their homes.[37]

Railways were not alone in cashing in on the eclipse; the following advertisement appeared in the *Liverpool Echo*:

ECLIPSE GOGGLES. To colleges, institutions and interested parties. Eclipse goggles, specification padded metal frames, with closed-in eye-pieces, blue tinted lenses and tape adjusters. Packed in velvet lined tin container. These glasses can also be used for motoring. Immediate application necessary. A pair of these super Eclipse Goggles sent post free for 1s.

How many Liverpudlians purchased these goggles is not recorded, but 50,000 of them are reported assembling on Bidston Hill on the Wirral, with 10,000 more at West Kirby, for whom the LMSR ran special trains which connected with trams from all parts of the city commencing at 3 am.

Altogether, the LMSR ran over 100 trains to the totality area which contributed to the 20,000 observers at Southport and 10,000 at Colwyn Bay where prayers were offered for a clear night! Much good their prayers did them, for at Colwyn Bay the eclipse was a total failure. 'It was the most hopeless eclipse I have ever taken part in,' said Dr Andrew Crommelin, the distinguished astronomer. 'From beginning to end the sun was out of sight behind heavy clouds, while the rain poured down continuously.'[38] On the summit of Snowdon, a Press Association special correspondent described the scene as a cheerless one where, drenched to the skin by heavy rain, watchers gulped down hot drinks in the refreshment hut.

In 1934, a 'tricky' innovation by the London Midland & Scottish Railway was Whist Drive excursions on Saturday afternoons, for which ten coaches with tables were provided. Twenty-four hands were played during the trip, which took players from Glasgow to Dumfries, Edinburgh to Ayr and another to Crieff, being a circular tour via Callandar and Gleneagles. The 5 shilling fare included entry in the whist drive for which the LMSR offered as prizes 3rd class return tickets to any station on the system to the first lady and gentleman, tickets to Llandudno, Blackpool or Southport as second, and to Oban or Inverness as third prize.[39]

Chapter 7
TRIP DAY

'. . . year after year the week which finishes with "TRIP" Saturday sees the growing excitement which reaches its height on Friday evening when the proud father sallies forth in quest of the tickets.'

Railway excursions gave 19th-century employers a new and welcome means by which to demonstrate their philanthropy. Welcome, because a rail trip to the seaside, accompanied by the family, was to be preferred by employers to the brutal sports and heavy drinking of the traditional fairs and wakes. What is more, the Victorians were obsessed with the health-giving effects of only one day in the clean air of seaside or moor, not to mention the alleged curative properties of sea-water which the well-off bought in casks transported by the Great Eastern Railway from the coast to London by rail.[1]

Richard Cobden, Member of Parliament, and famous for his agitation against the Corn Laws which were repealed in 1846, celebrated his success by granting all his employees in Chorley, Lancashire, a day's wage and a rail trip to Fleetwood over the Preston & Wyre Railway. Led by a band and banner, a thousand excursionists, many carrying flags, squeezed into 39 coaches for the memorable trip.[2]

Sir Titus Salt, Yorkshire woollen manufacturer and founder of the model industrial town of Saltaire, was the first employer in that area to take advantage of the newly opened Leeds & Bradford Railway (1847) when, in 1848, he gave

> . . . 2,000 of his hands an excursion to the country. Having taken up his own summer residence at Malham, amid the glorious scenery of Craven, he wished that those toilers, who had so few opportunities of healthy enjoyment, should breath for a day the mountain air, and ramble in the woods and fields to their heart's content.[3]

In that same year the *Blackburn Standard* reported that Messrs Hopwoods of that town took 1,200 of their workpeople to Blackpool, 'many of whom had never seen a sea-bathing place, been on a railway or passed through a tunnel'. The return fare was 1 shilling but 'to those in worst circumstances tickets were given or sold at reduced prices'. These excursionists were requested to provide themselves with refreshments, but the precaution was taken of storing 200 loaves, and 2-3 cwt of cheese, in a horsebox attached to the train, for those unable to cater for their own needs.

The novelty of the works outing by train is obvious from the number of such events reported in the mid-19th century. In 1849, another Chorley textile firm, R. Smethurst & Co, sent 500 of its workpeople to Blackpool, together with 300 friends, at a return fare of 1 shilling, and provided free refreshments. On leaving the train of 25 carriages, the trippers went in procession carrying banners and led by a band.

Workers living near the sea were taken on trips inland, as for example the 40 employees of hat and cap manufacturers Peel & Sons of Newcastle-upon-Tyne, who were taken by train to Hexham and who 'spent the day among the romantic scenery of Swallowship'.[4]

A band, banners and a procession were popular features of these early works outings, whilst the excursionists mostly made their own entertainment in the days before the resorts had become almost entirely commercialised. The workers from Blundell & Co's colour works at Hull, on their 1860 trip to Bridlington, danced at Dane's Dyke to music played by a bagpiper from among their party. The Brunswick band, which led the procession from the station to the pier, had been expected for dancing, but 'they did not find their way thither'. Could they have succumbed to the temptation of The Mermaid or The Jolly Fisherman? Class differences were strictly maintained on this trip, each to his own station so to speak, for, whilst the majority

> . . . refreshed themselves pic-nic fashion . . . the different foremen of the establishment and friends assembled at an adjoining inn where dinner was provided at the expense of the employers . . .

After making their appearance at the workpeoples' bagpipe knees-up,

> . . . Mr Blundell and the ladies and gentlemen of his party . . . assembled at the Britannia Hotel and partook of a sumptuous dinner . . .[5]

Such was the success of Blundell's outing that in the following year more excursionists than had been expected turned up at the station. 'Nevertheless, the servants of the railway company, somewhat perplexed', managed to provide 30 carriages for the 'living freight of more than 1,000 persons'.[6]

It was one thing for these merry groups of workpeople, with their bands and banners, to descend upon a seaside resort, but what must have been the impact of such a boisterous arrival upon the locals and other 'more select' visitors? Here is how the *Wimborne Journal* reported one such outing to Weymouth in 1873:

> On Saturday morning the Esplanade and St Thomas Street were startled from their propriety by the spirited sounds of a brass band played with more than common liveliness. Everybody rushed out and behold! about 300 men with their wives and families marched in grand procession down the street. They were connected with the Vobster quarries, Somerset, and the holiday treat was given by their employers. They started out about 5 in the morning from Vobster in 12 waggons and arrived at Frome about 20 past 8, hence they left by train and arrived at Weymouth about 10. Most of them left by the Portland Steamer for the Isle of Stone.[7]

In Scotland, the Edinburgh and Leith Trades Excursion must have been a most colourful event, attracting crowds to watch the various trades in procession to and from the station, as well as joining the excursions to several destinations.

> Yesterday was observed as a holiday by the bakers, grocers, fleshers and carters of Edinburgh, and the various excursions provided by the railway companies were largely taken advantage of. The bakers, numbering about 700, went to Dunfermline, by Queensferry; the grocers, to the number of about 400, visited Helensburgh, Dunoon and Kirn; and the carters, who mustered to the strength of about 750, made Galashiels and Melrose their rendezvous.

Although the various excursionists left the Waverley Station early in the morning, there was a considerable gathering along the streets, and the usual adjudication of prize horses took place . . .

A large number of the inhabitants [of Leith] left the town early in the day on pleasure excursions by road, rail and steamer. About 6 o'clock the porters, meters and weighers, who had decided to go to Dumfries this year, met in Dock Place, and proceeded by way of Leith Walk to the Caledonian Station, Edinburgh. They were accompanied by two brass bands, and displayed a number of models, and the flags and banners of the Corporation of Meters and Weighers. In previous years the carters joined the excursion of the porters, but on this occasion they elected to visit Galashiels and Melrose along with the Edinburgh carters. They formed into procession at the Corn Exchange shortly after 6 o'clock, and the gaily caparisoned horses, which had occupied a number of hands to get ready overnight, along with the models which were carried by members of the committee, had the effect as usual, not withstanding the early hour, of bringing out large crowds of spectators . . . In the evening, the Leith Walk was thronged with people who had assembled to witness the return of the procession to Leith . . .[8]

Dockyard employees at Portsmouth, not enjoying the advantages of a philanthropic employer, formed their own Portsmouth Dockyard Excursion Committee, and ran their first excursion on 13 October 1883 to the Fisheries Exhibition in London. The scheme covered Dockyard employees, their wives and children and, with a return fare to London

of 3 shillings for adults and 1s 6d for children, it is not surprising that 591 adults and 80 children travelled. Encouraged by this success, the Queen's Birthday the following year (a traditional Dockyard holiday) saw an excursion arranged to Oxford, Leamington and Birmingham. With a 5 am start and arrival back in Portsmouth at midnight, it was truly a 'day out'. Such was the growth in numbers patronising the PDEC excursions that difficulties were experienced by the railway company in running these trains without disrupting normal services. The table below indicates the facilities needed for these excursions on one Saturday in 1905:

Time	Railway	Destination	Platform	Coaches	Seats	Passengers
5.20 am	LSW	Birmingham	4	8(bogies)	488	373
5.45 am	LSW	West of England	5	10(bogies)	648	332
6.40 am	LBSC	Victoria	4	15(6-wheeler)	684	a
6.50 am	LBSC	Victoria	5	16(6-wheeler)	686	a
7.5am	LSW	Weymouth	4	14(mixed)	608	b
7.50 am	LBSC	London Bridge	HL	15(6-wheeler)	684	a
8.20 am	LSW	Bournemouth	4	16(mixed)	728	b
8.25 am	LSW	Windsor	5	10(bogies)	594	475
8.30 am	LBSC	Hastings	HL	15(6-wheeler)	684	556
9.20 am	LSW	Winchester	5	17(mixed)	684	460
9.30 am	LBSC	Arundel	4	12(mixed)	686	485
9.35 am	LBSC	Midhurst	5	12(mixed)	506	228
9.45 am	LSW	Haslemere	4	17(mixed)	670 }	1049
1.35 pm	LSW	Petersfield	4	17(mixed)	670 }	

(a) Total 1,596 passengers. (b) Total of 761 passengers.

Charles Kemp related how his grandfather, a railway official at Portsmouth, used a model railway to work out the complex train manoeuvres involved in dispatching all these excursion trains together with the normal traffic.[9]

Works outings did not always travel a great distance if, like Hull, the seaside was only 16 miles away at Withernsea, which is where Messrs C. G. Southcott took their employees by North Eastern Railway in 1897. Perhaps the shortness of the journey was compensated for by the provision of 'a special repast' in the public rooms. The afternoon was taken up with a cricket match, married men versus single, which ended in a draw. After tea and photographs, 'Mr Ellis and Mr Matthews enlivened the company by playing selections on the piano and violin, the younger members doing the light fantastic'.[10]

Not all works outings were large, sort of "appy 'amstead' affairs. In some firms, instead of one large outing, each department arranged its own, as did Cadbury Bros of Bourneville. For its Office Staff Excursion of 1902 the Midland Railway provided four spacious saloons to accommodate the 116 passengers. Luncheon was served en route to Bristol, and the day's programme included a steamer trip to Clevedon, and a 14-mile drive to Penpole Point.[11]

The day of the Office Staff Annual Excursion did not, however, exonerate the clerks from opening the mail and filling the 'IN' and 'PENDING' trays before setting off for Weston-super-Mare, as the programme for the 1903 outing (overleaf) shows.[12]

BOURNEVILLE
OFFICE STAFF ANNUAL EXCURSION
Saturday, May 16th, 1903,
to
WESTON-SUPER-MARE

'Double the labour of my task,
But give, oh! give me what I ask,
The sunlight and the mountain air.'   *Eliza Cook*

PROGRAMME

A.M.
8.0 Arrive Office
        'When my cue comes, call me, and I will answer.'   *Shakespeare*
9.25 Work ceases
        'I have just now other business in hand, which would seem idle to
                you, but it is with me the very stuff o' th' conscience.'   *Hazlitt*
9.40 Train leaves Bourneville
11.45 Luncheon en Route
        'They ordered luncheon in a canter,
            Cold or hot, it mattered not,
            Provided it was served instanter.'   *Horace Smith*

P.M.
12.50 Arrive Weston-super-Mare
        'Is this the mighty ocean?
        Is this all?'   *Gebir*
1.0 Char-a-Banc meets train for drive to Banwell, returning by a different
route to outward journey.
        'Hast thou a steed with a mane richly
        flowing?
        Hast thou a trumpet rich melodies
        blowing?'   *Keats*
4.0 Arrive Huntley's Restaurant, corner of Regents Street and Promenade.
5.30 Dinner
        'The busy cook-maids ranged full many a dish,
        Surcharged with rich variety of flesh and fish.'   *A. Melville Bell*
7.15 Boat from Pier Head to Cardiff, returning from Cardiff at 8.15
        'Aboard, aboard – for shame!
        The wind sits in the shoulder of your
        sail.'   *Shakespeare*
9.45 Train leaves Excursion Platform, Locking Road
        'I can no further crawl, no further go;
        My legs can keep no pace with my
        desires.'   *Shakespeare*
        'Good night! a kind good night to all.'   *Shakespeare*

An annual event was the Manchester Home Trade Picnic which, in 1912, the Great Central Railway conveyed to Stratford-on-Avon. To stimulate interest in the trip, the GCR put on a cinematograph film of their rail and motor tour through Shakespeare country. 'Atlantic' Class 4-4-2 No 258 hauled six corridor coaches, including a dining saloon, right through to Stratford-on-Avon via Woodford & Hinton and over the Stratford-upon-Avon & Midland Junction Railway's lines. Lunch was served on the outward journey and dinner on the return.[13]

The Great Central made a determined effort to attract excursion traffic, for which it built sets of saloon carriages of a most distinctive appearance, including a kitchen car, and with all seats having a folding table.[14]

In the way that the Lancashire mill towns had their Wakes Weeks, when mills closed down, maintenance was carried out, and workers went off on excursions, so too did several centres of engineering, particularly the railway towns such as Swindon and Crewe. These were known as Trip Weeks.

Lincoln's first Foundry Trip Week took place in 1871 and immediately generated railway excursion traffic amounting to 5,745 passengers. By 1885 the numbers had risen to 14,068, and by 1893 16,934 tickets were issued, when it was calculated that one third of the town's population went on Foundry Trips.[15]

Not everybody was convinced of the benefits to be derived from the Foundry Trips, one being 'Big Tom', in his column 'Lincoln Chimes' in a local newspaper:

> 'Next week at this time' that is the old saying, the anticipation of the coming trips which will be repeated by many in Lincoln this morning. I often wonder how it can be thought that a single day's outing is to do pater familias, mater familias and the brood 'the world of good' that is hoped for, but year after year the week which finishes with 'TRIP' Saturday sees the growing excitement which reaches its height on Friday evening when the proud father sallies forth in quest of the tickets. It is however, of the mother that I am thinking. All the week she has been making and mending, and it has seemed impossible for her to finish knitting and sewing by Friday night. As a matter of fact, she has not finished, but of course she cannot think of going to bed. The train goes in 'the wee sma hours' and it is a lengthy task to get the household to the station. And here the day has only begun. The ride in the train, the run on the seashore, the trying return journey – this is the Trip Saturday of many and many a Lincoln father and mother. And although it is a toil, the change is an acceptable one, and the full day's outing is followed by a good day's rest and the tiredness once overcome everybody is satisfied.[16]

The annual Trip of the employees of the Great Western Railway's Swindon workshops in the 1890s represented a tremendous feat of organisation by the railway staff when, for the conveyance of some 21,000 men, women and children, more than 500 carriages had to be employed, plus locomotives and train crews. At Swindon station, the Trip trains were loaded in numerous sidings, as well as at the usual platforms. This report of the 1912 Trip indicates the scope of this huge undertaking:

> For the first time in the history of the Trip the West of England working, which is amongst the heaviest, was appreciably relieved by the running of two special trains the night before. The trains were each formed of fourteen vehicles and the fact that they were heavily laden is proof that the concession met its object. On the Trip morning four trains composed of about fifteen coaches

The Great Western Railway's Swindon Works 'Trip' of 1910. Trippers had to climb aboard from ground level in the sidings outside the Works; not easily done in Edwardian ladies' costume!

each were run to Paddington between 5.15 am and 6.15 am. The Northern trains were despatched from the sidings outside the general offices. Each was very heavy consisting of fourteen or fifteen vehicles. In the case of the South West passengers three trains were required. These were made up of fifteen coaches each. Despite the overnight relief in the case of the West of England traffic on the morning of the trip 3 trains each of from fourteen to fifteen carriages were required to deal with the passengers. They were started between 5.5 am and 6.5 am from the Rodbourne Lane sidings. The Weston-super-Mare trains, which are always extensively patronised, were four in number and were worked from the Carriage Works sidings between 6.30 am and 7.0 am. Weymouth also had to be heavily provided for, five trains being required. These were despatched from another portion of the Carriage sidings between 4.55 am and 6.20 am. The trains arrived at their destinations in commendably good time and as usual everything passed off without a single hitch.[17]

North of the Border, the great railway works had their trips too, the largest being that of the Caledonian Railway from St Rollox Works, and popularly known as the Caley Trip.

It was a Saturday; in those days Saturday was a working day, but not that Saturday. Springburn had never known a day like it. By half past three the tenement windows were yellow with gaslight and in scores of kitchens porridge pots were simmering on the hobs. By half past four Springburn was athrob with activity. Whole families, merry and excited and dressed in their

The GWR Swindon Works 'Trip' in the 1930s. Fashions have changed but loading was still from ground level in the sidings.

Sunday best, emerged from tenement closes and pattered down Springburn Road in the first light. Springburn was going to England. Few families enjoyed a real holiday then, and a day outing was an event in most households. And England seemed so exciting and far away.

All roads led to St Rollox that morning. Special electric cars, one every two minutes, climbed up from the city and deposited their passengers at the station . . . Two hundred and fifty carriages, many of them the latest lavatory carriages, were made up into fourteen trains and McIntosh detailed fourteen (out of his thirty) Dunalastair Is and IIs to work them. And that on a Saturday. Each engine carried a disc bearing the train number in front of the chimney. The first departure was at 5.10 am, the train arriving in Carlisle fifteen minutes before train No 14 left St Rollox. To minimise confusion in handling the huge crowds, the trains were despatched alternately from St Rollox station and from the Cattle Bank adjoining it . . .

. . . Not since Prince Charlie's visit had Carlisle seen anything like it. The Mayor had instructed the townsfolk to decorate their houses and shops and 'Welcome to the St Rollox Visitors' signs hung out everywhere. The Carlisle eating houses were serving breakfasts by eight o'clock; tea or coffee with a choice of meats and all the bread and butter you wanted for a shilling. The invasion built up steadily as train after train rolled in and by mid-morning Springburn was in possession of Merrie Carlisle – and merrie was the word. Before the last train had arrived the band of the Glasgow Highlanders was dispensing the harmonies of Balfe in the public park, and in a hall not far away the Geisha Boys (brought specially from Scarborough for the occasion)

Fourteen Caledonian Railway 'Dunalistair' Class locomotives at Carlisle ready to work excursion trains northwards. *(National Railway Museum, York)*

were giving the first of three performances. Elsewhere the Springburn visitors danced the polka, the lancers and quadrilles or in a quieter mood listened to the Glasgow Male Voice Quartette . . .

. . . A few days after the excursion the Chief Constable of Carlisle wrote to St Rollox in the following terms: 'Your people behaved themselves in a most admirable manner, and I am pleased to say that no person was arrested by the Police during the day.' But somebody (an NB man no doubt) was churlish enought to inform the St Rollox and Springburn Express that 88 Caley men were locked up, drunk and incapable, in the station waiting room at Carlisle, and despatched to Glasgow on the Sunday morning.[18]

Not to be outdone, another Scottish railway, the North British, arranged a trip for its employees at the Cowlairs Works, Glasgow, but only ten trains were required to convey some 7,000 over the Border to Berwick-on-Tweed. This particular excursion does not appear to have been such a happy event as the Caley Trip, for not only did two trippers fall to their deaths from the castle ramparts, but a Berwick man wrote thus to the local newspaper:

The Cowlairs trip is over, and most people must be glad of it. The streets were disagreeable and crowded all day and when at night the rain came on it made one miserable to see the wretched plight of the poor souls. To them we would much rather say 'good-bye' as au revoir.[19]

Many sections of railway employees, other than the large works, arranged annual excursions, but an unusual feature of one London, Brighton & South Coast Railway society is interesting since there developed rivalry between the engine depots at New Cross and at Battersea over the decoration of the locomotives used to haul their annual excursions. In Queen Victoria's Diamond Jubilee Year, 1897, a prize of a huge marble clock was offered by an illustrated magazine for the best decorated engine. By a stroke of luck the Battersea District Locomotive Superintendent spotted two gilt figures of a boy and a girl at a local fair. He persuaded the showman to sell them, and these were included in the decoration of locomotive *Allen Sarle*, winner of the coveted clock.[20]

Obsession with cleanliness and whiteness by Victorian housewives consumed tons of both starch and blue, which swelled the profits of Reckitt's of Hull, and made the firm one of the largest employers in that city. Works outings had been run for several years before the First World War, and in 1913 seven excursion trains were required to carry 4,142 passengers for which the North Eastern Railway earned £639 6s 0d.[21]

Huntley & Palmers, the biscuit firm of Reading, ran its first outing for its employees in 1857, taking 450 by rail to the Crystal Palace where

> . . . they all spent a pleasant day. Such expressions of kind feeling by the employer towards the employed are always most gratifying to record.[22]

Works' excursions to the Crystal Palace were repeated in 1859, 1866 and 1886, by which time the numbers had increased to 1,530.

In 1862 this firm won an award for its display at the London Exhibition, and took 1,084 employees by train to see the winning entry. The *Grocer* magazine reported that a young man earning 16 shillings a week was reimbursed by the firm the sum of 30 shillings for damage to his girlfriend's dress whilst at the Exhibition.[23]

Huntley & Palmers' largest rail excursion took place in 1914, when all the schools in Reading closed for the day, enabling the children to accompany their parents. Five special trains conveyed some 4,000 to Ramsgate and Margate, whilst five more trains took some 3,000 to Portsmouth. Departures from Reading were between 3.30 am and 6 am, but the bleary-eyed were enlivened by the music of the Temperance Band playing at the station.

Among the many enamel signs adorning Victorian and Edwardian railway stations were those for 'Sunlight Soap', made by Lever Brothers at Port Sunlight on the Wirral, a firm which regularly arranged monster works' outings by train. In the Diamond Jubilee year of 1897, six special trains were required to convey 2,300 Port Sunlight employees from Bebington station to Euston. An early start at 4 am got the excursionists to London by 9 am, where they were met by brakes and waggonettes for a tour of the sights of London before visiting the Earls Court Exhibition.[24]

> What is beyond the reach of hundreds of thousands of British working men and women has been enjoyed by several hundred fortunate Sunlighters . . .

was how Lever Brothers' magazine began its report of 'the largest picnic on record', being the firm's excursion to the Paris Exhibition in 1900. Four special trains started from Birkenhead, picking up at Bebington and running right through, two to Dover and two to Folkestone, for a sea-crossing to Calais.

Refreshments were provided free on both journeys, as well as a 'knife and fork breakfast, wine lunch and wine dinner at the Exhibition'. In Paris, the 150 horse-drawn

Port Sunlight employees entraining at Bebington & New Ferry station for an excursion, probably in 1901. *(Port Sunlight Heritage Centre)*

brakes taking the party on a city tour were escorted by gendarmes on bicycles.[25] This excursion is said to have cost Levers £7,000.

For the Franco-British Exhibition at White City, London, in 1908, six special trains took 3,000 Port Sunlight workers to Uxbridge Road station on the West London line. Other employees, later in the year, were taken in three trains to Manchester for a visit to Belle Vue Gardens where

> . . . considerable amusement was afforded many of the excursionists who were able, by standing on a slight eminence, to witness many of their colleagues endeavouring to extricate themselves from the bewildering maze . . .[26]

Twelve special trains were involved in taking 6,000 of Levers' employees and families to Blackpool in 1909, but what lay behind the comment, 'even the late arrival and return of one or two of the Bebington trains have not left unpleasant reminiscences . . .'?[27]

IMPORTANT

AS SOME OF THE POINTS OF INTEREST etc. are distant from the Railway Terminus, all persons should allow themselves plenty of time to get to the Station to be comfortably seated in <u>THEIR OWN TRAIN</u> so that a punctual start on the return journey may be made.

This is just one example of the many pieces of sound advice for those travelling on Bass's Excursion to Great Yarmouth in 1893, and for which every one of the 8,000 passengers was provided with a 16-page programme. Fifteen trains were required from Burton-on-Trent, and one from St Pancras, London. From 3.50 am onwards, trains left Burton every 10 minutes until No 15 at 6.10 am. With a journey time of 4 hours 40 minutes for the 180-mile journey, many folk were in Yarmouth in time for breakfast, which was arranged at various Refreshment Houses, according to the programme, which also warned:

... let me advise all to get <u>substantial food</u> and so be fitted for the fatigue of such a long day. Avoid messes and odds and ends, the rather partaking of <u>MEALS</u> at proper hours as you do when at your ordinary employment.[28]

Organiser of this mammoth annual excursion was William Walters, Traffic Manager at Bass's Burton brewery, and his great attention to detail was no doubt fully justified when handling such a vast number of people.

Nothing was left to chance with the location of GENTLEMEN'S LAVATORIES and LADIES' RETIRING ROOMS at Yarmouth indicated. For those travelling in non-corridor carriages it must have been a welcome relief to reach Peterborough where

... passengers may alight for ten minutes both going and returning. They are earnestly requested to resume their seats promptly ... and to avoid leaving or joining the trains whilst in motion.

'Spending a Penny' at Peterborough – perhaps twopence – could also sustain the inner man, or woman, for the refreshment rooms offered:

Tea or Coffee (with slice of Bread & Butter)			2d per cup
Plain Bun	1d		
Bath Bun	2d	Ginger Beer	2d bottle
		Glass of Milk	$1^1/_2$d

Bass & Co's excursion trains await return departure from Blackpool in 1896. *(National Railway Museum, York)*

Sandwich	2d		Ale per Glass	
Sausage Roll	2d		Mild	$1^{1}/_{2}$d
Pork Pie	4d		Bitter	2d

Reflecting the public concern regarding railway accidents in the 1890s, Walters comforted relatives left behind in Burton with this promise:

> Upon arrival of the last Train at Yarmouth, I shall send a Telegram to Messrs Bass and Co announcing the same, which will be exhibited on their Old Brewery Yard Gates, in High St; a similar Telegram will also be sent to Mr Hawkins, at the Midland Railway Station, Burton. The information contained in these messages will be for the friends of the Excursionists, and may be relied upon as being true. These Telegrams should reach Burton about 11.30, if the Trains are running to time. The friends of the Excursionists are therefore advised to take no notice whatever of absurd rumours of accidents, &c (often circulated by unthinking people), but to wait for MY messages, which will be sent from Yarmouth as early as possible after I arrive in the last Train.

All the entertainments, amusements and attractions of Yarmouth were listed, together with sales outlets for 'BASS on DRAUGHT (Pale and Mild), our SPECIAL STOUT, and BASS in BOTTLE'.

Serving a largely agricultural East Anglia, the Great Eastern was nicknamed 'The Sweedey' and (quite unwarranted) given a reputation for unpunctuality. To allay any fears on the part of the Bass trippers that 'the Great Eastern is a wretched line to travel by', the programme assured them that 'the Great Eastern is the MOST PUNCTUAL line in the kingdom'.

After recommending Midsummer herring and a twopenny tram ride to Gorleston, 'to enjoy bracing air', William Walters concluded the programme:

> Travel Both Ways by your Own Train;
> Show your Railway Ticket, and everything I have referred to will be FREE.
> Be well-behaved and respectful to everyone.

The Austin Motor Company, in 1929, chartered nine special trains, five with restaurant cars, to convey 4,500 employees and their families from Birmingham to Blackpool for the famous Illuminations. On the same day, and also to Blackpool, the Tipton Labour Party travelled in three special trains comprised entirely of restaurant cars.[29]

Not only had the Labour Party abandoned its 'cloth cap and cattle truck' image by the 1920s, but the Co-operative movement had too. The Leicester Co-operative Society's Employees Annual Outing in 1931 took 700 to Skegness in 13 LMSR vestibule coaches. Arriving back in a huge city in the small hours of the morning could present a problem for reaching home, but 300 of this party wisely booked seats on the buses specially laid on by the Corporation.

Although the motor coach took much works' excursion traffic away from the railways from the 1930s onwards, not all such parties considered the coaches' facilities to compare favourably with those of rail travel. One such firm was Messrs C. & T. Painter of Harlesden who quitted the road for rail in 1933, when 56 of their staff chartered a saloon carriage for an outing to Brighton. They considered the advantages of rail travel to include more time by the sea and less on a char-a-banc, and the provision of a table for card playing.[30]

Employees of Ringtons Ltd at Newcastle-on-Tyne for the departure of the firm's outing to Scarborough in 1938. 1,500 travelled in two trains from Newcastle and one from Leeds.

A coach company certainly could not have provided the facilities required for Messrs Brown and Haigh's outing from Wigan to Scarborough in 1936, when the organisers requested a kitchen car, open vestibule carriages and a 61-foot luggage van fitted up as a dance saloon. The 500 excursionists had a choice of meals in the restaurant car or light refreshments at the buffet.[31]

In an article in the *Great Western Railway Magazine* headed 'Unbroken Bliss', the writer reports on his sampling of the facilities provided for a works' outing and purports to show 'Where the Railway Beats the Bus'. Here are some of his impressions:

> Despite such meals had on the way at other times, it was a novel experience when, with a party of 100 other workpeople upon their annual trip to the seaside, I answered the call to an en masse breakfast in one of the spacious restaurant cars attached to a Great Western train running from Cheltenham Spa to Brighton.
>
> I make no claim to Scotch ancestry and have never regarded porridge as a first-rate aperitif, but I am ready to confess that on this occasion I welcomed it with an avidity which could not have been exceeded anywhere north of the Tweed. From that I progressed to turbot manniere with a zest only paralleled by that of my vis-a-vis, who asked for grilled kippers. The alternative of the succeeding bacon and eggs, ham and potatoes, sausage and saute potatoes, and cold meats, was a veritable embarras de richesses in which, suffice it to say, I made a happy choice. It needed only the preserves and coffee to bring a state of beatitude worth all the early rising to attain. And then, how transformed did the scenery outside become, and with what calm contentment could one look forward to the end of the journey!

A Kettering clothing firm's outing to Blackpool in the 1950s. *(Northamptonshire Newspapers)*

At long last, having seen, according to our individual preferences, all that Brighton can show in 12 short hours, by devious ways we returned to the railway station to entrain for home. But what a different homecoming it proved, compared with some other journeys of the kind one remembers, for the last bit of anticipation had not on this occasion departed when we got on board and faced some six hours of night riding.

It was not long before the servants of the railway company (may blessings be on their devoted heads!) came round with clean towels and nice cakes of soap with 'G.W.R.' cunningly stamped on them, and much more desirable in every way than the cake the little boy had in the 'Jackdaw of Rheims', and invited us to have a wash. What boon can tired and travel-stained humanity crave more at such a time than soap and water? But that was merely by way of introduction to supper. And what a supper! I merely mention it in contrast to the buns carried back to the train in former days to sustain one through the night, and as an illustration of what the Great Western Railway Company can do for tired workers on a day's outing.

Imagine it, if you can. Time about 11 p.m. Scene: brightly but softly lit dining cars, with white napery and attractively laid tables. Chief actors: 100 holiday makers – hungry as hunters, attended by a dozen or so deft-footed and deft-handed waiters. Menu: roast leg of mutton, with a choice of several vegetables, redcurrant jelly, cold ham, ox tongue, compote of fruit, rice, custard, cheese and salad, coffee! With what unfeigned satisfaction we watched the skillful pouring of that coffee as our train glided along at some 60 miles an hour.

Between the wars, Reckitt's 'Sunshine Fund' arranged an outing for its retired employees and on one occasion 850 old people were taken by special train to Withernsea, an hour's journey. Four halls were booked enabling all the party to be seated for a meal. Each man received a gift of an ounce of tobacco, and each woman a quarter of a pound of tea.[32] An instance of 'His and Ours'!

Reckitt's house journal, Ours, after commenting that several excursionists were aged over 80, related:

> One old gentleman of 92 fainted on arrival at Withernsea and an attempt to procure a bathchair to take him to the sands failing, a cart was found and so he was borne to the beach, where he was instructed to stay until tea-time, when he was transported from the sands to the tearoom by motor car. After tea he voted to return to the sands and this time his friends begged a ride for him on a passing milk cart. Train time approaching, the old gentleman was taken to the station on a motor cycle![33]

It was no exaggeration to describe the Reckitt's Works Council outing to Blackpool in 1934 as 'an opportunity of seeing the lights and allowed members a long evening in Blackpool'. They were there from 5 pm on Saturday until 2 am on Sunday! This is how the scene at Blackpool was described:

> There pandemonium seemed to reign – engines puffed and tooted, megaphones bellowed instructions about times and platforms and throngs of people from every corner of the British Isles (so it appeared) rushed to and fro, talking, laughing, shouting, clutching sticks of rock and trophies won at the Pleasure Beach! . . . For anyone sufficiently wide awake to make the effort a stroll down the train on the homeward journey afforded a sucession of interesting studies in somnolent humanity, though the advent of an excellent supper brought new animation to many. One lady, however, slept so soundly between the courses that only a piercing whistle from the waiter brought her back to her roast mutton after the soup had been removed. Hull was reached at 7.0 am on Sunday morning and Corporation buses awaited arrival of the train and carried the travellers back to their homes.[34]

Claiming to be the biggest works' outing in the UK since the end of the war, Raleigh Industries Ltd of Nottingham took 5,000 to Blackpool in May 1949 and

> . . . everyone was there from the Managing Director to Works Managers. A 5 a.m. departure from Nottingham meant a very early rising for many trippers but as each one entered the platform they were handed a beaker of tea and a seat reservation ticket. Food rationing was still in force therefore no restaurant car meals could be provided, so each person received 'an appetising box lunch on the outward journey which was repeated on the homeward journey, and all employees received 15 shillings with the compliments of the Directors.

Train No 10 conveyed the Directors of the firm, who were given a civic reception by the Deputy Mayor of Blackpool, but afterwards 'our Directors were numbered among the hundreds of Raleigh people who "did" the Tower'. (They are human like us!)

Statistics for the packed meals were a mile of sausages in 10,000 sausage rolls, 20,000

The first of ten special trains conveying Raleigh Industries Ltd employees from Nottingham to Blackpool in 1949.

sandwiches and 10,000 cakes and, on top of all that, the *Nottingham Evening News* sent 5,000 copies of that day's edition by air to Blackpool so that the excursionists could read about their trip on the way home![35]

Excursion trains not only took factory workers on trips, but the general public took advantage of them to visit chocolate, biscuit, soap and engineering factories.

The first railway excursion to Fry's Somerdale factory in the early 1920s was a party from the Institute of Journalists. The popularity of such visits saw the number increase from 2,000 in 1923 to 9,000 in 1926, and by 1936 the 100,000 visitors required some 100 young lady guides. Excursion trains brought visitors from as far away as Belfast, Aberdeen and Penzance, and platforms at the Great Western's Keynsham station had to be extended to accommodate the ever-lengthening excursion trains which, in 1938, took 71,455 visitors to Fry's.[36]

Often these excursion trains followed unusual routes, an example being in June 1932, when an LMSR train ran from Northampton to Keynsham via Blisworth. Here it reversed to run over the ex-SMJR line to Broom Junction (reverse), and then to Ashchurch, to join the LMSR main line to Bristol, where it was handed over to the GWR for the final leg of this circuitous route.[37]

Cadbury Bros of Bourneville, home of the famous chocolate, was a magnet attracting thousands of excursionists by rail to the Model Factory and Garden Village. A return fare of a few shillings included a tour of the works and village, a tea and a small tin of chocolates. For special parties, such as the entire staff of the *Daily News* in 1906, a more extended programme included:

Reception at Bourneville Station
Swedish Drill display by boys and girls
Visit to Almshouses
Lunch in marquee and presentation of Illuminated Address to the Daily News

Visits to biscuit and chocolate factories were popular with the public – a free tea was included. GWR 'Hall' Class No 4937 poses with its passengers. (*National Railway Museum, York*)

Tour of the Village
Cricket and other games, swimming and water polo match.[38]

In the 1930s, the Southern Railway operated excursions to Cadbury Bros comprised of vestibuled coaches, and including a Pullman kitchen car serving luncheon and supper at 2s 6d per meal. The return fare from Brighton, inclusive of visit, was 10 shillings.[39]

The Great Western Railway ran the first of what would be a regular series of excursions to its Swindon Works in November 1927. Ticket sales had to be suspended two days before the day of departure when the number booked had reached 700. A second excursion was arranged a week later for the many disappointed applicants, and this train had to be run in two portions.

Additional publicity was got from some fast running on the return journey by 4-6-0 locomotive *King Edward VII*, which covered the 77 miles from Swindon to Paddington in 68 minutes.[40]

In 1953, to mark the centenary of the opening of the Great Northern Railway's Works at Doncaster, The Plant, the 'Plant Centenarian' excursion was chartered to run from King's Cross hauled by two ex-GNR 'Atlantic'-type locomotives, Nos 990 and 251. Five hundred people paid 55 shillings for a ticket which included meals served at every seat on both the outward and return journeys.[41]

Such customer care for excursionists contrasts with what many have experienced in recent times when either no catering facilities have been available, or trying to obtain a cup of tea has entailed a half-hour-long queue only to be told that supplies are exhausted.

A special train with 500 excursionists from Derby arriving at Bournville station for a tour of Cadbury's works and the Garden Village in 1929.

On 18 August 1854, Amy Jane Clark, daughter of James Clark, founder of the now famous shoe firm of Street, Somerset, wrote to her sister Fanny:

> . . . We went in next door at about ten to see the procession start from Street. All our men were collected opposite . . . they started at about half past ten to go up to the school for the school children, they had been waiting a long time for the band . . . Aubrey and Bessie had made a beautiful banner . . . there was no arch in all Glastonbury that we could see that matched the one opposite Uncle Cyrus's . . . We first of all went through the town to see the decorations. They were so beautiful – fir trees each side of all the streets and a great many arches and strings of flags etc . . . We then went into a field almost close to the station to see the procession pass and then the train come in . . .

Unfortunately much of Amy Jane's letter has been lost, but the *Illustrated London News* explained it all:

OPENING OF THE CENTRAL SOMERSET RAILWAY

The ceremonial of the opening of this line, which carries a road of iron into the very heart of pastoral Somerset, took place on Thursday . . . The station at Glastonbury was gaily decorated with flags and banners . . . the procession wended its way through the ruins of the Abbey, from which it crossed by a temporary bridge to a spacious tent in which a splendid cold collation for near 500 persons had been provided . . . about 800 of the working classes of

Glastonbury were entertained at dinner in another large tent. Some thousand or more operatives of Street were afterwards regaled with tea, besides which the committee, previous to the festival, distributed cake and tea to upwards of 1,500 females. The day, which will long be remembered by the inhabitants of Glastonbury, closed with a brilliant display of fireworks . . .

But what about an excursion? That took place on 28 August 1954, when the Clark family celebrated the centenary of the opening of the railway by chartering a special train to take 250 of their family from Glastonbury for a day at Burnham-on-Sea. In addition to the Clark family and relatives, large numbers of their employees, wives and children were on the train, as were numerous civic dignitaries. Many people were in period dress, and the 12-coach train was hauled by a 'period' Somerset & Dorset Joint Railway locomotive, an 0-6-0 No 43201, formerly No 64 of the S&DJR. Regular passenger services had been withdrawn from the Highbridge–Burnham section in 1951. A commemorative booklet concludes:

A great occasion, greatly celebrated – one which was worth travelling many miles to see and share in, and that will be long remembered.[42]

'Rock and Roll' is how some crews would describe the riding of their locomotives, but the 400 employees of John Beales of Nottingham were able to do just that, not on the engine, but in a converted parcels van, decorated and equipped with a piano. These excursionists danced their way to Blackpool and back on the occasion of their annual outing in June 1963.[43]

Young excursionists aboard 0-6-0 No 43201 which hauled the 'Centenary Celebration' train from Glastonbury to Burnham-on-Sea on 28 August 1954. (*Clark's Archives*)

Chapter 8
ALIVE WITH EXCURSION TRAINS

'The train now numbered 35 carriages and was computed to hold about 1,400, the largest train known to have passed this station since the opening of the Exhibition.'

What was 1,848 feet long, 408 feet broad, 66 feet high, with trancepts 108 feet high and enclosing some of the finest elms growing in Hyde Park, London? Why of course, the Great Exhibition Hall of 1851, or, as Punch named it, 'The Crystal Palace'.

> As though 'twere by a wizard's rod,
> A blazing arch of lucid glass
> Leaps like a fountain from the grass
> To meet the sun.

The 'Wizard' was Joseph Paxton, a director of the Midland Railway, who had doodled his design on a blotter whilst attending a directors' meeting and thereby won himself a prize of £5,000. However, the driving force behind the idea of a great international display of man's, especially British man's, achievement was the Prince Consort, Queen Victoria's husband, Albert.

Britain was the workshop of the world, and the Crystal Palace a symbol of the age, a symbol of capitalist entrepreneurial success, and of the rewards flowing from 'work'. Revolution haunted the rulers of Europe but, here in Britain, the Great Exhibition would demonstrate the superiority of not only British manufactures, but 'reveal to foreigners the attraction of the British constitution'.[1] However, if the gospel of work was to penetrate to those who created the products of British industry, then it had to be made possible for the working classes to visit that vast temple of industry.

To this end the Royal Commission, set up to arrange the Great Exhibition, requested the railway companies to make ample and detailed arrangements for the conveyance of excursionists to London during the summer of 1851. As early as 1842 the major railway companies had formed an association, the Railway Clearing House, which concerned itself mostly with attempts to standardise operations and equipment, and to allocate the revenue from through traffic between the various companies involved. Concerned at the growth of 3rd class travel, it is doubtful if the railway companies would have shown much enthusiasm for moving millions of excursionists to London, had not Prince Albert been behind the Commission's request.

Royal patronage of the Great Exhibition most certainly influenced the Railway Clearing House committee to resolve that

Queen Victoria opens the Great Exhibition of 1851. *(Progress, 1936)*

... the secretary be instructed to summon a meeting of General Managers for Saturday 22nd inst [March 1851] to consider the arrangements which it may be necessary to adopt with reference to excursion trains during the time the exhibition is open.[2]

The General Managers were not enthusiastic and at their first meeting saw insuperable difficulties and decided to 'defer the consideration of the matter to a future period'.[3] At the end of April, with the Exhibition opening on 1 May, it was decided to run no excursion trains to London before 1 July, but Paxton, a member of the Royal Commission, persuaded the railway General Managers to start running on 2 June.[4] Another factor influencing this decision was awareness that the steamship companies intended conveying visitors to the Exhibition from Scotland and East Coast ports at reduced fares.[5]

Excursion facilities were to be confined to working men's clubs, but it was later conceded that their families too should be conveyed, with children under 12 years of age paying only half the excursion fare. Needless to say, proof of membership of a working men's club was not insisted upon by the organisers of excursion trains. The *Railway Times* of June 1851 described the whole country as being 'alive with excursion trains'[6] and, when the exhibition closed after 22 weeks, no fewer than 6,200,000 separate visits had been made, and it was confidently believed that most visitors had arrived by train.

At the time of the Great Exhibition there was a rail network of some 6,600 miles linking most major towns and cities, and both East and West coast routes to Scotland had been completed. Even so, large areas of the West of England, Wales and Scotland were as yet unconnected, and hundreds of smaller towns and villages in England would not be rail connected until the end of the 19th century, when the total rail network reached 21,000 miles. The six million visitors to the exhibition collected from all over the rail system had eventually to be funnelled down the main lines of those companies having a London terminus. The volume of excursionists exceeded the availability of special carriages resulting in many being carried by ordinary trains[7], often to the discomfort of full-fare-paying passengers.

Admission to the Crystal Palace began at £1 (a week's wages for a working man), but was progressively reduced until, at 1 shilling, it was within the reach of all but the most downtrodden. Not only industrialists saw the wisdom of combining philanthropy with education by paying for their employees to travel to the Exhibition, but the squire and parson did too, as the following account illustrates:

EASTERN COUNTIES RAILWAY

On Wednesday last the inhabitants of the Borough of Maldon made arrangements for a general holiday by closing the shops and entirely suspending business. Upwards of 300 persons were conveyed by the early train for a day in the Crystal Palace. The clergy, gentry and inhabitants of Harlow met last week and made a liberal subscription to enable their servants and domestics – men, women and children – to visit the exhibition.[8]

That the Great Exhibition introduced many to the novelty of rail travel is in evidence from events at Colchester station:

On Monday last the Exhibition excursion trains left the Colchester station, the ticket department of which was literally beset with eager folk from the town and neighbourhood, and owing to the great number of excursionists, some totally innocent of railway travelling, caused some little merriment, and considerable delay . . . At Chelmsford, the number of carriages was increased and 284 with cheap tickets took their seats. The train now numbered 35 carriages and was computed to hold about 1,400, the largest train known to have passed this station since the opening of the exhibition.[9]

With such vast crowds travelling, it would have been surprising if no one got lost, but few could have anticipated being labelled!

On Tuesday fifty girls from Bath and the same number from Bristol were sent on a trip to the Great Exhibition by Sir John Hare of the Royal Crescent. Six of them, we hear, got lost in the crowd, and having been found by the police, were stowed away in the inner room of the police station, and labelled 'Bath' and 'Bristol'. They were made as comfortable as circumstances would permit and at last safely returned to the . . . party.[10]

Paxton had placed a vast glass roof over the Crystal Palace, but many excursionists to the Exhibition were conveyed in carriages without roofs:

On Monday last the number of passengers by the excursion train was 1,047 from Hungerford station alone; the whole number of passengers was greater than expected, exceeding 3,000. A want of sufficient carriages at this station caused a delay of nearly half an hour, after which some of the passengers were obliged to travel in open trucks. There is no doubt a complete arrangement will be made on future occasions.[11]

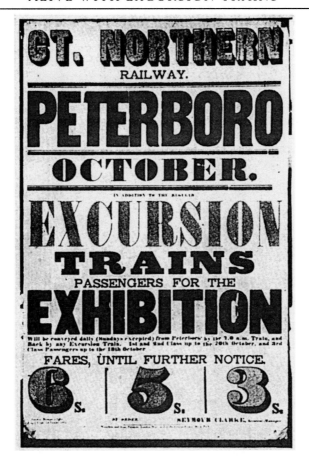

The Great Northern Railway's terminus at King's Cross was not ready for the Great Exhibition of 1851 so a temporary station at Maiden Lane was used.

In 1851, only two main lines connected London with the Midlands and the North of England, the London & North Western Railway and the Great Northern Railway. All the London-bound traffic from the Midland Railway at Rugby was funnelled into that of the LNWR from Scotland, Lancashire and North Wales, so that the LNWR's Euston terminus facilities were taxed beyond the limit.

At King's Cross, or York Road to be precise, because the Great Northern's new terminus was not yet completed, there were boisterous scenes, as this retired GNR employee recalled some 50 years later:

> We had brought up hundreds of north countrymen, chiefly Yorkshiremen to see 'T' Exhibition' and hadn't enough carriages to take them back . . . No promise of carriages could be given for some hours, and a wild time our Superintendent had of it . . . a night with a crowd of Yorkshiremen of half a century ago, combining the pertinacity of the cheap tripper who wants to get home and can't, with the radical methods of people who, in their native haunts, were said to be used to 'fettling' one another's 'mouts wi' bricks', was

objectionable from several points of view. He went out to endeavour to pacify them. They surrounded him in one surging clamourous mass; they shook in his face their unmailed fists, 'till I expected every moment . . . some serious injury to be done . . . Orders were sent in all directions, the telegraph needles clicked, news of 'more coaches' on the road was received. Many of the people adjourned to the slopes of a green embankment just outside the station; those who had ha'pence left sent for beer, some regaled themselves with the remnants of bread and cheese turned up from pockets or reticules; here and there a piece of German sausage or the contents of a tin travelling flask were shared with a neighbour, and the evening wore away, not unenlivened by the chorusing of the then 'last new' music hall song . . . Train after train of empties rolled into the station and were quickly loaded and started away; but not for hours did the last of those weary ones disappear through the tunnel . . .[12]

Some delay to returning excursionists was caused by the departure of Queen Victoria by Royal Train for Scotland. Her Majesty's request for a slow rate of travel added to the delay until some 3,000 excursionists attempted to board trains with a total capacity of only 1,000. The Chairman of the Great Northern Railway was on hand and threatened to dislodge those who had forced their way on to the wrong trains, making use of his walking stick! 'In such emergencies as this cattle trucks had not infrequently to be pressed into use for passenger service.'[13]

What did the six million visitors to the Crystal Palace see? Well, there was a 24-ton block of coal which the LNWR had conveyed from the Tipton Collieries, whilst two of its engines were on display, *Cornwall* built by Trevithick at Crewe, and Crampton's *Liverpool*. Both these engines were, however, eclipsed by the Great Western Railway's *Lord of the Isles*, broad gauge with 8-foot driving wheels, designed by Daniel Gooch. In green livery, with its highly polished metal and its copper dome, it towered over the other railway exhibits.

This was a time when the great engineers, men like Robert Stephenson, I. K. Brunel and Charles Vignoles, were spanning great river estuaries and carrying railways not only to the extremities of the United Kingdom, but across continents. There were models of the Britannia Bridge across the Menai Straits, the tubular bridge over the Wye at Chepstow and a British-built suspension bridge over the Dnieper at Kiev in Russia.

There were marine engines by Maudsley, stationary engines by James Watt & Co, and James Naysmith's steam hammer. Hydraulics were powering the machinery of the vast docks of the land and William Armstrong's hydraulic cranes and rams were on display. The intricate machinery of the textile mills rattled away beside a new mechanical printing press and a vast range of machine tools by the famous firm of Whitworths.

The exhibits were divided into four groups; raw materials, machinery, manufactures and fine arts. There were cotton spinning machines from Lancashire and the latest Singer sewing machines from the USA. Sèvres pottery was displayed along with Staffordshire's finest wares, and Honiton lace could be compared with Barcelona's fine black variety.

There were steam engines for agricultural work and a new reaping machine from the USA which would have aroused the interest of those farm workers able to visit the Crystal Palace as, for example, the 800 from the counties of Surrey and Sussex, 'conducted by the clergy at a cost of 2s 2d each person'.[14]

Not all the inventions were destined to catch on. For instance, nothing came of an 'alarm bedstead, causing a person to arise at any given hour', or of a 'Cricket catapulta, for propelling the ball in the absence of a first-class bowler'.

Queen Victoria was keenly interested in a medal-making machine to stamp out

50 million medals a week, and she 'had a go' with the electric telegraph, sending messages to her loyal subjects in Edinburgh and Manchester.[15]

To the denizens of the 'dark satanic mills' and dwellers in the back-to-back slums and courts of the industrial towns where the exhibits were produced, the bright, light, well-ventilated Crystal Palace must have seemed a real fairyland, but the astute Prince Consort, President of the Society for the Improvement of the Condition of the Labouring Classes, gave the labouring class visitors a glimpse of better things to come by arranging for a model house to be built close to the Exhibition.

After one visit to the Exhibition, Queen Victoria wrote in her journal:

> The tremendous cheering, the joy expressed in every face, the vastness of the building, the sound of the organ (with 200 instruments and 600 voices which seemed nothing) and my beloved husband, the creator of this peace festival, 'uniting the industry and art of all nations upon earth', all this was indeed moving, and a day to live forever. God bless my dearest Albert, and my dear country, which has shown itself so great today.[16]

Five weeks after the opening of the Great Exhibition, Cook's *Exhibition Herald and Excursion Advertiser* had to apologise for not being able to announce their first excursion:

> OUR FIRST TRIP. Various circumstances have delayed Our First Trip; but the principal hindrance has been the backwardness of the railway authorities in settling their terms . . . Even now on the 29th day of May, whilst tens of thousands are daily feasting on the gorgeous Hyde Park banquet of industry and skill, it is not positively known when the special arrangements of the railway companies for the industrial classes will come into operation, nor are the fares, we believe, definitely settled.[17]

In view of the fact that the Royal Commission had expressed its wish that the railways provide facilities for the labouring classes to be conveyed to the Exhibition, there must be suspicion as to why the companies dragged their feet. Was it collusion to keep the Crystal Palace select for the better classes? Was it reluctance to run excursion trains at excursion fares? Thomas Cook was quite outspoken on this:

> The Great Exhibition is mainly indebted for its astonishing interest to the skill and industry of the mechanics, artizans and others of the operative classes. And in many instances the honour of invention and execution which properly belongs to these classes is monopolised by the principals of manufactories (who may be mere noodles) or the wealthy millionaire, whose gold has made him the representative of the products of better men's brains and hands . . .
>
> DAY TRIPS TO LONDON AND BACK. With the view of meeting the circumstances of those who have but little time to spare from their occupations, and whose means are limited; and especially for the convenience of great numbers of young persons who could not with propriety be cast upon London for several days – SPECIAL EXPRESS DAY TRAINS . . . will leave Bradford 12.15 am; Leeds at 1; Normanton 1.30; Wakefield (by omnibus) 1.15; Barnsley (by omnibus) 1.30; Sheffield 1.40; Masboro 2.20; from whence it will proceed direct to London, only making necessary stoppages for water, refreshments etc. and arriving in London about 8.30 am, returning from Euston station at 9.0 pm.[18]

Excursionists, up from the country, at the Great Exhibition on a 'One Shilling' day. *(Illustrated London News)*

Here is one description of the scene on a 'One Shilling' day:

> [The working man] is waiting at the doors long before the opening time of ten has rung. He is there with his friends and his household – bundle in hand, and shilling in hand; through the glass he catches devious glimpses of fairy-land . . . Everyone stands on his tiptoes – mental and material – until chime goes the magic hour, down fall the barriers, round rush the turnstiles and [all] stand agape and wondering in Industrial Fairyland.
>
> . . . Where to begin, what to look at first, what to look at most, what to look at the closest? . . . Workers in wood, and in iron, and in stone, find the most congenial subjects for criticism in their own crafts; and accordingly, so long as each man confines himself to the examination of the branch of industry he understands, there is far more sound critisism flung about by the shillingers than by the five shillingers – far more real appreciation, and far more knowing remarks. [Mrs working man goes] backwards and forwards from compartment to compartment and aisle to aisle; up this gallery, down that, leaving a miraculous vision of dainty crystal for an extraordinary spectacle of gleaming pottery, hanging, oh how charmed and delighted, for many a rapt half-hour, over the pianofortes, and listening to those surprising musicians playing polkas and schottisches; . . .
>
> Dinner, thus, in all manner of dark holes and nooks and corners. A great untying of handkerchiefs and distribution of viands, and strange whiffs of rum and gin borne upon wandering zephyrs.
>
> After dinner and the scene is busier still. Humble, earnest, curious people are yet pouring in in continued streams from every turnstile. Groups of girls go giggling along together, and are only brought back to admiring gravity by

the sight of fine clothes. Boys whistle to their comrades . . . juveniles crying bitterly in consequence of having been lost, are taken to the station by benevolent policemen; charity schools walk in drab-coloured processions through the aisle; . . . Again we have groups collected around the Crystal Fountains; everybody waiting for somebody else – everybody looking for somebody else – separated families coming together – the occupants of excursion trains being mustered – greetings passing between townsmen or village men who have not met since morning – more whistling boys, more giggling girls, more lost children . . . [19]

As many as 74,122 visitors were admitted to the Exhibition on a 'Shilling Day' in July, but the record attendance occured in October when 109,760 seized almost their last chance to see the show. Such was the crush that the officials dispensed with the turnstiles.[20]

When the doors of the exhibition finally closed, it had made a profit of £186,437 which was used to found the museums which now stand in Exhibition Road, London. What of the railways which had made possible the conveyance of the multitudes in response to the Prince's appeal? The financial aspect of the Great Exhibition excursion traffic is considered in another chapter.

There can be no doubt but that the millions conveyed by rail to the Great Exhibition at very low fares triggered off a tremendous expansion of excursion travel, whilst the event itself stimulated enthusiasm for more exhibitions by both the organisers and the public. During the next half-century the railways ran excursion traffic to, among others, The Art Treasures Exhibition, Manchester (1857); The International Exhibition, London (1862); The Dublin Industrial Exhibition (1865); The International Exhibition (1872); The Fisheries Exhibition (1883); The International Health Exhibition (1884); International Inventions (1885); Indian and Colonial (1886), all in London; International Exhibitions at Liverpool and Manchester (1887) and Glasgow (1887 and 1888).

On and on went the exhibitions: Leeds (1887); The American at London's Earls Court (1887); The Anglo-Danish and The Italian (1888); The Spanish (1889); French (1890); Electric and Engineering at Edinburgh (1890); and the International Horticultural at Earls Court (1891).

For the International Exhibition in London in 1862, J. & J. Colman of Norwich took 500 of their workpeople by train, making an early start at 4.30 am and arriving at Liverpool Street at 9 am. Jeremiah James Colman wrote to his sister:

> If you had happened to be in London last Monday you would have liked to see the men – they were out for a day's frolic which they meant to enjoy, and enjoy it they did with no mistake about it . . . The day was unfortunately wet, but that did not matter much, and it did not make the men in love with London – most of them thought it a dirty place as they should not like to live in. They did not either fancy the people they saw, and one said he 'did not see a decently fat man all the time he was there' . . . Several told me they never enjoyed a day so much in their lives . . . I am especially glad that I made up my mind to go with the men in the same train.[21]

Glasgow's International Exhibition of 1888 generated a crop of excursion trains and the anticipated volume of traffic induced the North British Railway to increase the accommodation at its Finnieston station, the nearest to the Exhibition entrances. A new booking office, covered stairways to the platform and a new covered and glazed footbridge, together with 'ample lavatory accommodation for ladies and gentlemen with four drinking fountains' were provided.[22]

The Scotsman carried this description of the Exhibition:

> The main building, over a quarter of a mile in length, takes the form of a Moorish Palace and occupies with other erections, about 14 acres, being the largest exhibition since the London one of 1862 . . . One of the chief features of the design is a Kremlin-like dome at the intersection which attains the immense height of over 170 feet to the top of the vane.
>
> One of the principal features of the display is the grounds which extend to upwards of 50 acres. The southern bank of the Kelvin has the City Industrial Museum where the Queen's Jubilee presents are displayed; Van Houten's Dutch house, a working dairy, the Indian tea-room, a large number of conservatories, a bandstand, a terra-cotta fountain, which Messrs Doulton & Co have presented to the City, and an iron one which Messrs Dowell Steven & Co have erected. On the margin of the river steps lead to landing stages, used by those who patronise the gondolas, electric launches, torpedo boats and other craft which ply upon it.
>
> Provision is made for amusement by means of a 'switchback railway', a couple of shooting saloons and an equal number of bandstands. The grounds will be brilliantly illuminated after dark with coloured lamps as well as with electric light . . .
>
> The Machinery Court, which covers 160 square feet consists of nine bays, with a broad gallery carried around three sides of the square. It embraces probably one of the finest assortments of pieces of mechanism of all kinds ever witnessed . . .[23]

Excursion traffic was heavy throughout the Exhibition period, with 18 trains daily from Edinburgh and eight from towns in Fife.[24] However, attendance was apparently not up to the organisers' expectations for, when considering preparations for the 1901 Glasgow International Exhibition,

> . . . the Committee considered that during the Exhibition of 1888 the public throughout Scotland had not availed themselves of Excursion Trains so fully as they might have done, and the Committee had decided to send Canvassers to the larger centres of population to organise Excursions.[25]

The Caledonian Railway Company undertook to run excursion trains on any day, from all their stations in Scotland to Glasgow, and instructed that a footnote be added to all bills advertising bookings to Glasgow – 'Covered gangway direct from the Platform at Partick Central Station into the Exhibition'.[26]

Although the Great Exhibition of 1851 closed in October, the Crystal Palace building still had a future of some 85 years, but not in Hyde Park. A new Crystal Palace Company was formed in 1852 with Samuel Long as Chairman of both the new company and the London, Brighton & South Coast Railway. With an eye to future traffic, the LB&SCR made a substantial investment in the Crystal Palace Company, having the structure dismantled and re-erected on a hill at Sydenham in South London. In 1854, a branch line was opened to a new station built at the Crystal Palace.

Another railway, the London, Chatham & Dover, built a line to the Palace, completed in 1865, and opened its station known as High Level, which was alongside the Palace and connected by a subway.

The London, Chatham & Dover Railway's High Level station at Crystal Palace, opened in 1865. *(Illustrated London News)*

Excursionists travelled to the Crystal Palace in connection with exhibitions, music festivals and, in 1895, for Bostock and Wombwell's Royal National Menagerie. There were extensive grounds with gardens, lakes and huge, stone prehistoric monsters, whilst on summer evenings there were firework displays by Brocks.

When the Italian patriotic leader, Garibaldi, visited the Crystal Palace in 1864, special trains ran over LB&SCR metals from the MR, NER, LNWR, GWR and the North London Railway. It is interesting to note that 2nd class passengers still needed reassuring that covered carriages would be provided.

'Tens of thousands of SALVATIONISTS AND THEIR FRIENDS' is what the Salvation Army predicted for its 32nd anniversary gathering at the Crystal Palace in Queen Victoria's Jubilee year of 1897. The Salvation Army's newspaper, *War Cry*, displayed a list of over 1,200 stations from which excursion trains would run or excursion fares would operate, stretching from Carlisle to Penzance and from Pwllheli to Cromer, whilst from the Isle of Wight a special ferry boat left Ryde Pier at 5 am to connect with the excursion train to Crystal Palace.

For the Imperial Fruit Show in 1921, the Great Eastern Railway ran the Apple Show Express comprising 13 coaches and a restaurant car. On Monday it ran from Kings Lynn via Wisbech, March, Ely and Cambridge; on Wednesday from Kings Lynn via March, St Ives and Cambridge; and on Thursday from Norwich via Ipswich. On arrival at Liverpool Street station, the excursionists were conveyed by charabanc to the Crystal Palace. Locomotive No 1834, a 4-4-0, displayed a large, rosy apple on its smokebox and the legend 'Apple Show Express', whilst similar displays adorned the tender sides. Some 500 passengers travelled on the first excursion, 761 and 536 on the second and third respectively.[27]

Changing tastes in entertainment, and finally the First World War, brought to an end the Crystal Palace's role as an entertainment centre, but it continued to dominate the

THE COMING C.P. WILL THE BEAT THE RECORD !

WAR CRY

And Official Gazette of The Salvation Army.

INTERNATIONAL HEADQUARTERS.   [Registered at the General Post Office as a Newspaper.]   101, QUEEN VICTORIA STREET, E.C.

No. 1,595.   LONDON, SATURDAY, JULY 17, 1897.   PRICE ONE PENNY.

32ND Anniversary

Will You be There and I?

(Salvation Army Archives and Research Centre)

south London scene until it burned down in 1936.

Belle Vue Gardens, Manchester, to which so many excursion trains ran in connection with the variety of entertainment provided, was, in contrast to the Crystal Palace, the creation of one man and his family. In 1836 John Jennison bought Belle View House, a roadside inn on the outskirts of Manchester, and with it 36 acres of very rough ground. 'Old John' decided to have a Zoological Garden at Belle View and, in 1840, purchased the animals of a zoo which had closed down. There were monkeys, a reindeer and a chimpanzee that dressed up like a Victorian swell, smoked a pipe and drank tea. 'At enormous expense' Jennison purchased 'the King of Oudh's Fighting Tiger'.

'Novelty' became Belle Vue's (no longer 'View') slogan, and this resulted in 1852 in the first firework spectacular, 'The Bombardment of Algiers'. The Brass Band Competitions became an attraction, surviving until recent times, and in 1888 50 excursion trains ran to Belle Vue with bandsmen and supporters. Belle Vue scored several firsts – the first elephant seen in Lancashire and, in 1906, a 'spectacular new attraction', a helter-skelter tower.[28]

Served by Longsight station on the London & North Western Railway from 1842, and Ashburys on the Manchester, Sheffield & Lincolnshire from 1855, a third station named Belle Vue was opened in 1875 on the Sheffield & Manchester Joint line from Ashburys to New Mills.

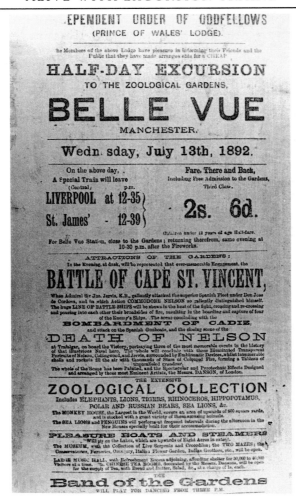

What a bargain! A battle, a bombardment and the death of Nelson for 2s 6d including the rail fare from Liverpool to Manchester.

When the Independent Order of Oddfellows (Prince of Wales Lodge) chartered a special train from Liverpool Central to Belle Vue in July 1892, the attractions included:

> In the evening at dusk will be represented that ever memorable Engagement, the

> BATTLE OF CAPE ST VINCENT

> When Admiral Sir Jno Jervis, KB, gallantly attacked the superior Spanish Fleet under Don JOSE de CORDOVA, and in which action COMMODORE NELSON so gallantly distinguished himself. The huge LINE OF BATTLESHIPS will be shown in the heat of the fight, crossing and recrossing and pouring into each other their broadsides of fire, resulting in the boarding and capture of four of the Enemy's Ships. The same concluding with the

BOMBARDMENT OF CADIZ and the attack on the Spanish Gunboats, and the closing scene of the
DEATH OF NELSON

For those seeking less bloodthirsty entertainments there was the Zoological Collection including

... ELEPHANTS, LIONS, TIGERS, RHINOCERUS, HIPPOPOTAMUS, POLAR AND RUSSIAN BEARS, SEA LIONS &c.

One could get lost in two mazes, and either listen to, or dance to, the Band of the Garden. Those taking their own refreshments could obtain

... Hot Water for Tea, Teapots, Teacups, Plates, Knives, Forks, Spoons, Trays &c ...

In 1889, M Eiffel engineered the world's tallest iron construction, a tower 984 feet high overlooking Paris. The success of the Eiffel Tower as a tourist attraction fired the imagination of a British railway magnate, Sir Edward Watkin, Chairman of the Metropolitan, MS&LR and South Eastern railway companies, for he planned a tower over 1,000 feet high to be erected on a site in north London. The Metropolitan Tower Company purchased 280 acres of land at Wembley in 1889 for the development of an amusement park, with the tower as a main attraction for the crowds of visitors which his railways hoped to convey.[29]

Watkin's tower never rose above the first stage, to which sightseers were admitted in 1896 and, with the demise of the whole scheme, the tower base was demolished in 1907. Another attempt to attract crowds to Wembley was more successful 17 years later with the opening of the British Empire Exhibition.

In the 1920s, every school boy and girl was taught that the sun never set on the British Empire but, in fact, just when the Empire covered a larger area than ever before, Britain's economy ceased to grow; instead it began to decline. What to do about it? In 1851 had not the Great Exhibition shown the world what Britain could do and stimulated pride among the population in their country's achievements?

So the idea of another great exhibition was floated and took concrete form as the British Empire Exhibition opened at Wembley on 23 April 1924 by His Majesty King George V. Costing £12 million, the pavilions, stadium and funfair covered 220 acres. The additional railway facilities provided have already been described in connection with football excursions.

As the crowds poured off the trains they entered the Exhibition ground through a massive West African fort of terracotta stucco, after which they made their choice of the vast pavilions housing the exhibits of the many lands comprising the British Empire. India's hall was an evocation of the Taj Mahal, whilst Australia displayed a mountain of butter, not to be confused with the EEC's butter mountain 60 years later!

The railway exhibits were a magnet for the boys, young and older, who stood dwarfed by the then giants of steam, the GWR's 4-6-0 No 4073 *Caerphilly Castle*, and the LNER's 4-6-2 No 4472 *Flying Scotsman*. The rival claims of the two companies for their locomotives led to one of the highlights of railway history, the locomotive trials of May 1925, when the superiority of the GWR principles of valve setting were established.

For those who could afford it, lunching, dining or just taking afternoon tea in the dining car of the South African Railways must have had quite an appeal, for some 60,000

The LNER's Wembley Exhibition station with a train composed of ex-Great Central coaches just arrived.

persons enjoyed this service. Since the car seated only 46 persons, the three or four sittings for each meal must have kept the staff busy.[30]

Of the 17 million visitors to Wembley, the majority arrived by train, with just one line alone, the LMSR, claiming to have carried six million. The Metropolitan Railway's trains shuttled to and fro from Baker Street, pouring in passengers at the rate of 1,000 per minute.[31] It was not quite a never-stop service, but inside the Exhibition there really was a 'Neverstop Railway' conveying sightseers around the grounds on an elevated track. The small cars were driven by a revolving continuous screw laid between the rails. The thread varied in pitch so that, through stations the cars crawled at walking pace, but between stations they travelled faster.

Regarded as a great educational opportunity by headmasters and parents, school parties poured in by the trainload, but were they all as well disciplined as these?

> A visit to the British Empire Exhibition which 400 Scarborough children of the elementary schools made during the past week is by far the greatest enterprise of its kind ever carried out under the auspices of the Local Education Authority . . . The railway authorities at Kings Cross said the train was absolutely clean from litter. They had seen nothing like it from any party travelling as we were . . . We took a supply of paper bags as waste paper baskets, and the children put their bits, orange peel, etc into the bags . . .[32]

Litter had become such a problem that *The Railway Magazine* described it as 'a very serious nuisance especially at the British Empire Exhibition', and the LNER produced a poster depicting a Boy Scout clearing litter under the caption 'His Day's Good Deed'.

Because of the 'special educational advantages offered at this exhibition', the directors of J. & J. Colman of Norwich decided to pay the expenses of any of their employees visiting the Wembley Exhibition, including admission. Three special trains were booked to carry the 1,971 employees to Liverpool Street station, London, where they transferred to special trains on the Metropolitan line to Wembley Stadium.

The editors of the Carrow Works magazine produced a special supplement to enable Colman's employees to derive the maximum pleasure from their visit:

WEMBLEY IN A DAY
THE EMPIRE IN A NUTSHELL
WONDERS AT WEMBLEY
THINGS WORTH NOTING

Among the wonders mentioned were: The World's Biggest Window, Bouncing Pottery from British Guiana and an Electric Farm powered by a 40-foot 'windmill'. Twenty tons of music were being used by the massed choirs, whilst the Aquarium used 50,000 gallons of sea water brought specially from the Dogger Bank.[33] The girls from the Starch Packing Department at Great Yarmouth wrote to the directors thanking them for 'one of the red letter days' of their lives.[34]

Boots (The Cash Chemists) took 5,800 employees to Wembley, the LNER providing eight special trains from Nottingham Victoria, departing between 5.47 and 9.02 am and the last due back at 2.36 am. Boots' magazine, *The Beacon*, described the visit as 'one never to be forgotten by any of Boots employees'.

It required five trains on each of five consecutive Mondays to convey 14,000 Lever Brothers' employees and their families from Port Sunlight to Wembley. Every adult and child was given a rail ticket and admission to the Exhibition, whilst unmarried employees and those men travelling without wives received 3 shillings, for refreshments, but married couples got 6 shillings. The *Port Sunlight News*, in giving details of the trip and advice on what to see, concluded:

> . . . As to the Exhibition . . . it is superfluous to advertise its magnificence of conception, the wonderful mirror it holds up to the energies of the British Empire . . . We shall all, in visiting it, become aware more truly than ever before of the greatness of the commonwealth of nations to which we belong . . . [35]

The British Empire proved to be in terminal decline, but in 1938 yet another Empire Exhibition was held, this time in Glasgow. Since it coincided with Lever Brothers' jubilee, the firm arranged to take its employees across the Border. Seventeen trains were involved, running on four consecutive Saturdays. Breakfast was served on the train on the outward journeys and supper on the return.

Not all these Lever excursionists were enthusiastic to witness '. . . the progress of the British Empire at home and overseas', or 'To emphasize to the world the peaceful aspirations of the people of the British Empire', as their *News* would have it. Many went off to Loch Lomond, others to Rothesay and Dunoon and some on a three lochs tour. 'A Young Man on the Staff' afterwards wrote a glowing account of the day and concluded:

> . . . Although our stay was in the nature of a flying visit it must have been sufficient to leave in the minds of all those from Port Sunlight a pleasant and lasting memory.

No doubt as to who is going where! *('The Beacon', Boots)*

The organisers congratulated the LMSR, and the LMSR congratulated Lever Brothers' organisers.[36]

'Special One Day Excursion to Glasgow Empire Exhibition' is how the Leicester Co-operative Society advertised their two trains, and leaving Leicester at 11 pm on Friday night and not arriving back before 6 am on Sunday, 'day' was no understatement. For 33 shillings, Tour No 1 included the rail journey in an 'LMS Vestibule Train', breakfast in Glasgow, a motor coach tour of Scottish beauty spots, admission to the Exhibition and a hot lunch. Tour No 2 at 20s 9d excluded the coach tour. A wise precaution was to purchase tickets for Leicester Corporation buses which met these trains upon their return.[37]

Pre-war excursion fares, at first sight, appear very cheap, but wages were equally low; consequently many people had to save up their money for a day out. The Leicester Co-operative Society sold sixpenny stamps which were applied to holiday savings cards. The LNER entered into an arrangement with the Yorkshire Penny Bank whereby depositors could make regular payments to a holiday fund. Instead of drawing cash for rail tickets, including excursion tickets, the depositor received a voucher exchangeable for a rail ticket, with a 5 per cent reduction on the cost.[38]

A century after the Great Exhibition, after the 'War to End All Wars' of 1914-1918 had been followed by the Second World War, the Festival of Britain was staged on London's South Bank in 1951. Whereas the 1851 exhibition had been of an international character with Britain dominating the scene, the 1951 Festival was intended as 'the people giving themselves a pat on the back', in the words of Herbert Morrison, Labour's Foreign Secretary, whose brainchild it was. After six years of war, followed by post-war austerity, thousands of visitors flocked to enjoy the 'fun, fantasy and colour' of the Festival, and the railways, now nationalised, carried large numbers by excursion trains, works outings and school trips, as well as by ordinary trains.

Railway exhibits were popular with the visitors, particularly a large 2-8-2 locomotive for the Indian Government Railways and British Railways' latest standard steam locomotive, *Britannia*, but a train that one could ride on was bound to appeal to all ages, and the 'Far Tottering and Oyster Creek Railway' was filled for every one of its third-of-a-mile circuits of the Festival Pleasure Gardens. Engine No 1, *Nellie*, improbably described as an 0-2-0, shared duties with *Neptune*, resembling a paddle steamer, and *Wild Goose*, looking like a hot-air balloon on rails!

The Far Tottering & Oyster Creek Railway at the Festival of Britain Fun Fair in 1951. Engine No 1, *Nellie*, took visitors on a third-of-a-mile run round the Pleasure Gardens.

Chapter 9
POLITICS, RELIGION AND TEMPERANCE

'Perhaps there is no class of British subjects who have availed themselves more of the facilities afforded by railway communication . . . than the abstainers from strong drinks . . .'

Perhaps the earliest use of the railway by a religious body was in the Spring of 1839, when the Society of Friends obtained special terms for the carriage of their party from Liverpool to Newton by the Liverpool & Manchester Railway.[1]

It has been shown how the Nonconformist Chapels were among the earliest organisations to take advantage of railway excursions for Sunday School Outings, and the Methodists of Diss, Norfolk, made their first trip to Great Yarmouth by train in 1853. 'When a man is tired of London he is tired of life,' wrote Dr Johnson, but what about tiring of Great Yarmouth? The Diss Methodists never once missed their excursion to that seaside resort in 59 years, and in 1912 their numbers reached 1,500.[2]

A grand temperance fete at which the pubs ran dry does seem to be something of a contradiction, but here is how one newspaper reported an event at Cleethorpes in 1863:

> A grand temperance fete and congregation of the Primitive Methodist body took place at Cleethorpes on Monday. People came in great numbers by railway (upwards of 12,000) and as many more by other conveyance. The cliff presented the appearance of a large pleasure fair, and every variety of stall and plentiful amusement was to be met with. Claude Duvalli, the rope-walker, again exhibited his agility, much to the annoyance of sober-minded persons who assembled on this occasion to take part in the open air preaching and praying, which was held close by . . . The bazaar and tea booths and collections on the cliffs realised something handsome towards paying off the debt on the Cleethorpes Chapel, and the vast concourse of people very much benefited the trade of the town. So great was the drain on the public houses that they were all dry before the crowds had cleared off, and such a profitable day Cleethorpes had never before experienced. Much credit is due to the promoters, and likewise to the millions who supported them. The behaviour of the latter was characterised by sobriety, order and patience, and there was abundant cause for exercise of this last virtue, many thousands being kept waiting at the station until a late hour. Notwithstanding the immense increase of traffic, the officials went through their work without the confusion or incivility too often the concomitants of these monster excursions.[3]

THE WELCOME HOME OF CAPTAIN DEANS AND LIEUTENANT MORRIS. MAY 9th 1887.

Part of the vast crowd at Buckingham which welcomed the two Salvation Army leaders back from prison in 1887. *(Salvation Army Archives & Research Centre)*

It would seem that there was sometimes a lack of 'Customer Care' 120 years before British Rail adopted the slogan.

When the leading citizens of Buckingham, aided by the police, attempted to intimidate those attending a Salvation Army meeting in the town in 1887, they little thought that their action would result in vast crowds descending on their town some 14 days later. Two of the Salvation Army men were charged with the unlawful playing of musical instruments and sentenced to 14 days' imprisonment at Aylesbury gaol.

Their subsequent release was the occasion for a planned reception back at Buckingham, with excursion trains from neighbouring towns conveying more than 800 Salvationists to join the crowds already thronging the approach to the station. To the beat of five brass bands they marched round the town and back to the station to meet the released prisoners – Captain Deans and Lieutenant Morris.

> . . . a quarter of an hour before the train arrived, and after the expected train had been signalled it was difficult to keep one's feet the excitement was so intense and the crushing to obtain a glimpse of the 'martyrs' as these two young men were termed, was simply indescribable . . . then an enthusiastic cry 'Here they come' arose, quickly followed by the appearance of the 'martyrs', who were immediately seized and carried bodily through the mob and in a surprisingly short space of time were placed upon two ponies which had been brought for the purpose. There it was that the whole assembly got a good sight

Crowds on Rushden station, Northamptonshire, await a special train taking them to a Billy Graham revivalist rally in 1955.

of them, and it also showed the imitation 'prison garb' with which Capt. Deans and Lieut Morris were clothed, to great advantage . . .

Through crowds estimated at 2,000 and more they proceeded to a field where tea was served, after which Commandant Booth told them that every Salvation Army corps within 40 miles was represented. Captain Deans said 'that the devil never knew that such a demonstraion would take place or he would never have sent them to prison . . .'[4]

Religious pilgrimages have generated considerable excursion traffic over the years, and often to otherwise little heard-of stations. In connection with St Winefride's Well at Holywell, North Wales, in the 1930s, trains left Euston at 9.30 am on a Sunday morning giving four hours at Holywell for a return fare of 22s 6d. There were also excursions from Selby, Leeds and Manchester. Other venues for pilgrimage excursions were Glastonbury, Somerset and Buckfastleigh Abbey, Devon. In 1935, two trains were required to convey pilgrims from London's Liverpool Street station to the Catholic Pilgrimage at Walsingham, Norfolk. In Scotland, in 1927, the LMSR opened a halt specially for pilgrim traffic to Holytown, situated on the ex-Caledonian Railway's line between Edinburgh and Glasgow. As many as 22 excursions called there on a day of pilgrimage.[5]

Undoubtedly the largest number ever conveyed on Britain's railways in connection with a religious event was for the visit of Pope John Paul II in 1982, when the train arrangements were comparable to those for the evacuation of children from our cities to safer areas in the Second World War. Special train arrangements were required for not just one but nine venues where Mass was to be celebrated, being Wembley, Coventry, Liverpool, Manchester, Cardiff, Edinburgh, Glasgow, Canterbury and York.

The visit coincided with the Spring Bank Holiday weekend, and the Pope arrived at

Gatwick on Friday 28 May to be conveyed in the Southern Region's General Manager's saloon, hauled by an electric locomotive of Class 73, *Broadlands*, to Victoria Station, London.

It is impossible to distinguish clearly between the strengthened normal services and extra trains operated to the various venues, but some idea of the scale of operations can be gained from the fact that the London Midland Region planned to run 750 trains, and the Western Region actually ran over 200 extra trains to Cardiff, and the Eastern Region nearly 100 to York.

British Rail carried through a really mammoth organisational task with few hitches, and this with a much depleted staff and very few spare coaches or locomotives to call upon. At York, for example, 60 clerical staff were recruited to act as stewards to marshal the crowds into their appropriate queues for the return trains. Additional carriage and station cleaners were on duty, whilst stand-by engineers were on hand at York and other strategic points in the region to deal with any emergency troubles.

Feeding the five thousand with five loaves and fishes must have been a miracle, but catering for the multitudes flocking by train to York racecourse for this Papal visit was little short of a miracle achieved by Travellers Fare, which had its York station buffet open continuously from 6 am on Saturday until 6 am on Tuesday, whilst a temporary buffet was set up beneath the station portico. Those hungry or thirsty pilgrims not being served in the buffets could purchase from platform trolleys or obtain buffet packs on sale on most of the special trains.

Not surprisingly, with such large crowds and a greatly increased sale of Travellers Fare drinks, 'Portakabins' were required to supplement the permanent toilet facilities.

Thomas Cook organised his first excursion from Leicester to Loughborough for a temperance demonstration on 5 July 1841, after which train travel made a great appeal to total abstainers.

> Perhaps there is no class of British subjects who have availed themselves more of the facilities afforded by railway communication, for the advancement of their purposes, than the abstainers from strong drinks; and it is an indisputable fact that no Pleasure Trains have proved more successful than Temperance Trains.[6]

This claim was made in a 36-page booklet produced by the Leicester Temperance Society and sold for twopence to passengers joining an excursion from Leicester, Loughborough, Derby and Burton-on-Trent to Birmingham on 30 April 1849. The fare from Leicester was 5 shillings 1st class, 3s 9d 2nd and 2s 9d open 3rd. The occasion was probably a Temperance rally because the booklet informed passengers that a brass band would

> . . . accompany the train from Leicester and will perform on the way, and at the head of a procession from the Railway station to the Bull Ring.

To celebrate his 'Tenth Excursion Season' in 1850, Thomas Cook arranged

A GREAT EXPERIMENTAL TRIP
> at lowest rates ever announced from Nottingham and all principal Midland stations to York, Scarborough, Bridlington and Hull, a circuit of about 350 miles for the ASTONISHINGLY LOW SUM OF SIX SHILLINGS in covered carriages . . .

During the previous decade Thomas Cook had conducted more than 100,000 tourists to various places in the British Isles without 'a single accident' occurring.[7]

Teetotallers were among the first groups to organise rail excursions in Scotland, and for the Glasgow Total Abstinence Society's Annual Pleasure Trip following the Glasgow Fair in 1845, the Edinburgh & Glasgow Railway provided a special train of 1st, 2nd, 3rd and 4th class carriages to convey the excursionists to Edinburgh.[8]

Shortly afterwards, the Rechabites and Teetotallers of Coatbridge arranged a combined rail and steamer trip. They began by walking in procession to the station to be conveyed by special train to Glasgow where they embarked on the *Engineer* for a trip round the Kyles of Bute.

> . . . After a pleasant excursion they returned in the evening and walked in procession from the steamer to the railway station, the juveniles, male and female, walking first, followed by their seniors who wore white sashes, and carrying flags, mottoes and appropriate emblems, and the various insignia of the order. They were accompanied with two bands, and their orderly and becoming conduct, as well as general appearance attracted attention.[9]

For a Temperance Gala at Hull's Zoological Gardens in August 1860, excursion trains ran from Boston, Newark, Nottingham, Lincoln, Sheffield, York and Leeds conveying some 3,000 abstainers.

> The Brothers Pentland performed several clever and daring feats . . . Brass bands were in attendance, and with the hippopotamus, the pleasure seeker found a good amount of attraction.[10]

Whilst teetotallers could cross the Scottish border with a clear conscience, others were less fortunate, for when the North British Railway connected Edinburgh with Berwick in 1846 Customs Duties were still payable on spirits crossing the frontier. Under a headline 'CAUTION TO RAILWAY TRAVELLERS FROM SCOTLAND', the *Edinburgh Evening Courant* related what happened when an excursion train from Edinburgh arrived at the Berwick terminus.

> . . . A lady and gentleman, on alighting from one of the carriages, brought out a small basket with them, when they were accosted by one of the excise officers belonging to Berwick, who seized it and searched it. A small bottle containing about a pint of whisky was found in it, which he seized . . . This case, we trust, will operate as a caution to travellers and may prevent many from being subjected to a similar annoyance.[11]

Belle Vue was the venue for the Centenary Celebrations of the Independent Order of Rechabites in June 1935, when the London Midland & Scottish and London & North Eastern railway companies ran over 120 special trains to convey some 70,000 excursionists from many parts of the country. Temperance was the aim of the Rechabite Order, founded in 1835, and their continued insistence on temperance led the Order to pay the Belle Vue authorities £2,000 as compensation for keeping the bars closed during the celebrations.

Enthusiasm for railway excursions by the Temperance movement must surely have been rivalled by the Friendly Societies, whose Lodges took their members by train, accompanied by their own bands and their colourful Lodge banners carried in procession to the station and through the streets of the resorts visited.

For the Foresters' Fete at Crystal Palace in 1859 the railways conveyed some 62,000 excursionists, and a state of siege was said to have existed at numerous stations; 'the rush for tickets was at times positively fearful'.[12] The weather was so good that most of the crowd stayed in the grounds where 'the fountains were in full play', and groups played kiss-in-the-ring among beds of bright red geraniums intermixed with yellow marigolds!

Getting away from the Palace appears to have been less pleasant than the fun in the gardens because the police allowed only certain exits to be used, which caused near panic among the huge crowds. Statistics for the volume of refreshments consumed are staggering: 8 tons of meat, 57,000 lbs of bread, 330 barrels of beer, 870 dozen bottles of beer, 14,786 quarts of tea, coffee and chocolate, 2,470 quarts of milk, 46 Cheddar cheeses, 400 lbs of butter, 213 lbs of mustard, 31,000 penny buns, 350 ice puddings, 340 dozen pastries, 500 Crystal Palace puddings, 8,000 Crystal Palace cakes, 2,340 Bath buns, $1^{1}/_{2}$ tons of sugar and 850 dozen mineral waters. A staff of 700 was employed to serve the refreshments.

The Good Templars were victims of a case of mistaken identity when chartering an excursion train to Stratford-on-Avon, but which they could not fill.

> On Tuesday last the ordinary serenity of our streets was completely upset by the influx of a gang of roughs – <u>pleasure</u>-seeking varlets – hailing from some benighted region of the brainless, under the banner, we believe, of teetotalism; but they proved themselves but weak disciples, if disciples at all, of that well conducted and flourishing order, for in less than two hours after their arrival . . . [they] were seen capering up and down the street in a state of beery hilarity, armed with long pipes and short pipes, shouting, screaming, and performing such fantastic tricks before high Heaven, enough as 'Punch' says, to make angels use their pocket-handkerchiefs . . .

> . . . Shakespeare must indeed occupy a sphere wonderfully remote from such comprehension . . .

> Since the above was in type we have been informed, on the most reliable authority, that the unruly mob which took possession of the town as above related were in no way connected with the Good Templars. It appears that a party of that Order, contemplating a visit to Stratford, had engaged a train, and had given to the Company a guarantee for a certain number of passengers, but in consequence of numerous disappointments were compelled to throw the train open to all comers. [13]

However, the following year the *Stratford Herald* was able to report a visit of a more dignified character, a Masonic Pilgrimage to Shakespeare's Town.

> There set forth from Paddington Station yesterday a pilgrimage of an unwonted character, the purpose being to offer, on part of the Masonic Brotherhood of England, a tribute to the memory of England's greatest poet . . .
> . . . after the brethren had been formally met in the Town Hall, a procession in 'clothing' was made in the church. A full choral service was held in the historic shrine . . . the window was unveiled, a tablet placed beneath it shown, and the pilgrims had the opportunity of once more looking upon the treasures of the erst Warwickshire hamlet, where the stone lies, which on pain of the poet's curse, stops human curiosity and all the posthumous honours which humanity would give . . . [14]

When, in 1857, the South Wales Railway issued a poster advertising a cheap excursion from Cardiff to Gloucester and Cheltenham for the benefit of the Widows and Orphans Fund of the Cardiff District of the Oddfellows, a glowing description of the attractions of the two towns included:

> Models of the pigeons which were seen to drink from a spring on the spot and so led to the discovery of the Mineral Properties of the Water . . . Lakes of Water with Majestic Swans of an immense size sporting on the surface, completely take the visitor by surprise and astonishment . . .

Political parties made early use of railway facilities, for in 1836 the Liverpool & Manchester Railway instructed Inspector Dixon to superintend the special trains conveying the South Lancashire Conservative Association's members from Liverpool to Newton for an annual dinner. Such distinguished passengers were not to be outraged by any misdemeanour on the part of railway servants, because Dixon was specifically instructed to watch the conduct of the enginemen on the return journey.[15]

The mid-19th century saw turbulent times in Europe when revolutionary situations developed in several countries. One patriot and fighter for freedom who came to Britain was Giuseppe Garibaldi, leader of the Italian Risorgimento, which established Italian independence from Austria. He was regarded as a hero by the champions of liberal democracy in Britain, so that when he was billed to speak at the Crystal Palace on 16 April 1864 large crowds travelled by excursion trains from many parts of the country.

Many of these excursionists were members of Working Men's Clubs, YMCAs,

Midland and North Eastern Railways.

GARIBALDI
DEMONSTRATION
AT THE CRYSTAL PALACE.

On SATURDAY, APRIL 16,

A Cheap Excursion Train will leave

HULL, SELBY, YORK

And the undermentioned Stations for

LONDON
(KING'S CROSS STATION)

FARES THERE AND BACK AND TIMES OF STARTING.

Stations	a.m.	FIRST CLASS	COVERED CARR.
Hull - - - dep. 6. 0			
Howden - " 6.54		25 0	12 6
Selby - - " 7.20			
York - - " 7.15			
Church Fenton " 7.43		21 0	10 6
Milford - " 8. 2			

LONDON (KING'S CROSS) ARRIVE ABOUT 4.45 P.M.

Children under Three years of Age Free; above Three and under Twelve, Half-fare.

The Return Train will leave the King's Cross Station, London, on Wednesday, April 20th, at 10.15 a.m.

Tickets are not transferable, and will be available for returning by this Train only.

Luggage must be conveyed under the Passengers' own care, as the Company will not be responsible.

Ten Minutes will be allowed at Trent Station for Refreshments both in going and returning.

Derby, April 1864.   BY ORDER

Bemrose and Sons, Printers by Steam Power, Derby.

Temperance Societies and Oddfellows parading their colourful banners to welcome Garibaldi to the demonstration. After a visit to Barclay & Perkin's Brewery at Southwark, Garibaldi was driven in the Duke of Sutherland's carriage to Crystal Palace and, as he alighted, the several bands struck up 'See the Conquering Hero Comes', followed by 'God save the Queen'.

> Stretched beneath the galleries along the transept as far as the eye could reach, east, west, north, south was one dense mass of human faces. As Garibaldi stepped into the box there was an ovation as would baffle any pen to describe. This enthusiasm continued for some ten minutes . . . Garibaldi was presented with a sword and a painting after which a concert followed.[16]

Ragley Park, near Alcester in Warwickshire, home of the 5th Marquess of Hertford, was the venue for the Coventry Conservative Club's picnic in August 1883 and it would seem that working class support for the Tories is not a recent phenomenon.

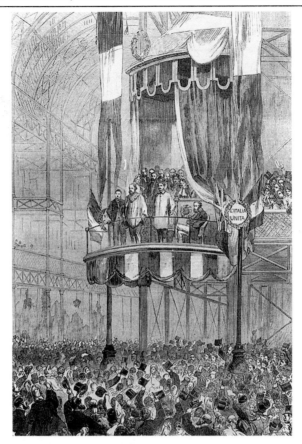

Garibaldi addressing the crowd of 20-30,000 at the Crystal Palace in 1864. *(Illustrated London News)*

... the Conservative working man turned up in strong force at the picnic of the Coventry Conservative Club on Monday. There was quite a lively crowd in Broadgate when the military band, engaged to furnish emphasis to the occasion, struck up a lively march and headed for the railway station. But the crowd who followed closely on the footsteps of the band in the hope of getting a choice of comfortable seats for the journey, were disappointed, hundreds of wide-awake Tories had been there before, and the train was already crowded.

It is doubtful if the Marquess of Hertford would have approved of his guests' behaviour on the train, had he been aware of it.

After a run of several miles an unexpected stoppage took place in the midst of green fields and far away from any signs of human dwellings. This was the signal for Tom, Dick and Jerry, who quickly left their carriages to walk up the line and enquire of the 'old 'oss', the engine driver, 'What's up?' For answer they got a short sharp whistle from the locomotive which compelled them to re-enter their carriages hastily, just in time to escape being left behind. At every stopping place and often whilst the train was tearing along at thirty miles an hour, there was a long row of heads out of carriage windows exchanging chaff and sending a ripple of laughter along the whole train.[17]

Stratford-on-Avon's East & West Junction Railway station seems an unlikely start for a journey to Scarborough, and to learn that this train made its last pick-up at Melton Mowbray must surely prompt railway enthusiasts to work out its devious route. After travelling 36 miles due east to Blisworth on the London & North Western main line, a reversal was made to proceed over the branch to Northampton Castle, then to Market Harborough and on to the Great Northern & London North Western Joint line as far as Bottesford to join the Great Northern main line to Doncaster and on to the North Eastern to York and Scarborough.

The intrepid party undertaking this 6-hour journey, which actually took 8 hours, was the Stratford-on-Avon Liberal Club, and their 300 members boarded their excursion train at 1 o'clock in the morning. Picking up other Liberals along the way, the train eventually comprised 17 carriages,

> . . . all on pleasure bent and eager to take advantage of the opportunity of visiting so cheaply a popular seaside resort . . . After the long journey a sea bathe proved very refreshing to many, and the varied delights of the 'Queen of Watering Places' were enjoyed to the full during the nine hours of the visit.[18]

They must have been a bleary-eyed lot of trippers who descended from the train at Stratford-on-Avon at 4 o'clock on Tuesday morning, having been away from home for 27 hours. That could certainly be called a 'Day Excursion'!

Hero worship, such as screaming teenage girls fighting to lay their hands on a tennis idol's sweatband, is not a new phenomenon; staid Liberals had their idol a century ago – Gladstone. A special train conveyed 250 Liberal members from the Stretford Division of South East Lancashire to Broughton Hall station on the London & North Western Railway for a visit to Gladstone's residence at Hawarden Park.[19]

> In the evening Mr Gladstone proceeded to the Hawarden Rectory, where, in the presence of a number of the excursionists, he doffed coat and vest, and, with all his old vigour, cut down a tree in the garden. The chips were eagerly seized upon as mementoes by the spectators, and one reverend gentleman who accompanied the party caused much amusement by deprecating hero-worship and idolatry and at the same moment eagerly seizing a branch of the tree and bearing it off in triumph. Mrs Gladstone distributed a number of flowers among the excursionists who returned to their homes much gratified with their reception at Hawarden.[20]

A Lancashire mill-owner and Member of Parliament, Mr Phillips, owned a large estate near Stratford-on-Avon known as Welcombe House, which became a LMSR hotel in 1931. In 1880 he invited the Radcliffe, Pilkington and Prestwich Liberal Club to hold their annual excursion and fete in his grounds. The Lancashire & Yorkshire Railway provided trains for 700 excursionists who were conveyed over the London & North Western system to Birmingham, then the Midland to Broom Junction and finally over the Evesham, Redditch & Stratford-upon-Avon Junction Railway to their destination.

Commenting that the excursionists usually visited a seaport or bathing place, the local paper described their 'delight with the change of scenery'. Having left their homes as early as 4 am, these Liberal excursionists arrived back in Lancashire at 1 am on Sunday morning, sound in the knowledge that 'A more orderly and respectable body of excursionists than those of Saturday last have never visited Stratford'.[21]

'BARNSLEY FIRM FOR THE BUDGET' read the banner carried at the head of a procession of 300 'ladies and gentlemen' from the Barnsley Liberal Association who had travelled by excursion train to Saltburn-by-the-Sea on the North Eastern Railway. The procession wended its way from the railway station to Rushford Hall, residence of Joseph Walton, MP for Barnsley, where several thousand had gathered to hear the Rt Hon Winston Churchill MP and the Rt Hon Herbert Samuel MP. As if hearing such able speakers were not sufficient, the excursionists were conducted over the charming grounds and palatial residence of Mr & Mrs Walton.

From the railway companies' point of view, excursions to political events were good business, whether Conservative or Liberal, but when the speaker was a republican, atheist, champion of civil liberties, advocate of birth control and a Radical, then perhaps a line should be drawn? The Great Western Railway Secretary's Report noted:

> THE PRACTICE OF RUNNING EXCURSIONS TO POLITICAL GATHERINGS.
>
> In January 1883 an application for excursion trains to be run to London on the occasion of the opening of Parliament in the following month was submitted to the superintendents at the Railway Clearing House and having regard to the great agitation which was taking place in the country at that time with reference to Mr Bradlaugh, it was thought desirable that such trains should not be run . . .
>
> . . . It appears to me that so long as the proper guarantee is given it is not for the company to question the object for which the train is run, and if the Directors confirm that view, instructions will be given to the officers to that effect.[22]

In June 1887, Gladstone, the Liberal statesman, visited Swansea, and the Great Western Railway had no hesitation in running excursions conveying 5,000 passengers, which was no doubt good business, although an application to run an excursion in connection with a Hyde Park demonstration against the Licensing Laws in 1890 was rejected by that company.

Cleethorpes was largely developed as a seaside resort by the Manchester, Sheffield & Lincolnshire Railway, so it is not surprising that its successor, the Great Central Railway, should encourage excursionists to visit that breezy East Coast town. The Brackley and Towcester Conservative Clubs jointly arranged an excursion starting from Banbury, then over the Northampton & Banbury Junction Railway, and from Stratford-on-Avon on the East & West Junction Railway, and joining at Woodford and Hinton to run via the Great Central to Grimsby and Cleethorpes.

Turn-of-the-century Tories were early risers, for this excursion departed from Banbury at 3.40 am and, almost 5 hours later, arrived in Cleethorpes in time for breakfast. After 11 hours of breezy seaside, or fishy Grimsby, these intrepid travellers rejoined their train at 7.50 pm and arrived back in Banbury about 1 am. Almost 24 hours away from home, 10 of them in a train, and all for 5 shillings.

'Oysters and ice-cream at 5 o'clock on a chilly morning would not suit every stomach,' is a sentiment with which most people would agree, but had they been coal miners in 1919 they might also have concurred with the Blackpool newspaper reporter who wrote that '. . . it was a change from dry bread and cold tea at the coal face'. This early

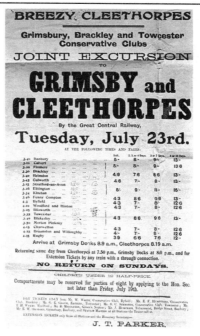

(Bernard Morris collection)

A miners' demonstration on Blackpool sands in 1919. 135 trains brought them from mining areas throughout the north. *(National Railway Museum, York)*

The miners and their wives took the train to Durham in 1947 to have a good time, as well as listen to Bevin, Morrison, Foot and Horner – speakers at the Durham Miners' Gala.

refreshment took place on the annual Joy Day and Demonstration of the Lancashire & Cheshire Miners' Federation in 1919, when politics were combined with a family outing.

Between 4 am and 10 am special trains from all parts of the two counties arrived at Blackpool's Talbot Road station every 3 or 4 minutes, until a total of 135 trains had disgorged 100,000 miners and their families. 'The biggest thing we've had to deal with for years,' said a Lancashire & Yorkshire Railway official.

The great parade of union lodges, with their colourful banners, included 25 bands and 'was a sight to be seen to be remembered. It took a full hour to pass,' commented one reporter.

Speakers at the demonstration on the Football Ground included the Secretary of the Labour Party, the Rt Hon Arthur Henderson, and the General Secretary of the Miners' Federation of Great Britain, Frank Hodges. A resolution called upon the Government to recognise the need for improving miners' conditions, for better housing and for the nationalisation of the mining industry.

This is how Blackpool catered for the thousands arriving at such early hours:

> . . . When the Tower buildings opened at 5 am there was a rush for that place of entertainment, and there were fair audiences at the picture halls, which commenced a continuous show an hour later . . . 'Jazzing' began on the Central Pier at 7 am, but long before that the Pleasure Beach was as busy as on a Bank Holiday afternoon . . . There were some strange spectacles early in the morning. Here and there were small impromptu concert parties, mouth organs and concertinas providing the music for those who were not fortunate

One thousand mothers and babies, guests of Horatio Bottomley, on arrival at Chingford station in 1920. *(Newham Library)*

enough to possess one of the full brass bands . . .

Wading was a favourite pastime . . . The water was cool and refreshing, and the ice-cream wafers carried by many paddlers were equally successful in the same direction . . .

The visitors spent freely . . . The Circular Tour toast-rack cars were out as early as 5 o'clock, and they did big business throughout the day . . .

. . . out of the huge throng of Saturday, there was not a single case of drunkenness to be dealt with by the magistrates . . .[23]

Such good behaviour together with the cash registers clocking up £50,000 spent by the visitors, must have gladdened the hearts of Blackpool tradespeople.

The annual Durham Miners' Gala in July was attended by some 250,000 visitors, at one time all arriving by train. In 1950, 90 special trains were required and Elvet station, closed to regular traffic in 1931, was re-opened to handle about half of these trains. Four miles of goods-only line were used for some trains for which a signal box at Sherburn House, otherwise closed, was brought into use.[24]

Two trains, each of 15 six-a-side four-wheeled carriages, were provided by the Great Eastern Railway to convey 1,000 mothers and babies from Liverpool Street to Chingford as the guests of the famous, or notorious, Horatio Bottomley, editor of that waspish weekly magazine *John Bull,* in 1920. Here is how one of the railwaymen involved described the event:

MR BOTTOMLEY'S LADY GUESTS AT CHINGFORD

Mine Host of the Forest Hotel was in something of a quandary. He had provided cakes and ale for one thousand of Mr Horatio Bottomley's guests on Tuesday, August 17th, but when he saw them marching on him nearly half of them 'armed' with babies, he was flabbergasted; to quote him he had 'not reckoned on babies' . . .

It was a beautiful day, not too hot for those who elected to dance – which they did to the accompaniment of a pipe of Pan – not too cold for those who chose to wander and lounge amid the leafy trees. The air and the country environment was worth gold to those who, as their host put it, had come from somewhat drab surroundings.

In our small way, we railwaymen conspired to add pleasure unto the good souls travelling on our line. Two trains were used each carriage being decorated with a large bow of red, white and blue bunting, and each engine with five flags and a shield bearing the Union Jack, while the trains were postered in large letters announcing that it was 'Bottomley's Outing' . . .

The good ladies added to the colour scheme, all of them wearing a yellow rosette. (Is this not our friend's election colour?) A stray fog signal or two found its way on to the line at Chingford, which some of the ladies thought meant an air-raid, until re-assured that it was a salute only.[24]

Whilst the mothers and offspring dined, the railwaymen were invited by Bottomley to partake of 'bread, cheese and an onion', and, typical of HB, he told the women that he had eaten some onion to prevent them kissing him!

Chapter 10
ROYALTY, FAIRS AND WAKES

'The band met every train, and played upon its arrival at the railway station, where the officials had erected a pretty arch of greenery and flags.'

Queen Victoria's Coronation in 1838 was too early to have generated any additional traffic, because the London & Birmingham Railway still had a gap in its line between the Denbigh Hall Inn, near Bletchley, and Rugby, whilst the Great Western had only reached Maidenhead from Paddington. Sixty-five years on, her son Edward VII spoiled elaborate plans for a Naval Review at Spithead by falling ill, otherwise the LSWR would have implemented its plans for the conveyance of thousands of excursionists from Waterloo to Southampton.

For the Coronation of George V in 1911, the main railway excursion activity was concerned with the entertainment of some 100,000 children at Crystal Palace, for which 96 specials were run. In 1937, this time for the Coronation of George VI, the conveyance of thousands of children by special day excursion trains presented a gigantic task for the railways. The Southern Railway carried 1,000 children to London for the Coronation procession, whilst the GWR organised combined rail and coach excursions for schools to travel to London, tour the decorated streets and visit such places of interest as the Tower and Madame Tussauds or the Zoo. A typical day saw as many as 140 motor coaches engaged to meet these trains when some 800 children were shepherded from train to coach in 10 minutes.

During the month of May, 1937, it was said that all records for the number of passengers carried by rail were broken. No fewer than 4,079 excursion trains were run during a month which included not only the Coronation but also the FA Cup Final, a Naval Review at Spithead and the Whitsun Bank Holiday.

On the LMSR, 24 long-distance excursions reached either Euston or St Pancras on the Sunday before Coronation Day, some 50 on Tuesday, which was the eve of the Coronation, 11 on the day after, with a further 95 during the following Whitsun weekend.

A 24-hour service, commencing at 3 am on Coronation Day, was operated by the Southern Railway, and from 7 am onwards 310 trains arrived at London termini. During the Whitsun holiday which followed, 74 specials left Waterloo and Victoria stations for Portsmouth, enabling passengers to see the Fleet assembled for the Naval Review.

The GWR too put on a 24-hour service of trains on Coronation Day and, in addition, between 12.30 am and 6 am, 25 excursion trains arrived at Paddington.

It has to be appreciated that, besides the extra Coronation traffic, the railways handled the usual additional holiday trains, many of which, like the 'Cornish Riviera Express', ran as four separate full-length trains.

During this momentous month for railway travel, the largest-ever single railway excursion carried 9,000 readers of the *Rochdale Observer* from that birthplace of Gracie Fields to Windsor and London. All four main-line companies, a steamer company and several coach operators were involved. Seven special trains, provided by the LMSR and the LNER, travelled via Brent on to the Southern Railway to Windsor, whilst the other six reached Windsor via Leamington Spa and the GWR. From Windsor this mammoth party took a steamer trip on the Thames, followed by coaches to the Alexandra Palace in North London. Here they were entertained by their very own 'Queen of Song' – Gracie Fields. Their return excursion trains left both Euston and Marylebone between 1.30 am and 2.30 am on Sunday morning.[1]

For the fifth Coronation to take place since the opening of the Liverpool & Manchester Railway in 1830, that of Queen Elizabeth II in 1953, British Railways ran excursion trains to London for both the event and during the period of street decorations which followed.

On the occasion of the Investiture of the Prince of Wales at Caernarvon on 1 July 1969, 11 specials were run from Euston, Cardiff and Crewe, but they were hardly 'Merrymakers', although the privileged elite who travelled in them no doubt did make merry in the Royal marquees. The Queen's own train had two colour TV sets installed to enable her to see what was going on before she arrived at Caernarvon. For Her Majesty's

Two special trains were needed to convey the employees of John White's shoe factory from Rushden, Northamptonshire, to St Pancras for the 1953 Coronation . . .

subjects of lower rank, there were three 12-car diesel multiple units and trains from Chester.[2]

Aldershot Military Tattoo attracted vast crowds by rail before the Second World War, and although excursion trains could come from far afield, all reached stations near the event over Southern Railway metals. In 1932, the SR handled 72,943 passengers at its four stations — Aldershot, Government Siding, North Camp and Fleet, excluding 11,000 children and 1,000 adults arriving in special trains for a Daylight Rehearsal put on

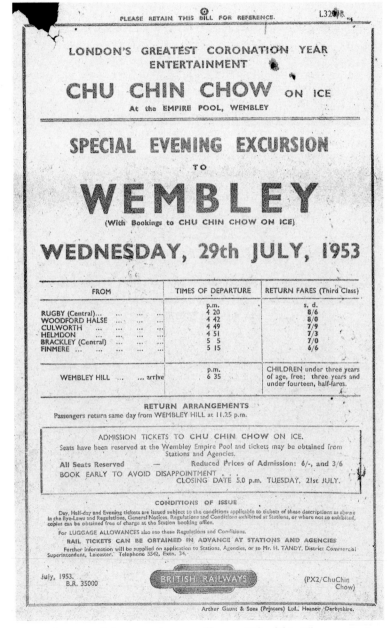

... when one of the attractions on offer was 'Chu Chin Chow on Ice'.

specially for schoolchildren. Twenty-three trains were involved in conveying these children, and a fleet of Aldershot and District Traction Company buses carried them from the station to the arena. On the first day of the Tattoo proper, 33 excursion trains carried 2,657 passengers to the event. On the final Saturday 36 trains arrived, several originating on the LMSR and GWR systems.[3]

An event, in 1934, prompted the *LNER Magazine* to report:

> A type of excursion unique in the history of transport left Newcastle on Sunday, February 25, at 10.15 for Southampton. Two trains were run. 750 devoted kinsfolk made the journey of 660 miles for a few hours reunion with their soldiermen. It was an occasion which stirred the soul of even a limited company . . . The Central Station was gaily decorated and the band of the 6th Territorial Battalion played the trains away amid scenes reminiscent of war time.

Cause of this long trek by the soldiers' families was the transfer of the 1st Battalion of the Northumberland Fusiliers from the West Indies to Egypt, and as additional drafts were to be picked up, the SS *Dorsetshire* was ordered to call at Southampton, although the men were not allowed time to visit their homes. The locomotives were bedecked with Union Jacks and headboards bearing the crest of the regiment. Seats were reserved, meals served *en route* and nurses were aboard.[4]

In October the following year, a similar troop movement took place involving the 1st Battalion the Manchester Regiment aboard the SS *Dorsetshire* which docked at Southampton for 6 hours only. This time it was two LMSR trains carrying 800 relatives from Manchester for a brief reunion with the soldiers. The Southern Railway's transhipment shed No 104 was gaily decorated for the lunch served to a total of 1,900 troops and relatives. As the SS *Dorsetshire* set sail, the band played 'The Girl I Left Behind Me' and 'Auld Lang Syne'. To reach Southampton these LMSR excursion trains took a route via Willesden and Addison Road over the West London Joint Railway to join the Southern Railway via East Putney.[5]

Once the Liverpool & Manchester Railway, opened in 1830, had established the superiority of rail transport for the speedy movement of troops, the government entered into an agreement with the L&MR regarding the carriage of the armed forces. To commemorate this event of 1831, British Rail ran a 13-coach excursion from Liverpool to York on 11 March 1981. Steam-hauled to York by ex-Southern Railway 4-6-0 locomotive No 850 *Lord Nelson*, the return journey via Doncaster, Sheffield and the Hope Valley to Manchester and back to Liverpool was behind Deltic No 55 002 *The King's Own Yorkshire Light Infantry*.[6]

Cheap railway excursions enabled increasing numbers of people to travel to the wakes and feasts which had their origin in the Saints' Days of medieval times, although growing numbers of town dwellers chose wakes weeks excursions to escape for a day from their dingy, depressing, industrial surroundings to the fresh breeze of the seaside or the clean air of the hills and moors.

> . . . The most remarkable feature of the Whitsuntide was the larger number leaving Manchester rather than spending the holiday in the traditional way at the Kensal Moor Races.[7]

One of the chief attractions of the Glasgow Fair Week in 1846 was a day excursion to Belfast, the journey taking only 8 hours in each direction. The Glasgow, Paisley, Kilmarnock & Ayr Railway conveyed the excursionists to Ardrossan where they embarked on the *Firefly* and the *Glow Worm*. Ticket sales were restricted to the capacity

of the boats, but twice the number could have been sold. The *Glasgow Herald* welcomed this new form of working class pleasure as

> ... a pleasing proof of what the railway and steamboat companies can do to induce the working classes to spend their holidays in a more rational way than among the shows and dram-shops ... [8]

For the Barnsley Feast of 1859, the attractions included the Alhambra Circus.

> ... The performers attached to this company eclipse those of any other. Pauline Newsome and young Hermandez, by their extraordinary feats, astonish all who see them, and Mr Wallett's mirth-provoking powers are of world-wide celebrity. [9]

A brass band contest and fireworks were also on the day's agenda, for which the Manchester, Sheffield & Lincolnshire Railway conveyed to Barnsley 2,500 passengers; there was also a large influx from Wakefield by the Lancashire & Yorkshire Railway. [10]

Thirty years later the emphasis was very much on getting away from Barnsley during Feast Week, as these advertisements showed:

Nearly 14 hours at Blackpool by the Barnsley Model Band's Trip. Barnsley Feast Monday. Fare 3s. Leave Barnsley 5.15 am. Leave Blackpool 9.50 pm after the fireworks.[11]

Blackpool. Messrs Craik & Co's work-people's special Express Excursion to Blackpool on Barnsley Feast Monday. Leaving Barnsley 4.55 am. Leaving Blackpool 8.58 pm. Fare 3s. Youths 1s 6d.[12]

Just how well patronised these and other excursions were can be seen from this report:

Never, we believe, on the occasion of any previous Barnsley Feast, has there been such a large exodus of holidaymakers, all like John Gilpin, 'on pleasure bent' as was witnessed on Saturday and Monday . . . [Saturday] being beautifully fine large numbers took advantage of the tempting facilities offered by the railway companies for visiting seaside and other places of popular resort . . . The following figures will enable our readers to form some idea as to the numbers who went to seaside and other pleasure resorts on Saturday and during the early part of the week. About 5,000 miners employed at various collieries in the South Yorkshire district visited Blackpool . . . A Trip, chartered by the Barnsley Temperance Society, was run to York and Scarborough by the Midland freighted with between 400 and 500 persons . . . The Lancashire & Yorkshire Railway Company also took the Model Band excursionists, who numbered over 800, to Blackpool. The MS&L had Ashburys (for Belle Vue) 562; Llandudno 120; Liverpool and Manchester 80; Temperance trip to Scarborough 600; Morecambe 24 . . . The incoming traffic also was heavy, so that, not-withstanding the exodus, the town was busy all day.[13]
. . . On Monday, Cooper's Royal Brass and Reed Band had promoted a cheap trip to Blackpool – Lancashire & Yorkshire – and some 1,400 people started at half past four in the morning for the favourite resort. They were to have 14 hours by the sea, starting home about 10 o'clock. The Barnsley Temperance Society had two trains to Scarborough, by the Midland route, conveying some 1,600 to 1,700 persons. The Oaks Colliery trip had about 500 by the Great Central Railway . . .[14]

Although, by the 1930s, motor coaches were taking many excursionists to the seaside, the LMSR ran 1,170 excursion trains from Lancashire and Yorkshire towns during 'Wakes' weeks in 1939. Top of the list were Halifax, Huddersfield, Bradford and Brighouse with 181 specials, next Preston, Bury and Stockport with 121, and third Todmorden, Horwich, Colne and Blackburn with 116.[15]

Barnsley Feast was officially dropped from 1971, although seven excursion trains still left the town on 'Feast Saturday' for Cleethorpes, Skegness, Blackpool, Yarmouth, Bournemouth and Scarborough.[16]

As we have seen, Belle Vue, Manchester, was a popular attraction for railway excursionists and, in 1914, the Great Central Railway, for the Staleybridge Wakes, offered

An ex-LMSR 'Crab' 2-6-0 speeds a 'Wakes Week' Blackpool excursion past Linthwaite signal box.

> . . . trips to Belle Vue and back. Fares including admission to Gardens 3rd 1s.2d. 1st 2s. On Wednesday July 22nd a special through train will leave Staleybridge at 2.35 pm returning from Ashburys at 10.20 pm after the Fireworks. The open-air panorama depicts the goal of the famous march from Kabul to Kandahar so finely led by Sir General Fred Roberts. The evening spectacle represents the Battle of Kandahar when Ayub Khan was completely defeated Sep 19th 1880.[17]

Many who enjoyed this glorification of war on 22 July 1914 would themselves be participating in the 'real thing' a few months later when the horror in the trenches of Flanders dispelled any illusions as to its glory.

In many town streets and on village greens today the 'rides', sideshows and stalls are all that remain of what were once much more important occasions. Some were great gatherings of merchants and craftsmen for several days of trading; others specialised in animal sales, horse, sheep and cattle fairs; whilst others were hiring fairs where farm servants sought new employers by displaying whip-cord or straw in their lapels to indicate their calling. Serving-maids carried mops for this purpose, and so originated the term 'Mop Fair'.

Claiming to be the largest one-day fair in the land, Stratford-on-Avon's Mop Fair filled (and still does) all the town centre streets with all the machinery, glitter and noise of the fairground. No excursion trains run to the Mop today, but during the 50 years preceeding the Second World War the two railways serving the town brought in thousands of factory workers and their families from industrial Birmingham and the Black Country.[18] For many of these workers, in the days before annual paid holidays, the 'Mop' was their only day out in the year. With a journey time of little more than an hour, other factory workers left work and flocked in large numbers to Stratford-on-Avon by the evening excursion

The 'Mop Fair' at Stratford-on-Avon, to which the LMSR and the GWR ran several excursion trains between the wars. *(Shakespeare Birthplace Trust)*

An East & West Junction Railway excursion train awaits returning 'Mop Fair' passengers at Stratford-on-Avon, behind Beyer Peacock 2-4-0T No 5.

East and West Junction and Stratford-on-Avon,
Towcester and Midland Junction Railways.

STRATFORD
MOP
AND
OX ROASTING
Saturday, Oct. 12th,
1907

CHEAP TICKETS

Will be issued by Special and ordinary Trains to Stratford as under:—

From		Times of Starting			Fares There and Back 3rd. Class		
		a.m.	a.m.	a.m.	p.m.	s.	d.
Blisworth	... ...		9. 3	10.47	2. 18	2	9
Towcester	... ...		9.13	10.57	2.28		
Blakesley	... ...		9.22	11. 6	2.37	2	6
Morton Pinkney	... ...		9.29	11. 13	2.44		
Byfield	... ...		9.40	11.40	2.55	2	3
Fenny Compton (by Train)			9.53	11.52	3. 7	1	9
Kineton	9. 55		...	12. 4	3.20	1	3
Ettington	10.6		...	12.12	3.30		9

Holders of these Tickets for Ettington and Kineton return from
Stratford-on-Avon at 6.10 p.m., and for other stations at 7.15
p.m., the same day.

Children under 12 years of age half-fare. Tickets not transferable. No luggage allowed.

Stratford-on-Avon, October, 1907.   BY ORDER.

(*Bernard Morris collection*)

trains, returning as late as midnight when the thousands of electric light bulbs were dimmed and the rides ceased whirling.

Nottingham Goose Fair lasted a week and included the showing and sale of horses, cattle, cheese and other produce as well as numerous fancy bazaars, stalls, side-shows and attractions which, in 1850, included:

> . . . Exhibition of all kinds of things, Saloons of Art, Fat Pigs, a Mammoth Ox and other monstrosities too tedious to mention. There are panoramas, illuminated models, conjuring shows and lastly, the funeral of the late Sir Robert Peel . . . At twelve o'clock the Exhibitions were in full swing – gongs, rattles, drums, trumpets etc are vying with each other . . . The special trains are pouring forth their thousands after thousands as the ponderous vehicles reach the station.[19]

Meanwhile, Edmunds' (late Wombwells) Royal Windsor Castle Menagerie offered:

> . . . A magnificent Collection of Wild Beasts, Birds and Reptiles, also that beautiful animal the Zebu, or Sacred Bull of India, late the property and idol of Nana Sahib, taken from the Temple at Lucknow, the day after the dreadful massacre . . . The Exhibition is also accompanied by that extraordinary race of men the Zulu Kaffirs, or Wild Men of Africa.

More than a century ago not everyone appreciated the contribution the railways would make, not only to keeping these fairs alive, but also swelling by thousands the number attending them. In 1874, Thomas Frost wrote:

... the railways connect the smaller towns, and most of the villages, with the larger ones in which amusements may be found superior to any ever presented by the old showman. What need then of fairs and shows? The last showman will soon be as great a curiosity as the dodo.[20]

Only one year after that prediction was made, Hull Fair, which lasted a whole week, attracted thousands more visitors conveyed by railway excursions. On the first day alone, the North Eastern Railway carried 7,500, the Hull & Barnsley 2,000, and the Manchester, Sheffield & Lincolnshire 3,000.[21] By 1905, an estimated attendance of 70,000 supported its claim to be the largest fair in England.[22]

What was it like at Hull Fair? A letter on the notepaper of the Hull Banking Company dated 18 October 1875, written to a friend, describes the event thus:

> ... usually first in order is a wild beast show, then come moving wax works, marrionettes and circuses, ghost shows, dancing dogs and goats, intelligent ponies and pigs. Enormously fat women said to weigh over 40 stones. The living skeleton is a great attraction to the class of people who attend this assemblage. There are also men who eat fire, swallow swords and hot bullets. Dogs with five legs and all kinds of freaks of nature. Some of these are dead and kept in spirits of wine. There are also boxing booths where some of the gaping country clowns get nicely knocked about, Cheap Jacks who profess to give several half-crowns, golden rings, watches etc. for one penny or one shilling as the case may be ... The field is one blaze of light from innumerable gas lights and naptha lamps, whilst the people heave to and fro like a seething cauldron or restless sea ... But the combined smell from the lamps, the people, the heat, the damp (Hull Fair is usually wet!) and the pea stalls and wild beasts is something sickening; oh the noise! ...[23]

Hull was still pulling in the crowds by rail in the 1930s when the LNER issued 100,000 handbills and put up 500 posters advertising excursions during Fair Week. Was this successful? Advertising Manager C. Dandridge commented, 'The result – a gain on both swings and roundabouts'.

Glasgow was linked to the Ayrshire coast from as early as 1839 when the Glasgow, Paisley, Kilmarnock & Ayr Railway was opened and excursion trains were run to the coast during Glasgow Fair Holidays each year. Clyde steamers had catered for Glaswegian excursionists for many years before the opening up of the railways, but now the latter brought other destinations within reach of day excursionists, as this report confirms:

> . The facilities of travelling afforded by railway communication have this year been extensively taken advantage of ... Yesterday morning a large pleasure train consisting of 20 carriages, arrived in Edinburgh, from Glasgow, on its way to Berwick, proceeding thither without changing carriages.[24]

Excursionists to the Lammas Fair at Melrose in 1849 made an early start, leaving Edinburgh by the North British Railway at

> o'clock Morning, calling at all stations along the line (eleven). The train will leave Melrose Returning at a Quarter past Eight PM.

The Preston Merchant Guild's origins lie in a Royal Charter granted to the burgesses of Preston, in 1175, to hold a fair. In 1752, the craftsmen of Preston began to organise in

Guilds or Friendly Societies as a means of affording protection and financial support for members in periods of trade depression, sickness and employers' lock-outs. In 1802 it was decided to mark the jubilee of the Guilds by holding a week of parades in which banners were carried, bands played, entertainments were provided and all to express the Guild members' pride in their crafts.

> ... The Wool-Combers and Cotton Workers ... were preceded by twenty-four young blooming handsome women, each bearing a branch of the cotton tree, then followed a spinning machine carried on men's shoulders, and afterwards a loom drawn on a sledge, each with work people busily employed on them.[25]

The same report listed the companies represented as including tanners, skinners, glovers, cordwainers, carpenters, butchers, vintners, tailors, smiths, mercers and drapers.

It was decided to repeat the celebration of the Guilds every 20 years, which gave the newly opened railways the opportunity to run excursion trains to 'Preston Guild' in 1842. The *Preston Pilot* carried this announcement:

PRESTON GUILD
Preston and Wyre Railway

For the accommodation of parties attending the Festivities of the Guild, SPECIAL TRAINS will run between Fleetwood and the Maudlands Station, Preston, during the week as follows:

on Tues from Preston, at 12 o'clock at night after the conclusion of the concert.

on Weds from Fleetwood, at 7 in the evening, returning from Preston at 3 in the morning.

on Thurs from Preston, at 8 in the evening, after the races, and 12 at night, after the concert.

on Fri from Preston, at 12 noon, with the school children, and from Fleetwood at 7 in the evening, returning from Preston at halfpast 8, after the Races, and at 3 in the morning after the costume Ball.

The regular trains will run as usual.
By Order
H. Bazett Jones, Secretary
Fleetwood Aug 30 1842.[26]

Such was the public response to this announcement that the railway's resources were stretched much beyond the limit with every available vehicle, including goods and cattle wagons, being brought into use to carry the crowds. Twenty years on, in 1862, 500,000 used the railway when one of the attractions swelling the number of excursionists to the Guild Week was the famous high-wire performer, Mr Blondin, as announced in this newspaper advertisement:

BLONDIN!! BLONDIN!! BLONDIN!!

FIREWORKS! FIREWORKS!

M. BLONDIN
(the hero of Niagara and the wonder of the age)
Has the honour to announce that he will appear in Preston on Monday

Evening (in the Guild Week) Sep. 1st 1862, and will make his Wonderful Night Descent on the high rope amidst the most gorgeous and magnificent Display of Fireworks ever exhibited.[27]

In 1882, anticipating even larger crowds during Guild week, the railway companies made advance preparations.

The Railway Companies have made extensive arrangements in connection with the great influx of visitors expected during the week. Cheap excursions have been arranged from various parts of the country and in addition to this the London & North Western Railway and the Lancashire & Yorkshire Railway Companies are running a very large number of relief trains. It is expected that one train will arrive at the station every two or three minutes. For the purpose of the LNW excursion traffic, the goods station in Charles Street has been utilised, and for the same traffic to the East Lancashire Railway the Butler Street goods station will be used. A new platform in Charles Street has been prepared. Special trains will be run at late hours to all places within thirty miles of Preston on the nights on which concerts are held.[28]

Because the West Lancashire Railway's line from Southport to Preston was not due to open until 16 September, special permission was granted by the Board of Trade for the company to run trains during Guild Week.

There can be no better description of the task facing the railway companies, and the efficiency with which they handled this traffic, than the account in the local newspaper after the event:

In addition to the very large number of people entering the town by vehicle the passenger traffic during the week has been extraordinary as will be seen from the following figures which have been supplied to us by the railway authorities. On Monday the number of persons estimated to have arrived in town was 10,000; Tuesday 25,000; Wednesday 175,000; Thursday 35,000 and Friday 25,000, being a total of 275,000. (Another 100,000 arrived on the Saturday!)

The arrangements of the companies were of the most complete and perfect character and although there was a constant incoming of trains the passengers were not incommoded in alighting. It is computed that on Wednesday no less than 2,000 persons left the station within the space of five minutes. The approaches to the station and the street leading into Fishergate were a complete mass of human beings and so great was the influx of visitors that the procession of the amalgamated trades was broken into by the great stream of people and it was impossible for some time to effect a juncture. The chief difficulty experienced by the officials was when the people wished to return home, and it was really surprising how efficiently they succeeded in despatching them. There was no stated time-table, trains being run as required and at an early hour visitors began to go home, indeed was this so much the case that at 8 o'clock in the evening more than half of them were on their return journey . . .

Between Euxton Junction and Preston the trains were so arranged that they should travel as fast as the block system would permit, namely follow each other every two minutes. The whole of the premises of the companies

The decorated arch through which excursionists passed on their way from Weldon & Corby station to the 1902 'Pole Fair'. (M. Waterfield collection)

were utilised for passenger traffic, the North Union goods yard and the Butler Street goods station having been fitted up for excursionists, also the cattle landing stage was brought into requisition. In the streets were boxes at which tickets were supplied.[29]

Five hundred and four special trains were run in connection with the 1922 Guild Week, conveying 555,434 passengers, or twice the number estimated to have attended the event in 1882. No Guild Week was held during the Second World War, but for the 1952 Guild 100 excursion trains were run. A sign of the changing mode of transport was this report: 'Police plan to cope with a threefold road traffic problem.'[30]

Another ancient custom marked by celebrations only once every 20 years is the Northamptonshire Corby Pole Fair. In 1902 and 1922, the Midland Railway poured crowds into its Weldon & Corby station by excursion as well as ordinary trains.

During the reign of Elizabeth I, probably in 1585, the small village of Corbei was granted a Charter which included the Queen's command:

> . . . We enjoin and command you and every one of you that you permit all and singular the men and tenants of the Manor of Corbei aforesaid to be quit from such Toll, Pannage, Murage and Passage to be paid on account of their goods or things throughout our whole realm aforesaid, and on account of the expenses of the Knights aforesaid . . .

Just how the granting of the Charter became incorporated in the 'Pole Fair' festivities is not known, but the ritual involves the placing of toll bars at the entrances to the town (ie the old village of Corby) and all entering the fair are called upon to pay a toll. Failure to pay results in a man being hoisted on a pole on which he is carried by strong men to the stocks.

Ladies are similarly conveyed, but in a chair. Only payment secures release from the stocks and, today, the proceeds are given to charities. Here is a description of the 1902 Pole Fair:

> Mainly by reason of the use of the stocks that call to mind the days of our forefathers, Corby Fair, which was celebrated on Whit Monday, was attended by several thousands of persons from all parts of the district. Crowded trains brought visitors from near and far, but chiefly of course, from the adjacent stations, and the unique historic occasion, which dates from the time of 'Good Queen Bess' was kept up with much enthusiasm.
>
> . . . At the entrance from Cottingham and from the Railway station, where was placed one of the barriers with a gate across the roadway to admit those who, on foot or in conveyances, had paid their toll, was quite a charming embellishment. The pillars of the arch were in red cloth, entwined with greenery, surmounted with large boxes of real flowers, while the arch itself had in red letters on a white ground on one side, 'Welcome to the Fair', and on the other, 'God Save the King'.
>
> The band met every train, and played upon its arrival at the railway station, where the officials had erected a pretty arch of greenery and flags. About 1,900 travelled from Kettering. Those who travelled by the midday trains experienced quite a crush in getting tickets; and nearly every carriage was overcrowded. At Corby many railway officials had assembled to prepare for the extraordinary traffic and the safety of the public. At Kettering extra carriages were put on, and empty trains sent to bring back many of the travellers much later than the time of the last ordinary . . . Despite all the precautions there was a terrible crush at Corby, and the platform became so full of people desiring to go back by the 6.37, that it was considered desirable not to let any more pass through the turnstile, even though they possessed tickets. The rush when the train came in can well be imagined . . . Even the guard's van was packed to capacity . . . the oscillation in the van when the train stopped caused more mirth than discomfiture.[31]

In 1040, Leofric, Earl of Mercia and Lord of Coventry, imposed exactions, harsh even for those times, on his tenants and which his wife beseeched him to remove. Legend has it that the Earl undertook to relieve the burden on his tenants only if Godiva, his lady, would ride naked through the city which, to his surprise, she did. This legend also asserts that the inhabitants of Coventry, out of respect for Godiva, remained behind shuttered windows as she passed. All except one, 'Peeping Tom', a tailor, who couldn't resist the spectacle, and so peeped through his shutters. Accounts vary as to his fate – either he was struck blind by the all-seeing God, that his eyes were put out by the townspeople, or that he was put to death by them.

Accustomed as we are today to mini-skirts, topless bathers and streakers, the Godiva incident seems hardly an event to warrant commemoration with a pageant, but such did take place from medieval times until its discontinuance in 1877. However, in 1883, a committee was formed to revive the pageant; whether to bring a little erotic excitement into the dull lives of Coventry's citizens or because pageants were good for business, is not clear. Perhaps understandably, the Pageant Committee anticipated the enthusiastic co-operation of the London & North Western Railway in arranging excursion trains to the event, for which an attendance of some 60,000 visitors was expected. However, the 'Premier Line', as the LNWR styled itself, declined to run trips to the Godiva Pageant giving as their reason that their rolling-stock was otherwise fully employed on that day. In fairness to the company, it should be appreciated that August Bank Holiday was the chosen day.

Another committee meeting was called at which 'several gentlemen addressed the meeting in favour of adhering to Bank Holiday', and expressing the opinion that 'the action of the LNW was anything but complimentary to Coventry and pointing out that it was unfortunate that the company had such a monopoly in Coventry'.[32]

Whether it was the accusation of a monopoly, or for some other reason, is not recorded, but the LNWR relented, for the *Coventry Independent Journal* reported that

> . . . as early as eight o'clock sightseers began to throng the streets and as trip after trip disgorged its human freight at the railway station, the crowd grew rapidly, until about eleven o'clock the principal streets were impassable. From the railway station to the Cross the streets were like a huge fair, hawkers, conjurors and ballad singers plying their peculiar vocations in every direction, whilst on all sides gaily coloured flags and banners streamed out in the gentle breeze.[33]

But what about the naked lady? Perhaps local beauties were reluctant to play the part of Godiva, for which a London actress was employed,

> . . . possessed of a commanding figure, her face being in repose, one admirably suited for the character she impersonated. She was dressed in a pink silk bodice, cut square and low on the bosom, no skirts but a kind of swallow-tail train, cut obliquely across the front, silk flashings, pink satin high boots and long pink kid gloves. Her hair, which was marvellously long, was a dead golden hue, falling in rippling masses on each of her shoulders, and spreading over the saddle-bow, was covered by a long tulle veil.[34]

Being 'sent to Coventry' could have its compensations!

Headboard for a special train from Liverpool Street to Colchester for the 'The Oyster Feast' on 27 October 1950. The characters are the Walrus and the Carpenter from Lewis Carroll's *Through the Looking Glass*.

Chapter 11
SEE THE SCENERY

'On we go until on our left the great panorama of the Cairngorms is stetched out before us . . . Passengers rise in their seats, and this is surely the most spectacular section of the trip . . .'

After the First World War the railway companies faced increasing competition from the 'charabanc' operators for excursion traffic. These new competitors offered several advantages to potential trippers – several pick-up points in residential areas, putting down on the seafront or other venue, and ease of stopping at wayside pubs. Many excursionists were, however, not attracted by this last facility, which some parties often abused to the displeasure of others. On the other hand, the railway excursion promised a more comfortable ride, the new excursion carriages had tables, and there were often buffet bar or restaurant car facilities provided. In the summer of 1934, the LMSR ran 1,616 half-day excursion trains, of which 260 had restaurant car facilities.

A feature of inter-war railway activity was the Evening Excursion, catering as it did for factory and office workers who could not get away before early evening. Of course, the outstanding evening excursion magnet was Blackpool, to which the LMSR began to run them in October 1933. In just three months, 47 such trains carrying 20,000 passengers were operated. By 1935, the figures had risen to 1,878 trains and 637,000 passengers.[1] An evening trip from Birmingham to Blackpool for the last night of the Illuminations was, at 4s 6d for 242 miles, considered 'one of the cheapest'.[2]

The LNER ran 781 evening excursions during the winter of 1934-5, mainly from outlying districts into such towns as Manchester, Sheffield, Nottingham, Leeds, Hull and Newcastle, patronized by some 300,000 passengers.[3]

Stratford-on-Avon and the Vale of Evesham were venues for LMSR 'Evening Cruise' trains from Birmingham and Wolverhampton in 1934, whilst the Peak District was also offered to Birmingham, as well as to Sheffield, Nottingham and Leicester patrons. Described by the LMSR as 'sightseeing trains for which exceptionally low fares are charged', they were composed of coaches 'suitable for observation purposes and will travel at reduced speed past the most beautiful stretches of scenery'.[4]

Every evening excursionist by the LMSR from London's Fenchurch Street, and stations east, paid only 2 shillings return to Southend, and that included free admission to the Kursaal and the Gardens.[5]

In Scotland, the LMSR introduced Evening Cruise trains in 1935, the first running from Glasgow to Alloway, where an hour was allowed to visit Burns' cottage and the kirk of Tam o' Shanter fame. The train then cruised 'at sightseeing speed' along the grass-strewn goods-only line, closed to passengers five years previously. Panoramic views of the Firth of Clyde were enjoyed on the way to Girvan, where another hour's break was allowed, before returning to Glasgow by a different route through Maybole. This 120-mile rail cruise cost only 2s 6d.

An evening cruise from Glasgow to St Fillans, on Loch Earn, took a route via Callender and Balquhidder outward and via Crieff and Gleneagles on returning. An unusual feature of this cruise was provision for 1st class passengers, fares being 4s 6d and 3 shillings, and a dining car served teas and light refreshments. 'Sightseeing speeds were maintained over the three lengths of line with the richest scenic attractions.'

Such was the popularity of these rail cruises that in subsequent years

> . . . a stream of trains which had to be pressed into service to cope with the rush, together with the difficulties of single line working, wrought havoc with the schedule.[6]

A 'See the Scenery' excursion was the LNER's offer to the people of Leeds in 1933, when two trains were required for the cruise 'at reduced speed throughout the picturesque scenery not otherwise accessible' on the Yorkshire Moors. Two weeks later two trains were employed for a similar cruise from York.[7]

The brand name 'See the Scenery' proved to be a good excursion train crowd-puller. For the Aberdeen Spring Holiday in 1936, two locomotives were attached to the nine-coach train, which included two restaurant cars, for a day circular cruise via Keith, Strathspey, Blair Atholl, Perth, Forfar and back to Aberdeen.

> The train is running smoothly, and Benachie with its Mither Tap and Oxen Craig arrest attention . . . past Keith on the Isla, by which time the stewards are dispensing the first luncheon . . . On we go until on our left the great panorama of the Cairngorms is stretched out before us, the spring snow giving the mountains a magnificent alpine appearance . . . Passengers rise in their seats, and this is surely the most spectacular section of the trip . . . Soon, in efficient hands, the engines prance to the summit of Drumochter Pass, 1,484 feet above sea level . . .

Sightseeing took place at Blair Atholl, and again at Perth, before commencing the return journey to Aberdeen. This ambitious excursion had covered some 250 miles over the lines of the former Great North of Scotland, Highland, and Caledonian companies. 'WSP' was well pleased:

> . . . With the tang of the ocean in their nostrils beyond Stonehaven, and the knowledge that they are nearing journey's end, the passengers spontaneously express opinions. Nothing but praise of the arrangements made for their enjoyment. . . . meals – first class and excellently served; train punctuality – perfect.
>
> Farewell for the present, 'Gordon Highlander'; and to you also, 'Hatton Castle' [the two locomotives] and many, many, thanks.[8]

Some 300 passengers embarked on an LNER 'Cruise Train' from Newcastle-on-Tyne for a 200-mile cruise via Kelso, Hawick and Hexham, with 1- or 2-hour stops at each. One satisfied 'cruiser' wrote to the Newcastle Stationmaster:

> I really do not know how to express in words the perfect service you gave. The train itself, luxury and comfort on wheels . . . the food served with fresh daintiness and deftness which would put many hotels amongst the non-runners . . . the stationmaster and porter where we stopped, seemed to radiate

that good fellowship which makes the difference between 'not too bad' and 'A jolly good time, would go again tomorrow if I had the chance'.[9]

'Customer Care' indeed.

Following the austerity of the war years, and with petrol rationing still in force, the idea of a rail cruise had appeal, so in 1951 British Rail offered a circular tour of North Wales starting from Llandudno and running via Rhyl, Denbigh and the Vale of Clwyd to Barmouth. After a sightseeing break, the train continued along the Cambrian coast and back to Llandudno. Seating was limited to 180, half of which was in easy chairs. Variously named 'North Wales Land Cruise', 'Coronation Land Cruise' and 'Cambrian Radio Cruise', there was a radio commentary along the route. The tour comprised 152 miles for which the fare was 13 shillings.[10] It is a sad thought that most of that scenic rail route has long been closed.

Mystery excursions, which had been a feature of the pre-war railway scene, were revived by British Rail and survived into the diesel era. In 1965, in the Bristol area, handbills proclaimed 'Mystery Destination' . . . 'Over 250 miles for £1'. Starting from Weston-super-Mare, the journey time to the mystery destination was to be 3 hours 25 minutes. Such was the public response that a second 11-coach relief train was commissioned to start from Bristol and proceed ahead of the train from Weston. Tenby proved to be the destination, but caterers there were taken by surprise, so the two cafeteria cars on the trains had to serve refreshments during the 5 hours their passengers were in Tenby.[11]

An unusual sight on the platform of Rutland's sole remaining railway station – Oakham – on a Sunday morning in July 1972 was a throng of people awaiting an 'Explore Britain by Train' mystery trip, for which a fare of £1 50p entitled them to a round journey time of 9 hours, plus $4^1/_2$ hours at an unknown destination. There was much speculation as to the train's route and destination:

> . . . But, when a little old lady loudly recalled a previous mystery trip to Rhyl, British Rail Passenger Network maps were quickly brought out from coat pockets, baskets and bags and consulted for possible routes to North Wales . . . 'Eric says we'll know where we are going when we get to the next station . . . if we turn right it'll be Bournemouth and if we go left Eastbourne' . . . Through Wing and Glaston tunnels, over the three abandoned lines radiating from Seaton Junction and across the imposing Welland Viaduct, we headed south . . . through Kettering and Wellingborough . . . for London . . . 'Southend,' said one lady. 'No, that's not far enough' . . . We started weaving through the maze of tracks around London . . . Clapham Junction . . . Hastings, or Folkestone, or Margate perhaps? . . . The BR rep . . . dropped a leaflet 'We hope you are enjoying the journey and have a pleasant time in Herne Bay' . . . It was a fine day out, with around 300 miles of comfortable travel for £1.50p apiece. And that can't be bad.[12]

British Rail's excursion brand names have been changed about as often as its management structure. In the 1960s, advertised excursions were 'Adex', football excursions 'Footex', and guaranteed excursions 'Garex', later changed to Chartex for chartered trains. In 1971, on the London Midland Region, a new name appeared — 'Merrymaker', and that summer 55 such trains carried 22,000 passengers. Such was the popularity of 'Merrymakers' that in the 1973-4 season, 173 trains were run, but they were too successful, and demand exceeded the capacity of the resources available. A new

MERRYMAKER

Excursion to Oban & Mull

Friday/Saturday/Sunday
20/21/22 August 1982

By Special train to Oban from Peterborough, Grantham, Newark, Retford and Doncaster, with connections from Lincoln and Gainsborough.

We are pleased to offer another in our series of Excursions into the beautiful Highlands and Islands of Western Scotland. Travel overnight Friday to Oban, arriving approximately 08.00 Saturday and spend the whole of the day in this premier Scottish resort. Or, as an optional extra, you can embark on the service steamer to Craignure, on the Inner Hebridean Isle of Mull, for a coach tour on this impressive island. The special train will return from Oban at about 20.00 on Saturday.

This is the age of the train

marketing strategy was thus introduced in 1980. However, by that time, 483,000 passengers had been booked on 'Merrymaker' trains over the previous ten years.

Since 1980, whilst some 'Merrymaker' trains have continued to be run, most seats for such travellers have been found on scheduled services, and the scope widened to provide more extensive facilities such as weekends inclusive of hotel and boat or coach trip, and even Continental destinations.

'Join the Merrymakers and get away for a break' was how BR wooed 1980s excursionists, and offered trips to Blackpool for the Illuminations, Spalding for the Tulip

Festival, a Scenic Tour to Carlisle via the Settle & Carlisle line, and a Mystery Excursion.

In a previous chapter, the trials and sufferings of excursionists returning from Blackpool were described, but 50 years later passengers on a 'Merrymaker' from Portsmouth to the Illuminations had a similar experience.

> . . . The journey home was not quite as scheduled . . . For practically ninety minutes the excursion stood immobile just outside Crewe . . . At last the train began to make slow progress southward . . . We weary excursionists returned three hours later than intended . . .

and then, philosophically, this 'Merrymaker' concluded that 'Merrymaker outings such as this are splendid value for money'.[13] But then, he was an enthusiast who had 'copped' lots of locomotive numbers!

A novelty on one 'Merrymaker' excursion, from St Pancras to York and Scarborough in 1980, was use of the 'Games Train' in which the tabletops of five coaches were printed with board games. Playing kits by the Waddington Playing Card Company were on sale from the buffet car staff.[14]

From the early days of railways, boat-trains connected with regular cross-Channel sailings and with the big liners at Liverpool and Southampton, but excursion trains taking crowds to look over the big ships became a feature of the railway scene in the inter-war years. Not surprisingly, the Southern Railway, with its extensive Southampton docks, led the way in 1927, when 3,280 Londoners were conveyed in six special trains to visit either the *Majestic* or the *Berengaria* liners. Each train included a dining car, and at an inclusive fare of only 5s 9d it is not surprising that these excursions remained popular right up until 1939.[15]

The LMSR promoted rail, steamer and coach excursions in Scotland. A LMSR charabanc meets the steamer at Ford Pier on Loch Awe.

L M S
LONDON MIDLAND AND SCOTTISH RAILWAY

Glasgow Weekly Herald

DAY EXCURSION

OVER THE SEA
TO SKYE

On Tuesday night, 19th July, 1932

OUTWARD JOURNEY.	Tuesday night.	RETURN JOURNEY.	Wed's'day night.
	p.m.		p.m.
GLASGOW (Buchanan Street)....... leave	11 50	PORTREE (Steamer) .... leave	8 15
	Wed's'day	BROADFORD (Steamer) .... „	9 25
	morning.	KYLE OF LOCHALSH (Steamer) .... arrive	10 0
STIRLING .... leave	12 35a	„ „ .... leave	10 30
PERTH.......................... „	1 30	PLOCKTON .... „	10 42
FORRES .... „	5 0	STROME FERRY .... „	10 54
NAIRN.......................... „	5 25	STRATHCARRON .... „	11 12
INVERNESS .... arrive	5 45	ACHNASHEEN................... „	11 50
„ „ .... leave	6 5		Thursday morning.
DINGWALL .... „	6 40		
GARVE .... „	7 20	GARVE .... „	12 28a
ACHNASHEEN .... „	7 50	DINGWALL .... „	12 51
STRATHCARRON................. „	8 25	INVERNESS ....arrive	1 35
STROME FERRY .... „	8 45	„ „ .... leave	1 45
PLOCKTON....................... „	8 55	NAIRN......................... „	2 8
KYLE OF LOCHALSH .... arrive	9 7	FORRES .... „	2 26
„ „ (Steamer) .... leave	9 35	PERTH.......................arrive	6 12
BROADFORD (Steamer)........... arrive	10 25	STIRLING .... „	7 15
PORTREE (Steamer) .... „	11 30	GLASGOW (Buchanan Street)..... „	8 5

RETURN FARE
22/-
GLASGOW TO SKYE

The First Day Excursion Glasgow to Skye

Truly a 'day' excursion – or a day and a half? Sleeping and dining cars were available and for £3 2s 6d a berth each way plus full breakfasts and suppers could be included.

However, 1936 saw a special event at Southampton, the maiden voyage of the *Queen Mary*. In addition to five boat trains for passengers sailing on the new liner, four excursions ran connecting with small vessels which would follow in the wake of the big ship down Southampton Water.[16]

In the previous April, when the *Queen Mary* arrived at Southampton from Clydeside, 18 special trains brought 6,984 passengers from as far afield as Bristol, Birmingham, Leicester, Bedford, South Wales, Dover, Brighton and, of course, London. On that day 18,000 visitors viewed the liner from the dock, and thousands more from other vantage points.[17]

A ship-launching on the Clyde, in 1931, attracted such vast crowds of Glaswegians that not only special Corporation buses and trains were put on, but also many special trains to any spot on the river from which a view of the new *Empress of Britain* might be had.[18]

Perhaps the earliest combined rail and steamer excursion was arranged by the

The Dingwall Stationmaster beside his own handiwork, advertising a Sunday excursion in 1930.

Birmingham & Derby Junction Railway in 1842, when trains from Birmingham, Tamworth and Burton-on-Trent ran to Ambergate on the North Midland line. Here passengers boarded canal boats for a cruise to Cromford Basin, from where horse-drawn coaches took them on to Matlock. Fares were 10 shillings 1st class and 6 shillings 2nd.[19]

Boston, Lincolnshire, is better known for its connection with the Pilgrim Fathers than as a pleasure resort, yet, long before the railway reached there in 1848, the paddle-steamers had done a brisk trade taking excursionists on trips across the Wash to Hunstanton, or round the coast to Skegness. There were bathing-machines in the estuary of the River Witham and at Freiston Shore, whilst in Skirbeck, the Vauxhall Gardens covered two acres, with a maze and a Theatre of Arts, or 'Cosmorama', with 'all the wonders of a magic lantern show'. In 1855, a baby show took place 'after the style of those held in New York by that king of showmen, Barnum'.[20]

Wet weather marred the first rail excursion from Nottingham to Boston on 25 April 1859[21], but better weather in July encouraged 6,000 rail excursionists to enjoy the attractions of the town:

A little after half-past eight the first of the excursion trains arrived bringing

This Great Eastern Railway's paddle steamer *Essex* was acquired in 1896 for excursion traffic on the River Orwell. *(Gerry Lewis collection)*

700 people from Nottingham. The train stopped at the Goods Department to unload instead of running into the passenger station. This departure from the regular order of things from a desire on the part of the managers of the line to afford an opportunity to pleasure seekers to secure a sea trip easily, the packets in Skirbeck Quarter being close to the spot and ready for sea at the time the train arrived.

Both the steamers were readily laden to excess and every available boat at hand was dragged into service. Those who could not get boat accommodation took 'bus' to Freiston Shore. Scarcely however, had this batch of people got out of the way when another train from the same direction arrived with another 700 visitors. This was speedily followed by one from Hitchin and Peterborough bearing about 1,000 more. Then came a third one from the Nottingham line, from Sleaford and stations between that place and Boston bearing another 300. The next one was from Hull, Grimsby and Louth bringing upwards of 900. This was followed by a second from Peterborough and stations in that direction bringing 450. Then there came a monster one of 40 carriages from Doncaster, Lincoln etc bearing upwards of 1,500. This completed the list of morning trains.

There was an afternoon train from Sleaford to accommodate those people who could not come by the early ones owing to it being Sleaford market. The number brought by this train made the total of railway importations to 6,000.[22]

An ambitious rail and steamer excursion was run by the GWR in 1925. The train left Paddington at 7.50 pm on Friday evening on a journey to Killarney, which was reached at

Whitley Bay Chamber of Trade excursionists at Larne Harbour, Northern Ireland, in September 1932. Two trains conveyed the party to Stranraer for the crossing in RMS *Princess Margaret*.

10.30 am the following morning. The sea-crossing was by GWR steamer from Fishguard to Rosslare, whilst the rail journey to Killarney was over the Great Southern & Western Railway. Returning at 6.15 pm, by the same route, the excursionists arrived back at Paddington at 9 am on Sunday morning.[23]

Northern Ireland was the venue for the Whitley Bay Chamber of Trade's excursion by the LNER in 1932, when the 750 passengers travelled in two corridor trains with dining cars. At Stranraer, the party boarded RMS *Princess Margaret* for the crossing to Larne. After breakfast at the LMSR's Laharna Hotel, motor coaches took them on a tour which included the Giant's Causeway, followed by luncheon at the LMSR's Portrush hotel.[24]

Colonel Baldwin Webb MP organised a mammoth combined rail and steamer trip for his constituents in the Wrekin Division of Shropshire in July 1936. Eight special trains took over 4,000 of his supporters to Southampton, where they embarked on five steamers chartered for a cruise round the Isle of Wight. Afterwards these 'Shropshire Lads and Lassies' rejoined their trains to be taken to Aldershot for the Military Tattoo.[25]

Another combined rail and river excursion, when the passengers stood on the banks and watched the river go by, was certainly different. In April 1936, the LMSR advertised an excursion from Wolverhampton and Birmingham to witness 'The SEVERNTH WONDER OF THE WORLD', for which a fare of 3s 9d would include train travel to Gloucester and coach to Stonebench to see the Severn Bore, when a wall of water 9 feet high would roll up the river. There was a 'flood' of passengers, so much so that a duplicate train was run.[26]

Combined rail and theatre excursions were another innovation of the inter-war years.

Fourth Annual Visit

A special evening excursion
with reserved accommodation
has been arranged for

SLEEPING BEAUTY

at the Birmingham Theatre Royal

THURSDAY, MARCH 23rd, 1939

Prices from 4/6 to 8/6 including rail fare,
reserved seats and light refreshments.
Party bookings now accepted, apply

L·C·S TRAVEL BUREAU
Union Street   Telephone 20431

(Leicester Co-operative Society)

The LMSR ran these from Stratford-on-Avon, picking up at eight stations on the way, to Northampton for performances at the Royal Theatre. Stratford-on-Avon itself was the venue for excursion trains from London, Hereford, Bristol and Newport on the GWR, and from Northampton on the LMSR for the opening of the new Shakespeare Memorial Theatre by the Prince of Wales in 1932. Between 3 and 4 miles of bunting and ceremonial shields were used to decorate the GWR station.[27]

In 1937 the GWR claimed to have run possibly the first excursion to a film studio. A train from Bristol ran to Slough where motor coaches conveyed the party to the Pinewood Film Studios, 'the largest and most up-to-date in Europe.' As well as a conducted tour of all the studios, the party saw a film in the making before being served tea. Back in Bristol, these excursionists were able, by visiting local cinemas, to see themselves on a film made during their visit, and all this for 10s 6d return fare.[28]

Twenty years later, British Rail ran an Amateur Photographers' Excursion from Glasgow over the West Highland line, with stops for photography and slow running at several points to enable pictures to be taken from the moving train. On board was a photographic information bureau, and prizes ranging from photographic equipment to 'runabout' tickets were offered by British Rail for the best prints submitted, which were then publicly exhibited at Glasgow Central station.

The Scottish Region of BR introduced a Television Train over the West Highland line, each coach having a screen mounted above the central gangway. Excursionists were invited to the 'studio' in the guard's van to entertain their fellow travellers. Perhaps this TV train was put to better use when chartered by an education authority to give several hundred schoolchildren a practical geography lesson along the line.[29]

When Wiggins Teape Ltd chartered a special train for 120 guests to run from Paddington to Sudbrooke, Monmouthshire, the Western Region of BR adapted a dining car as a cinema coach enabling four film shows to be given during the journey.[30]

'Talking of Trains' is the title of a Workers' Educational Association course started at Kingston, Surrey, in 1961, and still running! Numerous special trains have been chartered by this group since their first in 1967. In 1970 they hired the 'Blue Pullman' diesel-electric train for a 570-mile trip for 212 people from Surbiton and Guildford to Carmarthen, with a separate diesel multiple unit used for a tour of goods-only lines in North Wales.[31]

As early as 1929, the LNER introduced excursions using Pullman Car Company coaches. Known as the 'Eastern Belle', these trains ran from Liverpool Street station non-stop to Felixstowe on Mondays, to Clacton on Tuesdays, to Frinton and Walton on Wednesdays, to Harwich on Thursdays and to Thorpeness and Aldeburgh on Fridays. The fare, including the Pullman supplement, was 10s 6d 1st class and 6s 6d 3rd class, with all seats numbered.[32]

Music festivals, choral festivals, brass band contests, even fife and drum contests have generated excursion traffic since early railway days. However, the first time a Pullman train had been used for such a purpose was in 1972, when the organisers of the Brighton Festival chartered the 'Brighton Belle' for a musical trip from Victoria station to Brighton. The 200 passengers were served dinner in the Royal Pavilion, followed by a performance of Berlioz's 'Railroad Song' by military bands and choirs on the concourse of Brighton station.

In that same year British Rail, in association with the Royal Philharmonic Orchestra, arranged a series of concerts in the Royal Albert Hall under the title 'Journeys Through Music'. More than 4,000 young people from 148 schools were conveyed in special trains from within a 100-mile radius of London.[33]

A moving hide for birdwatching sounds a bit unlikely, but the Cornwall Birdwatching and Preservation Society hired a special train to travel slowly along the bank of the River Fowey between Par and Fowey in October 1972.[34] They would have spotted some 'rails' if nothing else!

The 'Holiday Preview Express' was run from Paddington to Weston-super-Mare in March 1970, the idea being to whet people's appetites for a holiday in that resort. Publicity wallets were handed to each of the 230 passengers who paid only £1 for the return trip. However, blizzard conditions for the first part of the journey, together with an icy blast from the Bristol Channel, can have done little to stimulate enthusiasm for a longer stay in the resort.[35]

The Scottish Region of BR chose 'Look and Book' as the title for its holiday preview excursions in February 1980 when, on four successive Saturdays, trains ran from Glasgow to Blackpool (2), Southport and Morecambe, all at a fare of £5 50p.[36]

An event which a retired GWR Superintendent said he was always glad to see over was Shrewsbury Floral Fete, when as many as 40,000 excursionists arrived from Leeds, Liverpool, Bristol, Birmingham and intermediate stations.

> Return trains had to be compressed into a few hours, sixteen of them had to be started from the goods yard. There were no platforms; the illumination was a few oil lamps. Passengers had to cross the lines of rails to reach their trains, . . . some would creep between the carriages. I was relieved when midnight arrived and no mishap occurred.[34]

Railway station gardens, particularly in rural areas, were once not only a source of pleasure for passengers, but also the cause of much rivalry between station staff in the Best Kept Station competitions organised by the companies. In 1936 the LNER ran excursions to enable the public to see some of its station gardens in the Northern District, and so successful was this innovation that, in the following year, eight such excursions were arranged and 1,700 people catered for. The company's latest tourist coaches with buffet facilities were provided. This appears to have been a very successful public relations exercise, when many of the passengers took the opportunity to have many details of railway operating explained to them.[38]

It was the rapid transit to distant towns and markets provided by the railways which encouraged the growth of the cut-flower and bulb industry in the Lincolnshire Fens, and

Passengers on a LNER excursion visiting wayside station gardens in 1937 admire the First Class prize winner at North Grimston, Yorkshire.

it was the railways which popularised the bulb fields as a choice of venue for excursions. The LNER's association with the Eastern Counties Omnibus Company made possible a tour of the bulb fields following a train journey to Spalding. To promote these excursions from London, the LNER had a display of blooms in its Regent Street office window.[39] The annual Spalding Flower Parade, with its many floats decorated with thousands of flower heads, still attracts huge crowds, but today few special trains. As recently as the 1970s excursion trains were run from points as far distant as Brighton, Liverpool, Derby and, of course, London. The sidings at Spalding could not accommodate so many trains, so several were sent to Peterborough and March to wait until required for the return journeys.

Hop-picking in Kent began in the last week of August and continued for about two weeks. Some 30,000 London 'Eastenders' were conveyed by the Southern Railway in special trains mainly from London Bridge and New Cross stations. The pickers comprised whole families with many children, and for them it was a working holiday, and hardly an 'Away Day'. However, the 'Hop-pickers' Friends' specials were 'Away Days' when as many as 43,412 (in 1925) relatives and friends from London visited the pickers in the hop-fields on a Sunday.

Guinness was not only 'Good for you' but its hop-fields around Bodiam were good for Colonel Stephens's Kent & East Sussex Railway, which ran 24 miles from Robertsbridge to Headcorn, linking with the Southern Railway at both ends. A K&ESR train usually comprised one passenger coach plus goods wagons, but a 'Hop-pickers' Friends' special could see as many as 15 SR bogie coaches plus two old K&ESR six-wheelers, all hauled by an ancient ex-LSWR saddle-tank locomotive.[40]

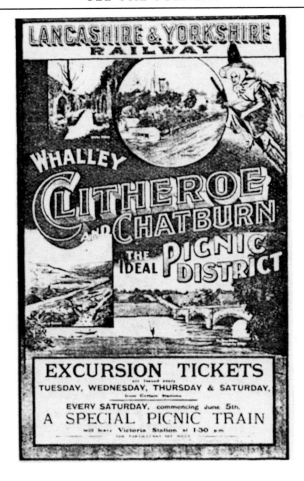

A 'Special Picnic Train' was used by the Lancashire & Yorkshire Railway to entice its customers into the countryside.

An innovation by the North Eastern Region of BR in 1955 was to arrange a special type of excursion train from Tyneside, Teeside and Hull districts during the peak local holiday week, and intended for the holidaymaker who preferred to sleep at home. These trains travelled to three different holiday resorts on three successive days for a fare which included a reserved seat. The 'Northern Venturer' from Newcastle, the 'Teeside Nomad' from Middlesbrough, and the 'Humber Rover' from Hull were names selected from suggestions submitted by the public, with a prize of two tickets for the winning entries.[41]

This idea caught on and, in 1957, the London Midland Region ran holiday expresses from Midland towns to North Wales on Monday, Southend on Tuesday, Skegness on Wednesday, London on Thursday, and Blackpool on Friday, all for an inclusive fare of only 50 shillings.[42]

In 1964 the Western Region promoted its holiday expresses as 'Bucket and Spade' specials, on which each child passenger received a free bucket and spade, and there was a chance to win cash prizes. For 65 shillings, 'sleep-at-home' holidaymakers could visit Paignton, Weymouth, Minehead, Bournemouth and London. Not surprisingly the

Hiking became popular in the 1930s and ramblers' specials took shorts-clad and rucksack-toting walkers to the country.

scheme proved to be a sell-out.[43]

A new word came to the fore in the late 1920s – 'hiking' – and those who did it were 'hikers'. There was a popular song:

> I'm happy when I'm hiking
> With a rucksack on my back,
> I'm happy when I'm hiking
> Off the beaten track.

Bovril, the beef extract manufacturers, claimed that 'HIKERS' SPECIAL DELIGHT IS BOVRIL', and the railways were soon running hikers' excursion trains carrying city dwellers to the countryside for a day's rambling. In 1928 the LNER reported:

> . . .Young men in khaki shorts and young women attired in anything from
> football kit to raiment of a more (or less!) orthodox character throng London
> Road Station every Sunday morning, all clamouring for walking-out tickets.[44]

A year later, 1,000 hikers travelled by special train from Glasgow, Queen Street, to

Balloch Pier, where they boarded a steamer to Rowardennan, and from there climbed Ben Lomond, on which an 'indicator', presented by the *Glasgow Daily Record*, was accepted on behalf of the public by the Secretary of the Federation of Ramblers.[45]

Rambles in the Chiltern Country was a GWR publication in 1932, following which two special 'Hikers' Mystery Expresses' were organised from Paddington. These trains comprised 12 3rd class corridor coaches to carry some 2,000 ramblers, when the mystery destinations proved to be Pangbourne and Henley-on-Thames.

Ramblers' excursion trains after the Second World War often took unusual routes, or travelled over lines no longer used by scheduled passenger trains. The 'John Milton Special' in 1956 was run from Crystal Palace to Chesham, Bucks. Steam power hauled this train to New Cross Gate, where an electric locomotive took it via the East London line to the St Mary's curve, then on the old Metropolitan Railway line as far as Rickmansworth. Here an ex-Metropolitan steam engine took the train forward to Chesham.[46]

Another ramblers' excursion, the 'West Sussex Downsman' in 1958, ran from Charing Cross to Midhurst, travelling over the Pulborough to Midhurst line which had closed to passengers three years earlier.[47]

The Ryedale Railway, linking Gilling with Pickering, North Yorkshire, closed to passengers in 1953, but ramblers' specials continued to call there until 1964. Likewise the line from Northallerton to Hawes, which was closed to passengers in 1954, had a ramblers' special along the line in 1976, and this prompted the Yorkshire Dales National Park Committee to promote a 'Dalesrail' shopping excursion from Redmire, a station on this line, to York, returning with ramblers who wished to walk in Wensleydale.[48]

'Drive your own excursion train' could be expected to attract the steam addicts, but the Southern Railway did not go that far. It did, however, in April 1939, run an excursion from Waterloo to Brookwood for a return fare of 7s 6d which included a footplate ride down the Bisley branch. Two Drummond 0-4-4 tank engines, coupled back to back, trundled their appreciative cargo back and forth and, although a driver was heard to tell his captive audience that his engine was capable of 70 mph, the speed restriction was in fact 10 mph. A 'Lord Nelson' Class 4-6-0 locomotive, standing unsteamed in Brookwood station, was admired, crawled over, and its controls handled by the starry-eyed would-be drivers.[49]

'The Half & Half Excursion' was how the *Lincoln Echo* described excursion trains which started from the one-time Midland station, St Marks, which was closed in 1984. Because the two platforms butted up close to a level crossing on a busy street, a long excursion train could not load up at a platform without fouling the crossing. Instead, six coaches of a 12-coach train were placed in the up platform and six in the down. At departure time, the front half of the train pulled forward, reversed on to the other half and coupled up, before the final 'Right Away' to the seaside.[50]

Excursion trains sometimes came as a surprise, not only to the public, but also to railwaymen. In 1934, an excursion from Leicester to Brighton was routed via Market Harborough, Kettering, both Wellingborough stations, Northampton Bridge Street, Bletchley and Kensington. Indeed an interesting route, but the surprise was to come on the return journey when, between Northampton and Wellingborough, a level-crossing gate-keeper had gone to bed, leaving his gates closed across the line and his signals firmly at 'Danger'.[51]

Chapter 12
THE SOUND OF MUSIC

'This was IT, whether we liked it or not, this was the end of steam . . . yet it was unbelievable. No-one could really grasp that this was The End.'

It has been mostly for purposes of enjoying the seaside, scenery, sport or other forms of entertainment that the excursion trains so far considered have been arranged, but interest in railways themselves, and particularly nostalgia for steam locomotives, has prompted the arranging of many excursion trains.

Various organisations, among them the Stephenson Locomotive Society, the Railway Correspondence and Travel Society and the Locomotive Club of Great Britain, have chartered trains to travel over closed lines, or to commemorate the opening or closing of a railway, as well as the return to steam operation of locomotives rescued from breakers' yards, or those in the care of the National Railway Museum.

Particularly since the demise of steam operation on British Railways, the number of

On August Bank Holiday, 1959, LMSR Compound 4-4-0 No 41101 was allocated to haul a *Daily Mirror* excursion from Manchester Victoria to Blackpool. Painted in yellow and black for this trip, the engine was withdrawn from service immediately afterwards.

such special trains has reached such proportions as to make it impossible to cover the subject fully in this general survey of the railway day excursion. Consequently, only examples of a few of the more significant events are to be referred to here.

In May 1888, the West Coast Route to Edinburgh – the LNWR plus the Caledonian Railway – cut the journey time from London by 1 hour to just 9 hours. The East Coast route – the Great Northern Railway plus the North Eastern Railway plus the North British Railway – retaliated with a reduction to only 8^1/$_2$ hours. From 1 August both routes cut their times back to 8 hours. However, the East Coast route then announced that its train would only take 7^3/$_4$ hours on 10 August but, on that very day, the West Coast train was into Edinburgh in 7 hours and 32 minutes.

The achievement of the Great Northern's locomotives, the Stirling 8-foot 'single' 4-2-2s and 7 ft 7 ins 2-2-2s, in this historic 'Race to the North' was commemorated, in August 1938, by the LNER arranging a half-day excursion from King's Cross to Cambridge in a train of ex-GNR coaches hauled by ex-GNR locomotive No 1 from the Railway Museum. Billed as 'The Flying Scotsman', departure from London was timed for 11.04 am with arrival back at 8.14 pm – a long half-day indeed. Some passengers wore costumes of the 1880 period. One participant considered that

> ... a large proportion of the passengers clearly consisted of those sufficiently old to be sampling afresh a railway experience they must have thought gone for ever – that of travelling in six-wheel coaches behind a single driver locomotive ... On the return journey, indeed, No 1 showed herself still abreast of the times by touching about 74 mph near Wood Green.[1]

Patrick Stirling's engine, and her East Coast Joint Stock coaches, went on exhibition at Sheffield in the following September, and from there an excursion comprising this train was run to Lincoln when, on the return journey, this veteran was credited with attaining 65 mph 'to the delight of the passengers and the press representatives on board'.[2]

> Records crowd upon records in this remarkable year of railway history. But the Great Western Railway's greatest feat really does look something like a climax which may be expected to remain unassailed for a long time to come ...

wrote Charles Rous Marten, that prolific train recorder for *The Railway Magazine* in 1904.[3] He had travelled on the GWR Ocean Mails special from Plymouth to Paddington on 9 May and, based upon his timings, it was afterwards claimed that *City of Truro*, 4-4-0 locomotive No 3440, had attained 102.3 mph, though admittedly down Wellington Bank.

Well, here was a steam locomotive achievement the 60th anniversary of which was worth recognising when, in 1964, the end of steam was already forecast. An Ian Allan Rail Tour ran to do just that, from Paddington to Plymouth, hauled by ex-GWR 4-6-0 No 4079 *Pendennis Castle*. A mishap with firebars caused this locomotive to be taken off at Taunton and replaced by No 7025 *Sudeley Castle*, which completed the run to Plymouth and returned the train as far as Bristol. Here 4-6-0 No 7034 *Earl of Ducie* took over for the final leg of the tour back to Paddington. The 334 seats available were sold at a price of £5 15s which included lunch and high tea. One of the organisers afterwards wrote '. . . but the magic 100 eluded us . . . there was a strong cross wind which didn't help . . . It was a triumphant day for everyone.'[4]

Anticipating the ending of steam-hauled trains by British Railways in August 1968, the Ian Allan publishing company also organised two special trains from Paddington to Birkenhead, for which *Clun Castle* and *Pendennis Castle* attracted full loadings of their

Ex-GWR 4-6-0 No 4079 *Pendennis Castle* backs on to an Ian Allan excursion for a run from Paddington to Plymouth in 1964, marking 60 years since *City of Truro* achieved a speed claimed to be over 102 mph.

trains, whilst thousands lined the route or waited on station platforms to observe the passing of steam.[5]

Under a headline, 'The Nostalgia Line or a 200 MILE JOURNEY to the AGE of STEAM', the *Liverpool Daily Post* reported an excursion arranged by the Railway Correspondence and Travel Society in 1967, to record for posterity the last journey by a passenger train to Brymbo, near Wrexham. The regular passenger service between Wrexham and Brymbo had been withdrawn in 1950. During a 12-hour round trip, four steam locomotives were employed: Class '8F' 2-8-0 No 48697; two Class '4' 2-6-4Ts, Nos 42616 and 42647; and Class '9F' 2-10-0 No 92058.

Any and every excuse for running steam-hauled trains was sought as the dreaded end of steam on BR approached, but not everyone was sorry to see the last of steam locomotives, as a letter from a driver's wife in 1967 explained:

> So Mr J. B. L. is sorry to see steam locomotives stopped. I'm one of a large number who will not be sorry. We are the wives of drivers who have their washing to do. You go a few miles on a footplate and see the coal-dust get down to your underclothes . . . see how happy your lady clothes-washer is. We women are not attached to steam trains and would not feel very happy about paying more fares just to travel on a steam-hissing, vibrating, dirty train.[6]

A quarter of a century later, steam-hauled trains are filled with 'enthusiasts', paying high fares, who are disappointed if they go home with clean faces – or underclothes!

To celebrate the 40th anniversary of non-stop trains between King's Cross and Edinburgh, special trains were run in May 1968. Ex-LNER 4-6-2 locomotive No 4472 *Flying Scotsman*, hauled its train from King's Cross's platform 10 at 10 am, just as a diesel-

British Rail
runs out of steam

Last steam train makes
historic special farewell journey
Sunday August 11th

Liverpool/Manchester
to Carlisle & back

This will be the very last train to operate on
standard gauge track headed by a B.R. steam locomotive. 314 nostalgic miles, 10½ happy hours, with
luncheon, high tea, other refreshments, souvenir
ticket and souvenir scroll. 15 guineas.
Liverpool Lime Street Dep 09.10 – Arr 19.50
Manchester Victoria Dep 11.06 – Arr 18.48
For Tickets. Write quickly to Passenger
Marketing Manager, British Rail, London Midland
Region, Euston House, London NW1. Mark your
envelope Personal and enclose £15.15 per ticket
required. Money immediately refunded if the 470
seats have already been sold.

British Rail

electric 'Deltic' departed with BR's 'Flying Scotsman' train from platform 8.

With only a few hours to go before the departure of the last scheduled steam-hauled passenger train on British Railways, here is how one saddened mourner recorded his impressions of the scene at Preston:

Preston station at six o'clock in the evening of Saturday August 3rd, 1968. Already groups of fanatics were gathering, and throughout the station – on the platforms, in the refreshment rooms, out by the ticket barrier – there was only one word that mattered: Steam. This was IT, whether we liked it or not, this was the end of steam . . . This was the last we'd ever see of passenger steam – <u>proper</u> passenger steam – for the next day's tour would be too clean and too artificial to be valued – this was the last working steam on BR: yet it was unbelievable. No-one could really grasp that this was The End.[7]

The following day the Locomotive Club of Great Britain ran an excursion from St Pancras to Carnforth hauled by Standard Class '7' 4-6-2 No 70013 *Oliver Cromwell* and Stanier Class '5' 4-6-0 No 44781 as a farewell to steam. The Stephenson Locomotive

Society also ran two farewell tours utilising two Class '5' 4-6-0s, Nos 45017 and 44874, whilst Great Central Enterprises' excursion from Stockport to Carnforth was behind Class '5' 4-6-0 No 45156 *Ayrshire Yeomanry*. The Railway Correspondence and Travel Society also ran a special to Carnforth utilising Class '8F' 2-8-0 No 48476 and Class '5' 4-6-0 No 73069.

Steam was a long time ending for, on 11 August, British Rail ran its own 15 guinea (£15 15s 0d) special from Liverpool and Manchester to Carnforth, and advertised by posters which read:

BRITISH RAIL
runs out of steam
Last steam train makes
historic special farewell journey
Sunday August 11th

From Liverpool to Manchester, Class '5' 4-6-0 No 45110 was in charge, but from Manchester to Carnforth 'Britannia' Class '7' 4-6-2 No 70013 *Oliver Cromwell* took over.

After this, BR management banned all steam working on its system, so that rescued and restored locomotives were restricted to the short lengths of line of preserved railways where they hauled Santa Specials, or were decorated in various garbs for advertising films. Agitation for the lifting of the steam ban was sustained, and some support came from those in high places.

At last, on 2 October 1971, it seemed that BR's ban was to be relaxed, for the ex-GWR 4-6-0 express locomotive *King George V* was to be allowed out of the Bulmer Cider works at Hereford to haul, not only the Bulmer Cider Exhibition train, but also a number of excursion trains.

Accommodation was in the five Pullman cars comprising the Bulmer's train and

The last steam-hauled train of 1968 behind Class '7' No 70013 *Oliver Cromwell*, passing Whalley between Manchester and Carlisle.

No 4472 *Flying Scotsman* with the 'Fair Maid Pullman' at Gleneagles on 1 October 1983. Chartered by the Steam Locomotive Operators' Association, this special ran from Euston to Perth via Motherwell, returning via Edinburgh. (*Jim Wade*)

strengthened by an additional pair of BR Mk 1 coaches. The first excursion ran from Birmingham Moor Street station to Kensington Olympia on 4 October, for which 115 passengers paid £7 50p each. The Pullman cars of the Cider Train were on exhibition to the public whilst at Olympia. On 7 October, *King George* V took the Pullmans, plus three BR 2nd class open carriages, with some 120 fare-paying passengers, from Olympia to Swindon, where the Cider Train remained on show until the final experimental run was made from Swindon to Hereford on 9 October. This time the Pullmans were stengthened by four BR coaches, and 210 passengers paid £5 for this trip.[8]

Following the Bulmer's specials, British Rail further relaxed its ban on steam and, early in 1972, routes authorised for steam operation were: Birmingham Moor Street to Didcot, 77 miles; Shrewsbury to Newport, 94 miles; York to Scarborough, 42 miles; Newcastle to Carlisle, 60 miles; and Carnforth to Barrow, 28 miles. Quick off the mark was the *Birmingham Post* on 10 June with a steam tour from its city to Didcot–Severn Tunnel–Hereford and home. Ex-GWR 4-6-0 No 7029 *Clun Castle* was used between Birmingham and Didcot. Others organising steam specials after the lifting of the ban included the Great Western Society, running *Clun Castle* between Birmingham and Didcot, and the A4 Locomotive Society operating ex-LNER 'A4', 4-6-2 No 4498 *Sir Nigel Gresley* between Newcastle and Carlisle.

It was September 1972 before the first steam-hauled excursion ran between York and Scarborough, when the York Department of Tourism arranged with the A4 Locomotive

Society to have No 60019 *Bittern* haul its 'Salute to Steam' special of 12 coaches conveying 600 passengers. From Scarborough, these excursionists went by road to the preserved North Yorkshire Moors Railway.

An unusual reason for organising day excursion trains occurred in September 1978, following the death of the well-known railway photographer the Right Reverend Eric Treacy, Lord Bishop of Wakefield. From London, the 'Lord Bishop' special ran to Hellifield, from which point ex-LNER 4-6-2 No 4472 *Flying Scotsman* took over for the section to Appleby, where a memorial service took place in the goods yard. No 92220 *Evening Star* hauled the 'Bishop Treacy' special from Wakefield to Appleby. After the ceremony of unveiling a plaque at Appleby station, *Evening Star* took its train to Armathwaite, from where *Clun Castle* returned the train to Hellifield.[9]

Commemorative special trains can be expensive; for example, in 1979 the day return fare from Paddington to Didcot was £3 46p, but for a special marking the 125th anniversary of the rebuilding of Paddington station, the fare was £12 50p. Ex-GWR 4-6-0 No 6000 *King George V* stood at the head of this special ready for departure from platform 3 at 11.20 am when, at the same time, a High Speed Train 'InterCity 125' would pull out for Bristol. As one observer wrote:

> . . . Railway enthusiasts had had their treat . . . there was an infectious air of goodwill which was echoed by railway staff, some dressed in period GWR uniforms . . . even Paddington Bear, the children's favourite, stood on his plinth . . . watching the 'Paddington Party'.[10]

What is the connection between a whiff of steam and inhaling menthol? Hall Brothers of Whitefield, makers of Mentholyptus, the throat lozenge, considered there to be a close connection and so chartered No 4472 *Flying Scotsman* to haul the 12-coach 'Mentholyptus Special' to Chester in 1987.

The programme for the day, marking the 60th anniversary of the firm, included a send-off by the Mayor and Mayoress of Bury, some 300 excursionists dressed in a variety of 1920s fashions, the Bolton Barber Shop Quartet Singers and, at Chester, a vintage Fowler steam lorry in Mentholyptus livery. Large crowds gathered at Chester to view the train, whilst others watched from the lineside. Regrettably, far too many so-called enthusiasts stood in the path of the train taking photographs or making recordings – a foolish practice which it has so far proved impossible to discourage. The Quartet sang 'Chattanooga Choo-Choo' – ugh![11]

In the aftermath of the Beeching line and station closures, from 1964 onwards, many 'last train' excursions were organised, but even more special trains have been arranged as part of campaigns to secure re-openings of closed stations, or the opening of new ones to serve new housing developments, and to provide alternative transport to the car. Leading most of these campaigns, which have resulted in 173 stations being opened since 1970, has been the Railway Development Society.

Typical of 'last train' specials was the 'Standard Special' organised by the *Lincolnshire Standard* newspaper in October 1970, when the Grimsby to Firsby line was closed. With 687 readers on board, this 12-coach excursion train headed for King's Cross, but hundreds more 'mourners' lined the route – a thousand at Louth alone. On the return journey, the special left King's Cross a few minutes before the last scheduled train to Grimsby but, between Sandy and Huntingdon, the special was allowed to drop behind the scheduled train so that it could in truth be the very 'last train' over the line. The day ended with 'the doffing of hats, the explosion of detonators and the sounding of the Last Post, whilst the enginemen autographed souvenir brochures'.[12]

The last train, specially chartered by the Welland Valley Rail Revival Group, traverses the Market Harborough to Northampton line on 15 August 1981. A wreath is carried in the front window. *(Jim Wade)*

In 1972, the scenic Kyle of Lochalsh line was threatened with closure and, as part of a campaign to keep it open, the *Aberdeen Evening Express* chartered two 'Lifeline' charity specials over the threatened line. Tickets for the 380 mile round trip cost £2 50p, and for the first train all were sold out within 24 hours; for the second train all were sold within half an hour. More than 1,200 people made the trip and so demonstrated their support for saving the line. Nor were the inhabitants of Kyle and Skye overlooked, for a Saturday 'Shopper's Special' ran to Aberdeen, departing from Kyle of Lochalsh at 6 am and arriving back at 10.30 pm. A long day but worth it, for the line was saved and the glens continue to echo to the throb of diesels and two-tone horns.[13]

Corby, Northamptonshire, with a population of 55,000, lost its passenger service in 1966, the station being demolished except for the down platform. Local members of the Railway Development Society formed 'Corbyrail' to campaign for the restoration of a passenger service, and one of its activities was to organise excursions from the old station to York and Scarborough (1984), Liverpool International Garden Festival (1984), Llandudno (1985), Portsmouth and Southsea (1986), York and Scarborough (1987) and Bristol and Weston-super-Mare (1988). In addition, Christmas shopping trips were organised to Nottingham with Father Christmas aboard and gifts for the children. The train to Llandudno was apparently not expected on the North Wales line because it arrived at Mostyn to find that the engineers had the track lifted! On board the Corby special was a British Rail Area Manager, which was fortunate indeed, because a later

Class '40' No 40 365 heads one of two specials from Aberdeen to Kyle of Lochalsh when the line was threatened with closure in 1972.

return from the resort was hastily arranged to compensate for the late arrival caused by this 'oversight' by the engineers.

These excursions gave very many Corby folk their first opportunity to sample a rail outing, and after their station was re-opened in April 1987, there was good usage of the shuttle service to Kettering giving connections to London and Leicester.

Twenty or so years after banning steam from its system, British Rail now runs its own steam-hauled trains on a regular schedule during the summer months, but these do not fall within our category of day excursions.

Hundreds of diesel-electric and diesel-hydraulic locomotives, which replaced steam from 1957 onwards, have themselves now been withdrawn. A few are preserved, but most have gone to demolition yards. There are as many enthusiasts finding the money to purchase and preserve diesels, or paying to ride on excursions hauled by threatened species, as there are for steam locomotives.

From the 1980s onwards there have been so many special excursion trains organised by numerous societies supporting or enthusiastic about various classes of diesel locomotives that it is somewhat invidious to single out any particular occasion. However, the end of what has gone down in railway history as 'The Deltic Era' is as good an example as any of the never-failing support for 'farewell' specials.

These 3,300 hp diesel-electric locomotives, capable of 100 mph, revolutionised the East Coast Main Line express services from 1961 onwards. When their total withdrawal from service was approaching in 1981, almost every weekend saw a 'Deltic' railtour, and not only over their usual racing ground, the East Coast Main Line, but over such routes as the Settle & Carlisle line, the ex-GWR line to Paignton, and even on to the preserved Nene Valley Railway at Peterborough.

British Rail surprised everybody, in August 1981, by allocating 'Deltic' No 55 021 *Argyll and Sutherland Highlander* to haul two of its excursion trains from Edinburgh to Oban over the former West Highland line. One passenger observed that the

Passengers boarding the 'Corbyrail' Christmas Shopping trip to Nottingham at Corby station, Northamptonshire, on 6 December 1986. Father Christmas, otherwise known as BR Leicester Area Manager Alan Peel, talks to the driver. *(Jim Wade)*

trains were filled not with camera and recorder-toting enthusiasts but with 'families and older couples – the classic Merrymakers'.[14]

The last 'Deltic' turns on ordinary passenger service were on 31 December 1981 when No 55 017 *The Durham Light Infantry* made the final northbound trip from Kings Cross to York carrying a wreath and a headboard announcing '1961–1981. 20 YEARS SERVICE. ECML'. Two days later, BR arranged a 'Deltic Farewell' special round trip from King's Cross to Edinburgh, when No 55 012 *Royal Scots Grey* entered the London station for the last time.

As one 'Deltic' fan mourned, 'The Sound of Music will be heard no more'.

Chapter 13
TOO AWFUL TO DESCRIBE

'Railway traffic worked under such conditions cannot, whatever the system employed, be expected to be carried on without serious accidents.'

In its issue of 2 December 1840, the *Derby Mercury* carried the following encouraging advertisement:

> The Public still have the opportunity of going by coaches combining safety and expedition with comfort and economy . . . it must be evident to all that the Old Mode of Travelling is still the most preferable and the only one to escape the Dreadful Railway Accidents too awful to describe.

Following an accident involving an excursion train at Bolton in 1852, *The Times* thundered:

> The first remedy that should be applied is an introduction of an extensive change in the system of excursion trains, if indeed they should not be abolished altogether. Let the regular fare be lowered so that passengers may go on what excursions they will by regular trains . . . This will constitute our best security against danger.[1]

Because excursion trains so often proved very popular it was common practice for more and more carriages to be added, and when the load was too much for one engine, a second and even three or four more were employed. The strain on the couplings was enormous, and being loose-coupled, stopping and restarting such long trains caused snatching of couplings which frequently broke. As early as 1844, the Railway Department of the Board of Trade circulated a letter to a number of railway companies as follows:

> The attention of the Lords of the Committee of Privy Council for Trade having been called to the extent and character of Trains for Excursions of pleasure, and eminent Engineers and Managers of Railways having represented, in reply to their Lordships' enquiries, that much danger to the Passengers is incurred, on these occasions, from the unmanagable size of the trains, travelling at a high rate of speed, and without guards in proportion to the number of Carriages and Passengers, I am directed to request that you will be so good as to bring under the notice of the Board of Directors of the Stockton and Darlington Company, the great importance of conducting these Excursions in a manner which shall diminish the chances of accidents.
>
> Their Lordships do not propose to advise your Company to adopt any particular arrangement, but they direct me to inform you that the professional

gentlemen above mentioned whose opinions on this subject are worthy of the gravest consideration have stated their conviction in which their Lordships entirely concur, that danger is to be apprehended, unless the size of the Trains be considerably diminished, or their rate of speed lessened.

Some of these gentlemen recommend that the Excursion Trains should be divided into Sections, of a size suitable to the powers of one Locomotive Engine only. Others are of the opinion that two Locomotive Engines, coupled with a proportional number of Carriages, are not objectionable.

In these instances, the usual speed may be kept up, provided great precautions are taken to prevent collision.

Again there are others who do not object to the use of a greater number of Engines, but who strongly insist on the necessity of restricting the speed to 15 miles per hour. These gentlemen, however, admit that, on such occasions, it is difficult to regulate the speed and bring it within due limits. All of them agree that the Carriages, for this purpose, should be provided with bearing and drawing springs, that a number of guards, adequate to enforce the Company's regulations, and preserve order, should be attached to the Trains; and that arrangements should be made for preventing the Platforms at Stations being crowded to excess.

In conveying these sentiments, My Lords desire that it may be clearly understood, that they by no means wish to suppress Excursions of this character: their Lordships are aware of their useful influence on the portions of the community who profit by them; but, my Lords are most anxious that their very utility, and consequent magnitude, should not lead to the disastrous results, which must ensue, if the practice of conveying great multitudes along

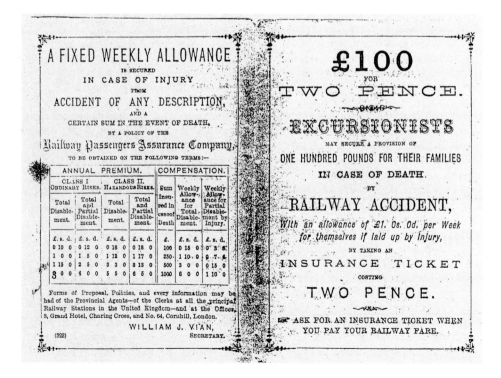

Railways be not accompanied by a better system than that which has hitherto prevailed.

My Lords take this opportunity of stating also, that the primary object of each Company is to convey passengers, generally, according to the Published Time-tables; and their Lordships conceive that, in no case should the trains so published be postponed or delayed, or otherwise interferred with, by casual trains, however beneficial to a particular section of the Public or profitable to the Railway Company.[2]

At most stations the Railway Passengers Assurance Company offered 'EXCURSIONISTS £100 for TWO PENCE in case of death by Railway Accident', whilst newspaper reports of excursion trains frequently concluded, 'The whole proceeding passed off without a mishap', or '. . . but all safely arrived without any accident or unpleasantness of any kind'.[3] It was almost as if an accident were to be expected on a rail journey, and more especially if it were an excursion train.

The Victorian public, press and Parliament were increasingly alarmed by the frequency of rail accidents and their increasing severity, but, in retrospect, it is amazing that the carnage was not far greater. Above all, that the accident record was not far worse is a tribute to the loyal, conscientious attention to duty of the overworked, underpaid railwaymen. In fact, by the 1880s public alarm at the long hours worked by railwaymen in such responsible positions as drivers, guards and signalmen was reflected in letters to the press. Members of Parliament took up the matter, among them F. Channing, whose exposure resulted, in 1890, in a Select Committee on Railway Servants' Hours of Labour, and M. T. Bass, the brewer, who, in giving evidence in the House of Commons, cited the Midland Railway engine drivers as having worked 'nearly double the time assigned to them'.[4] Their normal working day was 10 hours, but they were averaging $19^1/_2$ hours, and in one instance $29^1/_2$ hours.

> . . . Overwork is no doubt the cause of most railway accidents. From the very birth of the service the companies have overworked their servants, and the results have been disastrous to passengers and still more so to the railway men.[5]

Not until the latter part of the 19th century did locomotives have brakes, yet speeds of 60 mph were being attained by express trains. Brakes were applied by guards riding in the carriages, perhaps four guards to 20 carriages.

In 1855, the North Eastern Railway issued Special Instructions for Excursion and Special Trains which required

> . . . Breakvans [sic] to be attached in the following proportions – up to 9 coaches, 1 van; 10 to 24 coaches, 2 vans; and 25 to 30 coaches, 3 vans. No excursion train to run more than 20 miles without stopping [bringing relief no doubt to many!]. Doors on the offside of excursion trains to be locked.[6]

Continuous brakes applied by the driver, or automatically if a train became split into two parts, were not made compulsory until the Regulation of Railways Act in 1889. In early railway years, points and signals were not interlocked, so that a signal might indicate 'All Clear' for the main line whereas the points were set to turn the train into a siding. Communication between one signalman and another was impossible until the adoption of the electric telegraph. Consequently trains were permitted to follow one another on a

'Time Interval' system: for example, 5 minutes after the passing of one train, the signalman assumed that it was safe for the next train to follow – and frequently IT WAS NOT!

An example of a rear-end accident to an excursion train was that at Cowlairs, Glasgow, on 1 August 1850, when three excursion trains of some 35 coaches each were following at 5-minute intervals. So many excursionists wished to attend the Highland Agricultural Show that, when all carriages were filled, they climbed to the roofs from which they refused to descend. Finally, a number of open trucks, fitted with hurdles, were attached to the first train and the offenders came off the carriage roofs. The first train was delayed, thus reducing the time interval between it and the following excursion. Next, before descending the steep Cowlairs incline into Glasgow, this first train halted to allow the engine to uncouple and run round to the rear of its train, which was customary.

Owing to the exceptional length of this train, the engine could not complete this manoeuvre, whereupon the second train drew up behind the first train, making in all a line of some 70 carriages! No steps were taken to protect this obstruction; consequently the third train, unaware of events ahead, crashed into the halted carriages. Many passengers leapt to safety but five were killed and many seriously injured.[7]

A rear-end collision caused by faulty judgement occurred at Bristol on the Great Western Railway in 1876, when an excursion to Weston-super-Mare, standing at the platform, was run into by a train from Swindon with such force as to push the excursion train 20 yards along the line. Sixteen excursionists were cut and bruised. A railway official explained that the platform was a very long one so it was thought there was room for two trains![8]

Children are, or were, well aware that 'puff-puffs' pull trains, but at Wootton Bassett in 1850 it was the wind which blew a horsebox out of a siding and into the path of an excursion train![9]

An example of the dangers resulting from overlong excursion trains, and the use of goods wagons to carry passengers, occurred on the Manchester & Birmingham Railway in 1844, involving a cheap trip from Manchester to Alderley Edge. More than 2,000 excursionists wished to travel, and so the train

> . . . consisted principally of box wagons, opening behind. On arriving at Alderley, the fore part of the train being required to go forward, the carriages were unshackled, and directly after an order given for that part of the train to proceed forward. After the usual signal by the engine whistle had been twice given, the train started, when it was found that some person without any authority, had reshackled the train, in consequence of which a woman, of the name of Mary Bealey, who was in the act of getting out of the wagon, was thrown down under the wheel, which passed over the lower part of her head. An inquest was held on the following day, and a verdict of 'accidental death' returned, no blame being in any manner attached to the servants of the company.[10]

Following this accident, the Directors of the Manchester & Birmingham Railway resolved that box wagons opening at the end should not again be used for the conveyance of passengers.

As already noted, the North British Railway connected Edinburgh to Berwick in 1846, and immediately arranged numerous excursion trains over the line. One of these special trains was involved in an accident at Musselburgh station in the line's opening year when a train of 42 carriages was required to convey 1,300 members of the Caledonian Youth Society to Berwick.

... For the purpose of allowing another train behind it to pass, the train was being backed up another set of rails, when, owing to the intense mist that prevailed, it came upon the other locomotive with so much force as to throw the last carriage completely across the line, injuring some of the passengers, though not severely. After things were adjusted, the train moved on till it reached the tunnel at Carlton Hill, where another delay took place, owing, it is supposed, to deficiency of power. An additional locomotive having been procured, it was attached behind, and the passengers landed at the station.[11]

In September 1866, the Calvanistic Methodists of South Wales held their quarterly meeting at Caernarvon, and because the line was newly constructed and the station not yet completed, several excursion trains were run into a temporary platform. On the last evening of the meeting, a train heavily loaded with excursionists returning to Portmadoc was approaching Brynkir when the engine kept to the main line but its tender, and the trucks in which the excursionists were riding, took a siding. Although the train was travelling slowly, the tender toppled over and the heavily laden trucks piled over it.

... In a moment the air was filled with the shrieks of terrified passengers. After a few moments of confusion those who found themselves uninjured set to work to release their less fortunate companions who were jammed up in the overturned carriages. In the course of half an hour five dead persons were picked out of the smashed carriages, the shocking appearance of the bodies showing that death, if painful, must have been instantaneous.[12]

At a subsequent Board of Trade enquiry it was stated that the newly constructed line had not yet been handed over to the Carnarvonshire Railway by the contractors, and that authority to convey goods or passengers had not been given. The contractor's brother told the enquiry that

... the people of Portmadoc and the district were constantly teasing me to run an excursion train on this occasion and at length I yielded ... We have not had time to make arrangements about points on the Carnarvonshire Railway ... the points are not locked.[13]

The virgins were wise to keep oil in their lamps, and excursionists from Oakham to London for the International Exhibition in 1862 were fortunate to have purchased two candles whilst in London with which to illuminate their unlit carriages at Euston station. On the return journey, the train conveying 103 Oakham passengers crashed at Market Harborough. In the search for injured passengers, the candles of the Oakham bookseller's wife were to prove extremely useful. Following this disaster there were complaints to the Midland Railway for not lighting its carriages, and for keeping Oakham people waiting in Leicester tunnel after all they had suffered in the accident.[14]

A terrible disaster involving excursion trains on the LB&SCR line occurred in the Clayton Tunnel, near Brighton, on 25 August 1861, when 23 persons were killed and 175 injured. About 300 yards from the Brighton end the tunnel was

... blocked up to the roof with a horrible mass in which were mingled dead and dying men, women and children buried beneath and amidst heaps of broken carriages, with the engine and tender crowning and pressing down the whole. To add to the suffering of the unfortunates, the steam and boiling

207

water descended in showers upon them, scalding those whose bodies were at all exposed.[15]

Since the accident happened on a Sunday, it inflamed the controversy over Sunday travel, and particularly excursions. A memorial was sent from the Brighton clergy to the Directors of the railway complaining of Sunday excursion trains. But from the Metropolitan Tabernacle there came repudiation of any suggestion that the Clayton Tunnel accident was some kind of divine punishment for Sunday travel since railway accidents took place on any day of the week.[16]

Three factors contributed to this accident: excessive hours of duty by the signalman, a faulty signal mechanism, and misleading telegraph instruments. Involved were an excursion train from Portsmouth to London, another excursion from Brighton and the regular express from Brighton. The instructions were to dispatch trains at 5-minute intervals. As the first train, the Portsmouth excursion, passed the signal protecting the tunnel, the treadle device, which should have placed that signal at STOP for a following train, failed to do so. The South Box signalman sent the 'Train in Tunnel' message on the telegraph to his colleague at the north end of the tunnel. Almost immediately the second train, the Brighton excursion, passed the faulty signal at 'All Clear', whereupon the South signalman, realising the danger, dashed out of his cabin to wave a red flag at the driver. Although he had not received the 'Tunnel Clear' message from the North box he again sent the 'train in tunnel' message, followed by 'Is Tunnel Clear?'.

The North Box signalman was puzzled, but as the Portsmouth train emerged from the tunnel he telegraphed 'Tunnel clear', whereas there was, unbeknown to him, a second train in the tunnel. This train, the Brighton excursion, had now stopped in response to the South Box signalman's red flag warning, and the driver began to ease his train in reverse to ascertain the problem from the signalman.

The South signalman took the 'Tunnel Clear' message to apply to the second train, whereas it was in respect only of the first. His next, and fatal mistake was to show an 'All Clear' flag to the driver of the third train, which sped on to collide with the reversing train inside the tunnel![17]

In order to enjoy one day's rest in a week, it was necessary for the South Box signalmen to work one shift of 24 hours, a practice not conducive to clear thinking in a position of enormous responsibility.

A safer method of working was known as 'space interval block', and this the Board of Trade Inspectorate advised railways to adopt, but 28 years were to elapse before this advice could be legally enforced. Following this accident, it was decided to light the tunnel, resulting in the town of Hassocks getting a gas works.

Another signalman's error was the cause of an accident to a Cup Final excursion conveying Aston Villa supporters for the match against Newcastle United in 1924. Their train was entering Euston station at 7.53 am when an electric train collided with its rear, killing five and injuring 68. At the subsequent enquiry it transpired that a signalman had made the mistake of giving the 'Line Clear' signal for the Scotch express on the 'Up Slow' instead of on the 'Up Fast' line, as a result of which he accepted the local electric train on the line occupied by the football excursion.[18]

In that same year, another LMSR excursion train was involved in a collision, this time at Lime Street station, Liverpool, although no blame attached to the excursion train crew. A regular service train had arrived, unusually drawn by two engines, and when the empty carriages were drawn out of the platform, one of the two engines remained coupled and pushing from the rear. The second of the two engines began to move slowly back along the platform line when the driver spotted an excursion train heading towards him, whereupon he reversed his engine in order to lessen the force of the collision. Blame appeared to rest with either the signalman, a foreman or an inspector.[19] Sixteen people, although injured, were able to go home, but Mrs Evans of Beaufort Street, Liverpool, who had suffered shock and concussion, declared 'I shall not go to London again if I can help it'.[20]

At Retford, the Great Northern Railway's main line was crossed on the level by the metals of the Manchester, Sheffield & Lincolnshire Railway, and here an excursion train came to grief in 1873. A works' outing of 17 carriages, conveying some 300 employees with their families and friends, was proceeding along the MS&LR eastwards towards Cleethorpes. Upon approaching the Retford level crossing, the driver of this train was horrified to see a Great Northern fish train speeding along the main line. Desperately attempting to avoid a collision, the driver of the excursion train accelerated to get his train clear of the crossing, but to no avail. The fish train engine struck the sixth excursion coach and smashed it to matchwood, after which the signal gantry collapsed upon the wreckage. Three passengers were killed and 40 injured.[21]

Main lines usually have separate tracks for up and for down trains, but there were several thousand miles of single line used by trains travelling in both directions. Various methods of working were devised in an endeavour to ensure that not more than one train was on any section of single line at any one time but, particularly in early railway days, all depended eventually on the human element.

'What a way to run a railway!' could be a fair comment on the circumstances involving an excursion train on the single line of the Somerset & Dorset Joint Railway in 1876. Here is what the Board of Trade report had to say:

> . . . but, whatever the system of working, or the apparatus employed (as Captain Tyler observed in his summing-up), safety must more or less depend upon adherence to simple rules, and on the employment of responsible

Carriages of an excursion train guarded by police after the 1876 accident near Radstock on the Somerset & Dorset Railway. *(Bath & Wilts Chronicle & Herald)*

agents, carefully selected and closely watched . . . The risk of working must be materially increased when, as in the present instance, the regulations do not apply to the mode or the appliances of working; when the rules as regards the mode of telegraphing trains, or the use of crossing-orders or telegraph-passes, are not faithfully carried out; when there are too many telegraph-instruments on one wire; when signal lamps cannot be lighted for want of oil; when special trains are run without printed notices, or even proper telegraphic advices; when wrangling takes place, and important messages are improperly checked from headquarters on the telegraph-instruments; and when the duties supposed to be performed by responsible stationmasters are allowed, in practice, to devolve upon telegraph-clerks of immature age or experience, employed for long hours, and taken away constantly to duties incompatible with their proper attention to the simple details prescribed with a view to safety. Railway traffic worked under such conditions cannot, whatever the system employed, be expected to be carried on without serious accidents.[22]

It was revealed that a youth aged 18 was in charge of Radstock station, working from 6.30 am to 9.30 pm for 17s 6d a week. The signalman at Foxcote was also a youth who had been in the company's employ for only four months, unable to read the telegraph instruments, and too weak to pull over the levers! On the night of the accident, the Foxcote distant signal lamp was out, and the arm limp between 'Caution' and 'All Clear', which the driver said was not unusual. The young signalman gave this driver of the excursion train a handlamp signal to proceed on the single line section, unaware of the fact that another train was approaching towards it. Twelve passengers and the guard were killed, 28 passengers and six railwaymen injured. Children losing one parent in this collision received a bible, those losing both parents 5 shillings in addition.

A Great Northern main-line excursion train, which attempted to go down the Underground, featured in an accident at King's Cross in June 1860. This again was a long train, 35 carriages, entirely dependent on the guard for braking, which charged into this London terminus,

> . . . leaped the platform at the end of it, a height of between 5 and 6 feet, carrying with it the brake and one or two carriages, and proceeding on its course ran down the incline plane immediately under the clock tower and across the Old Pancras Road, burst through the enclosure of the Metropolitan Railway works, and but for the immense quantity of earth lying there (the stuff excavated from the New Road tunnel) would have buried itself in the shaft of the undertaking . . . [23]

The driver said that on approaching King's Cross he had cut off steam and signalled to the guard to put on the brakes. That the guard failed to do so was not surprising, for it transpired that he had drunk four glasses of ale and one of gin at Peterborough and was intoxicated!

Excursionists often regarded the train journey as a fun run, engaging in pranks and behaving irresponsibly. Unfortunately railwaymen were very occasionally drawn into these antics, as appears to have been a contributory cause of an accident at Round Oak, near Stourbridge, on the then Oxford, Worcester & Wolverhampton Railway in 1858. The excursion was run from Wolverhampton to Worcester, being advertised for schoolchildren only, although this condition was not complied with, for of the 1,506 passengers only 739 were children.[24] Such a vast crowd required 37 carriages and two vans, into one of which the guard, Cook, admitted several passengers and joined them in drinking and smoking, permitting them to screw the brake on and off. Several times couplings were broken, so that on the return journey, facing a steep gradient of 1 in 75, it was decided to run the train in two parts. Guard Cook and his drinking companions were in the van at the rear of the front portion of the train when it came to a stand in Round Oak station, whereupon Cook alighted on the platform. At that moment another coupling snapped and Cook's van, together with 17 coaches carrying 450 passengers, started to run back down the gradient. By this time the second part of the train had left the previous station at Brettell Lane, and was climbing the incline, when the engine crew saw the runaway coaches heading towards them! Fourteen passengers died, 50 were badly injured and 170 less so.

Throughout the enquiry, Cook maintained that he was in his van, attempting to apply the brake, shouting to passengers to 'jump for their lives', finally leaping to safety himself. The Board of Trade Inspector, Captain Tyler, was not convinced by Cook's version, and eventually established that he was not in the van of the runaway train, but standing on the platform. Captain Tyler considered this to have been 'Decidedly the worst railway accident that has ever occurred in this country'.[25]

Another instance of a coupling breaking, and the coaches running back to collide with an oncoming train, occurred on the Lancashire & Yorkshire Railway in 1860, when an excursion was run from various East Lancashire stations to Manchester's Belle Vue Gardens. Three specials started from Colne, and such was the pressure on the company's rolling-stock that it utilized 'some of the old carriages of the Chester & Birkenhead Railway'.[26] For the return journey, the first train left Manchester at 11.30 pm and proceeded safely, but the second train of some 30 carriages, conveying 1,000 passengers, had reached Helmshore when a coupling broke and 16 carriages ran back down the line to collide with another train from Salford ascending the incline. Ten people were killed, 26 were seriously injured and 30 less so. Two hours after the mishap a man was found to be asleep in a compartment of the Salford train unaware of the accident – he was drunk!

Questioned in Parliament as to the likely outcome of a steam locomotive encountering a cow on the line, George Stephenson laconically replied 'It would be a poor look out for the coo!' When in 1863, an excursion train on the Great Eastern Railway struck a bullock, the train was derailed, five passengers killed and 25 injured. The *Grimsby Herald* described it as the worst accident to have occurred in that part of England since the introduction of railways, and reported:

> The excursion . . . from Wisbech and Lynn to that rapidly improving watering place, Hunstanton, consisted of fifteen carriages. It left Hunstanton on the return journey at 7 pm and when nearing Wootton station the driver saw a bullock roaming on the same line upon which the train was proceeding at the rate of 25–30 mph. He instantly sounded the whistle . . . the steam was shut off and the breaks [sic] applied . . . the beast was at once struck to the ground. The engine and tender and the first three carriages passed safely over the carcase but the next three were thrown off the line with a frightful crash, the fifth being toppled over and literally shivered to pieces . . . The screams and cries which arose were of the most piercing description.[27]

An unhesitating verdict of accidental death on the five persons deceased was recorded, accompanied by accusations of

> . . . gross negligence of the authorities of the Great Eastern Railway and their

officers first, by not putting the fence in that state of safety that the public require; secondly, by not putting the bullock off the line where the accident occurred; thirdly, by the disgraceful state of the carriages used for the conveyance of those unfortunate persons.[28]

This last criticism arose from Captain Tyler's inquiry revealing that the carriage in which the deceased were riding 'contained some wood in an advanced state of decay'.

Fortunately, surprisingly few accidents occurred to the Great Exhibition excursion traffic of 1851, but one which could have been more serious befell a GWR train from Gloucester carrying 1,500 passengers in 23 carriages. Two locomotives were employed to haul this monster load up the 1 in 75 incline between Stroud and Swindon, which leads into Sapperton Tunnel. As the excursion emerged from the tunnel it was discovered that 11 carriages were

> . . . nowhere to be seen. The utmost consternation was caused by the discovery, especially as it was known the detached carriages must of necessity rush back down the incline, and as there was but one guard to control their speed, it was feared that they would run into the up mail train, which was known to be following close behind. A pilot engine was despatched on the down rails to overtake the runaway carriages and give warning of their approach at the bottom of the incline. Very fortunately as the pilot engine was proceeding down the incline the mail train was next slowly ascending, and the engine driver having been apprised of the danger, he immediately reversed his engine and backed his train down the incline, thus allowing the runaway carriages to descend upon him without any serious collision, and both trains arrived at the bottom of the incline in safety. The passengers were greatly alarmed and two or three of them who leaped from the carriages as they were descending received rather serious contusions . . .[29]

Returning from Euston to Oxford, a London & North Western Railway excursion taking Great Exhibition visitors home on 6 September 1851 was involved in an accident killing six and injuring many more. As the train approached Bicester station at a good speed, the engine separated from the tender, left the rails, and knocked down the gatepost at the side of the turnpike road. Careering close to the Stationmaster's house, the engine was finally brought to a stand when a length of rail wrapped itself around the wheels. One carriage fell on its side into the roadway, and a second rolled completely over before being crushed by other debris, whilst a third had its undercarriage and floor torn away.[30]

'A somewhat laughable mishap' is how one newspaper reported an incident connected with a Great Western Railway excursion train to the Royal Agricultural Show at Salisbury in 1857. A train of 29 carriages stalled on an incline, but let the reporter describe the event in his own colourful language:

> . . . For several miles beyond Westbury the line rises, and hence presented an increased resistance for the engines to overcome. On getting about halfway up the incline, such was the weight of the carriages and their occupants, that they overpowered the strength of the engines, and the train gradually returned to the station. After some little further delay an additional engine was attached, and the train ultimately reached its destination . . .[31]

All's well that ends well! For the 'two or three hundred good folk of Warminster' who

212

were left behind by this train, the day did not end so well.

A prank, for which it is impossible to show any enthusiasm, was minuted by the Northern Sub-committee of the London & North Western Railway in 1860:

> . . . A man named Leather who went with an excursion train from Earlstown Wagon Works to Bangor turned up with two pigeons on the journey with notes attached to their legs to the following effect 'That the train had met with an accident in Chester Tunnel, that nine persons were killed and many wounded', which false news caused great alarm in the neighbourhood of Earlstown.[32]

Mr Leather deserved to have his hide tanned!

Three race specials, returning from Chester to Manchester on 30 April 1851, were involved in a collision killing eight passengers and causing fractures to 35 others. It appears that the first train came to a standstill in the $1^1/2$-mile long tunnel between Frodsham and Sutton, on the Birkenhead Joint line. A second special train, travelling slowly, ran into the rear of the stationary train. Next, a third special, travelling at 'a fearful speed', collided with the rear vehicles of the now halted second train. According to the press account,

> . . . the cries of 'Murder' and 'Help' were frightful. People were seeking wives, husbands and friends in all directions . . . At or near the end of the train was an open truck crowded with a great number of people standing, and which the engine must have struck, and over which it was supposed to have passed .
> . . Mrs Ridgeway's private carriage was being conveyed on a flat truck behind the train and her liveried servant riding in it, was killed.[33]

Because the volume of traffic was so great for the Doncaster race week, the normal method of signalling, known as absolute block working, was suspended over the $1^1/2$-mile section between Hexthorpe Junction and Cherry Tree Lane, on which was situated a special platform for the collection of tickets. Two men with flags were positioned to control the trains under a system known as permissive block working. All train staff were issued with a voluminous document detailing the arrangements for race week, but it is doubtful if all, or many, men really understood the instructions, instead relying on the signals they were given.

On this day, in 1887, two Midland Railway excursions followed each other through Hexthorpe Junction; the first stopped at the ticket platform and the second a short distance behind. The first train drew out and the second pulled into the ticket platform. Behind came a Manchester, Sheffield & Lincolnshire Railway train heavily loaded with racegoers, the driver of which noted first the Distant signal at 'Caution', and next the Home signal at 'Danger'. As he approached the Home signal it was lowered, which the driver interpreted as 'All Clear' to Cherry Lane, so he put on steam to reach between 30–40 mph. As this train rounded a curve, the driver spotted the Midland excursion at the ticket platform ahead, whereupon he applied the 'simple' vacuum brake. He even threw the engine into reverse in a desperate attempt to stop.

Unfortunately, the 'simple' vacuum brake had a serious weakness, because if the train pipe was broken, no brakes would be applied to the rear carriages, and this happened at Hexthorpe. Although the locomotive was halted, the impetus of the rear carriages drove them on to destruction. Twenty-five passengers were killed and 95 injured.[34] The driver and fireman of the Manchester, Sheffield & Lincolnshire train were charged with manslaughter and their employers refused to provide them with a legal defence. The men's Trade Union, ASLEF, did, after which membership increased to 2,000.

One of four Midland Railway excursion trains returning to Leicester from the Nottingham Goose Fair in 1869 was halted in dense fog by a blocked line ahead. A mail train, which left Nottingham 5 minutes after the excursion, and travelling at 35 mph, ran into the rear of the excursion, despite the driver having put his engine into reverse gear in an effort to stop. The last two of the 35 excursion carriages were wrecked and the mail train engine derailed. Eight deaths and numerous injuries resulted.

At the inquest, the jury recommended that the absolute block system of signalling be adopted by the Midland Railway Company.[35] This system of signalling ensured that no trains could be signalled to enter the section ahead unless and until the signalman was certain that the section was clear of trains. Not until the Railway Act of 1889 was this safe method of operation enforced.

Every railway accident involving members of the public had to be, and still is, investigated by a member of the Railway Inspectorate, a department of the then Board of

Rescuing survivors from the race special at Hexthorpe, near Doncaster, in 1887 when a Manchester, Sheffield & Lincolnshire Railway train ran into the rear of a Midland Railway train. (Illustrated London News)

An artist's impression of an excursion train accident at Trent Bridge in 1869. (*Illustrated Midland News*)

Trade. These inspectors have always been military men, but their findings have not always found acceptance by the railway fraternity, and this was the case following an accident to a Cambrian Railways excursion train at Welshampton on 11 June 1897.

> The inquiry into the cause of the recent fatal accident near Welshampton, on the Cambrian Railways, forcibly shows the defects in the method now employed in conducting the enquiries. The military officer directing the proceedings, judging from the newspaper reports, appears to have already made up his mind that the accident resulted from the bad condition of the permanent way. All his questions tended to this one conclusion.[36]

This Sunday School excursion originating from Royston, Lancashire, consisted of Lancashire & Yorkshire Railway rolling-stock which included a four-wheeled brake van positioned next to the two engines on the return journey from Barmouth. On the outward journey the guard complained of the rough riding of this brake van. Near Welshampton the brake van and several coaches left the rails, overturned and telescoped, which resulted in nine children killed, two dying later, and many injuries. Lt Col Yorke's report concluded:

> . . . It is not, of course, possible to describe with certainty the exact sequence in which the different portions of the train became derailed. But most careful consideration of all the circumstances confirms me in the belief that this most serious accident was certainly due to the dislocation of the permanent way produced by the high speed and the consequent oscillation of the two heavy engines and tenders of the train; that the second tender was probably the first

The wreckage of the Cambrian Railways excursion train at Welshampton on 11 June 1897.

> vehicle to leave the rails; and that the derailment would have occurred, even
> if a brake van had not been present . . . it is evident that the condition of the
> road demands the immediate attention of the Cambrian Company. The
> company have entered with much spirit into competition for holiday and
> excursion traffic, and it behoves them to spare no expense in rendering their line
> strong enough to support the heavy engines and rolling stock now in use . . . [37]

A feature of this accident which stimulated interest among the superstitious public was
that *Old Moore's Almanac* had predicted a terrible railway collision in mid-June!

During dense fog in the early morning of 19 October 1900, an excursion train from
Wolverhampton to London on the London & North Western Railway was in collision
with a goods train at Portobello Junction, near Wolverhampton. The goods train had run
past signals at 'Danger' and in doing so had fouled the path of the excursion train so as to
overturn the locomotive and derail all its carriages. Although the driver and fireman of
the excursion train were killed, only ten passengers complained of slight injuries.[38]

Near Whiteacre Junction, on the Midland Railway, in 1903, a goods train was diverted
into a siding to enable an excursion train returning from Bristol to Lancashire to pass.
The goods train failed to stop before colliding with the buffer stop, demolishing it, and
ploughing along the track beside the main line for 30 yards. Nine wagons were wrecked
and two thrown across the main line.

On what was described as 'a wild night' the driver of the excursion train did not see the
obstruction until it was too late for his brake application to avert a collision. The
excursion engine ploughed into the wrecked goods wagons, breaking all the windows
along one side of the carriages. Although many passengers were thrown from their seats,
none were seriously injured.[39]

Fortunately few railway accidents have been in tunnels, but an excursion from
Swansea to Weston-super-Mare in 1906 came to grief in the $4^1/_2$-mile Severn Tunnel.

The breakdown gang clearing the line at Portobello Junction, Wolverhampton, after an accident to a London & North Western Railway excursion train in 1899.

Although there were no casualties, the passengers were subjected to a long wait in the tunnel. A side-rod of the locomotive became disconnected, causing it to leave the rails and come to a dead stop. Neither the driver nor the fireman was injured and the guard cut the emergency wire which ran through the entire length of the tunnel, so causing the tell-tale bells to ring at either end. On hearing these bells the signalmen threw all signals to 'Danger', so preventing other trains from entering the tunnel.[40]

In a tunnel accident at Birkenhead Woodside in 1911, a LNWR 2-4-2 tank engine derailed, slewed across the rails and blocked the station throat completely. As a consequence the empty coaches of a Sunday School outing could not be taken into the platform. A railway Inspector, carrying a handlamp, led a 'crocodile' of white-dressed children in Pied Piper fashion along the street to the Town station to join their train.[41]

Mistaking an excursion train from Wolverhampton for the regular railmotor service which terminated in a bay platform, a signalman at Henley-in-Arden, in 1911, caused the excursion, travelling at 40 mph, to crash into the buffer stops. The driver and fireman were badly scalded and 11 passengers injured, but having regard to the severity of the collision, the outcome could have been worse, for the engine and tender were thrown off the rails on their side and the first three carriages derailed. The engine, named *Mafeking*, had 'met its Waterloo', and never entered service again.[42]

Realising that she was in the wrong train as it passed through Rainhill, a nurse from Rainhill Asylum jumped from the excursion train she had mistakenly boarded at Liverpool, and was seriously injured.[43] Another leaping fatality occurred

> . . . as a Midland excursion train from London to the north was passing Wingfield station two young men leaped out notwithstanding that the train was then at full speed. One escaped with a few bruises but the life of the other was the forfeit of his temerity. Falling between the platform and the rails, his body was much crushed by the passing carriages, whilst his head, lying across

the rails was literally smashed to atoms and his brains scattered in all directions ... The mutilated remains of the young man were gathered up and removed to a neighbouring Inn to await the Coroner's inquiry.[44]

A more understandable case of leaping was that of a young lady travelling in an excursion train from Nottingham to Grimsby. As the train started

> ... some of the foremost carriages got off the line, and occasioned great alarm to all the passengers. Miss Brewster, in her fright, opened the carriage door and jumped out. Her head struck against one of the telegraph poles and she sustained such a frightful fracture of the skull that she died instantly.[45]

An instance of excursionists being killed and injured before joining their train occurred at Hampstead Heath, on the North London Railway, in 1892. A threatening storm led large crowds to leave the famous Heath and return to the station for shelter, and to join returning excursion trains. Only one narrow staircase led down to the platform whilst a projecting ticket collector's booth left a gap of only 3 ft 6in for the vast hurrying crowd to pass through. A wedge of human beings was forced ever more tightly by the ever-increasing pressure of the throng behind. A boy was strangled as his head was forced through the window of the ticket booth and other people tripped over him. In a few minutes eight people had lost their lives by suffocation and 22 were injured.[46]

An engine driver, misreading complicated signals at a busy and complex station, was the cause of an accident involving an excursion train at Darlington on 27 June 1928. A combined passenger and parcels train drew up at the south end of Darlington station, then, after discharging its passengers, began its scheduled shunting procedure before going forward as a parcels-only train. The train's engine, 4-6-0 No 2369 of the LNER, collected a rake of vans and pulled out of a siding towards the main line. However, the small-arm 'Calling-On' signal authorized this train only to pull forward a short distance and not to go so far as to foul the main line. The driver mistook the signal and pulled out over the crossover into the path of an excursion train returning from Scarborough to Newcastle. Locomotive No 2164, a 4-4-2, ploughed into the parcels train and its 11 coaches were derailed and telescoped, killing 25 and seriously injuring 45 other passengers.[47]

At Miles Platting, Manchester, a similar instance of a driver misreading a signal resulted in a LMSR light engine, 4-4-0 No 356, passing a signal at 'Danger', and colliding with the rear of a LNER excursion train from Hull to Blackpool, killing two guards and injuring several passengers.[48]

Unauthorized people on the footplate of the locomotive may have contributed to an accident resulting from excessive speed by an excursion train in 1955. This occurred on the ex-North British section of British Railways, at Wormit station, near the Tay Bridge in Scotland. A 4-6-0 engine was running tender first with eight non-corridor coaches when it became derailed on a sharp curve in a tunnel at the approach to Wormit station. As the train emerged from the tunnel, the tender and engine mounted the platform, overturned, and four coaches were derailed, two of them overturning. Of the three people killed, one was the fireman, the others a man and a boy irregularly riding on the footplate. The driver and 14 passengers were seriously injured. The enquiry concluded that excessive speed caused the accident.[49]

Excessive speed was also the cause of an accident to an excursion train from Treherbert, South Wales, to Paddington on Sunday 20 November 1955. At Milton, between Steventon and Didcot, the train was diverted from the up main line to the up

The wreckage after the head-on collision involving an excursion train at Darlington on 27 June 1928. Twelve passengers were killed and 24 seriously injured.

BR 'Britannia' Class 4-6-2 No 70026 *Polar Star* on Sunday 20 November 1955, with an excursion train from South Wales to Paddington. The photograph was taken about 1 hour before the train crashed near Didcot.

***Polar Star* about to be hauled upright after the Didcot accident.**

goods loop line to avoid engineering works. 'Britannia' Class locomotive No 70026 *Polar Star* took the crossover at speed, derailed and plunged down a 20-foot embankment, taking the first four coaches with it; the next three coaches were derailed. Ten people were killed and 96 taken to hospital, although the driver and fireman were not seriously harmed. At the enquiry, the driver admitted that he had overlooked the Weekly Notice advising of the diversion and of the speed restriction through the diversion.[50]

An excursion train chartered by the Kentish Town Railwaymen's Club for a trip to Margate in June 1972 came to grief on the return journey. Once again, excessive speed on a 20 mph restricted curve at Eltham Well Hall station, on the Southern Region, caused the Class '47' diesel-electric locomotive No 1630 to jump the track and plough 100 yards into a coal yard. The driver was one of the four killed.[51]

Unauthorized people riding in the driving cab of a diesel multiple unit was considered by the Inspecting Officer to have contributed to an accident involving an excursion train chartered by the Blackburn Rovers Supporters Club on 18 January 1986. This train was returning from Carlisle to Accrington when it failed to respond to a brake application on approaching Preston station, continued through the station and passed two more signals at 'Danger' before colliding violently with a stationary diesel-electric locomotive, No 47 111. Forty-four of the 115 passengers on the train were injured. The Inspecting Officer attributed the train's failure to stop to a lack of vacuum in its braking system, and that the driver had inadvertently destroyed the vacuum during the journey, probably because his attention was disturbed by the presence of one of the Club's organisers and a boy in the cab of the unit.[52]

It was railwaymen, working alongside the path of an excursion train, who were in danger from jettisoned missiles, as this warning to Huntley & Palmers' employees on their 1898 outing indicates:

A Kentish Town Railwaymen's Club special returning from Margate crashed at Eltham Well Hall on 11 June 1972. Class '47' No 1630 jumped the track on a 20 mph restricted curve; four were killed and many injured.

A GLASS BOTTLE WAS THROWN FROM ONE OF THE CARRIAGES DURING THE JOURNEY TO RAMSGATE, NEARLY HITTING A PLATELAYER.

Bass's Brewery considered it necessary to warn their employees on their monster outings against such dangerous practices.

CAUTION

IT IS HOPED THAT NONE OF THE MEN WILL THROW EMPTY BOTTLES, ETC., OUT OF THE CARRIAGE WINDOWS, ESPECIALLY WHILE THE TRAINS ARE IN MOTION, AS SUCH A PROCEEDING IS HIGHLY DANGEROUS TO THE PLATELAYERS AND OTHERS EMPLOYED ON THE RAILWAY.

Chapter 14
DID IT PAY?

'. . . but now they are all travelling at Exhibition fares, a great boon to the public, but not so to the shareholders . . .'

A minute of the Newcastle & North Shields Railway, in 1840, recorded the following resolution:

> That the Rev Mr Atkinson be permitted to take scholars and the teachers of the Gateshead Fell National School to Tynemouth on Saturday next, or any other day, at half price, namely, free one way and pay the other.[1]

This apparent generosity on the part of the Company was, in fact, a means of circumventing the Government duty imposed on railways in 1832, which amounted to one halfpenny per mile for every four passengers carried. By its ruse, the NNSR paid duty for each passenger on only 6.75 miles instead of 13.5 miles.

In 1842, the Government tax on rail travel was changed to a duty of 5 per cent on the gross receipts from all passengers conveyed. This meant that the 5 per cent duty was especially onerous on traffic for which working expenses formed a high proportion of gross revenue, and excursion traffic, more often than not, fell into this category. The reason was that railway managers considered it sound policy to employ resources at a low rate of profit rather than leaving them idle. This tax imposed on rail travel partly explains the reluctance of some early railway managements to encourage excursion traffic at low fares.

Yet another Act, of 1844, compelled all companies to operate at least one train every weekday from end to end of the line, in each direction, calling at every station, at a fare not exceeding one penny per mile. These were known as Parliamentary trains, and for these the companies had remitted to them the duty otherwise payable.

The position regarding excursion trains was further complicated by a difference of opinion, between the Railway Department of the Board of Trade and the Board of Inland Revenue, over the remission of duty on excursion trains. The Department's policy was to class excursion trains as Parliamentary trains, and so allow remission of duty, whereas the Inland Revenue ruled against excursion trains.[2]

Refusal to approve excursion trains for remission of duty on the ground that 'details of an excursion had not been received before the date on which it was run', inhibited companies from arranging such trains at short notice. In Parliament, attempts to get the duty removed or alleviated continued throughout the 19th century, but not until 1929 was it abolished.

In 1849 the Secretary of the Bristol & Exeter Railway wrote to the South Devon Railway as follows:

> . . . I have seen your note of this morning. We have three cheap trains during

BRISTOL & EXETER RAILWAY.

CHEAP EXCURSION

TO

WESTON.

On MONDAY, MAY 31st, 1869,

A CHEAP EXCURSION

WILL RUN AS UNDER

LEAVING	A.M.	FARES TO AND FRO. on this occasion, COV. CARS.
Exeter - - - -	8. 0	
Hele and Bradninch	8.23	
Collumpton - - -	8.35	
Tiverton Junction -	8.44	**1s. 6d.**
Tiverton - - - -	8. 0	
Wellington - - -	9. 7	

Arriving at Weston about 10.30 a.m. Returning from Weston at 6 p.m.

The Tickets are not transferable, and are not available by any other Train or for any other Station.

NO LUGGAGE ALLOWED.

By order,

HENRY DYKES,

Terminus, Bristol, May 17th, 1869.   SUPERINTENDENT.

Exeter: Printed at the " Flying Post " Office, Little Queen Street.

'These trains . . . afford conveyance on very low terms . . .'

the present week. I would rather not have any more. About 1,500 persons are gone to Weston today, we expect some hundreds from Exeter tomorrow. I shall have to convey about 1,500 to Weston on Saturday.

These trains do indirect good in encouraging Railway Travelling: but they afford conveyance on very low terms to many who would otherwise pay the usual fares, and they interfere a good deal with regular business . . .[3]

Evidently there was no enthusiasm for excursion traffic.

For the Great Exhibition of 1851, the organisers had urged the railways to make arrangements for the conveyance of the working classes, and this led to a meeting of railway General Managers at which it was resolved:

That the attention of the Committee of the Railway Clearing House be respectfully called to the unsatisfactory position of this question [ie excursion fares] the Railway Companies now being refused all exemptions from tax on excursion fares, though under one penny per mile, except on the lowest fare – that is to say, if in an excursion train running 100 miles the fares are 7s, 5s and 3s, it is only on the 3s fare that the Commissioners will grant exemption from tax. A penalty is thus practically imposed on giving any but the worst class of carriage accommodation.

This would be much more severely felt in a pecuniary shape, as the excursion traffic to the Exhibition increases, and should therefore, it is submitted, be looked to before such excursions commence.[4]

Although railway management was expected, by the shareholders, to operate in such a manner as to provide the anticipated rate of profit, there is much evidence of a conflict of interest between management and shareholders and, indeed, between different types of shareholders. One railway shareholder complained:

> Sir: Will you permit me through your wide-spreading paper, to call the attention of my brother shareholders to the great folly of bringing passengers to London at very low fares (for I understand such is contemplated), we all know that we get but a small return (and in some cases none) for the money we have advanced to provide a safe, quick and cheap mode of transit, and why should we now, that large numbers will come to London to see the Exhibition etc at our regular charges, we wish to give away our chance? I do not say we ought to raise the fares, but in justice to ourselves, they ought not to be lowered.
>
> I am, Sir, your constant reader,
> JUSTICE[5]

Another railway shareholder complained:

> Sir: Before your columns begin to be crowded with reports of the half-yearly meetings, I must crave a small space for some remarks upon a subject at this moment of vital importance to shareholders; I allude to the greatly reduced charges adopted by several of the railways for conveying passengers to and from London during the time of the Exhibition . . . The system adopted [on the Eastern Counties] has been reduction upon a most lavish scale; besides excursion trains, special trains (including the conveyance of passengers through town and home again at less than half price) all the usual fares have been greatly reduced; three times a week the charges for 1st and 2nd class from the country and back, have been half price only, besides return tickets to and from London extending over several days . . . To excursion trains at intervals, especially for the lower classes, I see no objection, but to this regular and general reduction at all times and for all classes, I see the greatest. The Eastern Counties district is essentially agricultural, the population thin, and spread over a large surface; with the exception of Norwich and Halstead there is no place having any pretention to the name of manufacturing town. The description of persons who use these lines are men of business, masters, millers, tradesmen, farmers etc; whether the fare to London is 6s or 10s: they must go, or their business is neglected . . . but now they are all travelling at Exhibition fares, a great boon to the public, but not so to the shareholders . . .[6]

These shareholders' appeals were in vain for, as has been shown, the railways were 'alive with excursions' in the Great Exhibition year. It appears to have been a case of swings and roundabouts, because very many of the otherwise full-fare-paying passengers who visited the Exhibition did not make their usual journeys to the seaside and watering places. The Chairman of the Midland Railway gave an example of this:

> The year 1851 was in some respects both remarkable and disappointing. The opening of the Great Exhibition created the expectation that the receipts by the railways would be unusually large. These anticipations, however, were not realized. A multitude of passengers were conveyed to and from the metropolis, but the competition of the Great Northern Company led to the adoption of such low rates that the wonder was that the lines payed at all. But the extraordinary flow of passengers to and from London greatly diminished the traffic elsewhere. The Birmingham and Gloucester traffic, for instance, which was untouched by the Great Northern competition, was affected in a remarkable degree. In one week in August the receipts on that line were £400 less than in the corresponding week of 1850, and in another week were £550 less, though on that line there had been no reduction in fares. 'The fact is,' said the Chairman, 'there has been nobody going to Cheltenham this year; scarcely anybody to Scarborough; and the little Matlock line has experienced a decline in its receipts this year amounting to 20%. All this is entirely owing to the Exhibition.'[7]

The Chairman of the Great Northern Railway, reporting to the shareholders on the financial results for 1851, explained:

> With respect to the working expenses they are undoubtedly large. In round numbers they are 50 per cent . . . Another way of accounting for it is that during the excursion period highly respectable persons – I am sorry to say it for your sakes – took advantage of the excursion trains, and our ordinary trains often went very nearly empty, so that at that particular period we were running double trains and receiving very low fares . . .[8]

Contrary to the impression conveyed by some railway historians, the companies were not always locked in contests of rivalry and competition. Far more often they co-operated, combined or pooled receipts to eliminate what was regarded as wasteful competition. However, an example of the latter occurred during the Great Exhibition of 1851, for which a temporary agreement to charge equal fares from the West Riding of Yorkshire was reached between the London & North Western, the Midland and the Great Northern companies. From 15 shillings return, there was a reduction to 10 shillings, then to 5 shillings, by which time the Great Northern company was carrying excursionists at a loss. This was because the Great Northern trains ran over a section of the Manchester, Sheffield & Lincolnshire Company's line for which a sum in excess of 5 shillings per passenger was liable to be paid. Not surprisingly, the Great Northern withdrew from the competition!

> Severe as it was, however, the competition on the whole was not so 'ruinous' financially as had been expected beforehand, because the great number who travelled made up, to a huge extent, for the very low fares they paid.[9]

Mark Huish, Manager of the London & North Western Railway, claimed that his company had carried 775,000 people to and from London during the Great Exhibition, and that 90,000 had travelled in special excursion trains.[10]

For the railway companies serving London, ie the Eastern Counties, the Great Western, the Great Northern, the London & North Western, the London & Blackwall, the London, Brighton & South Coast, the London & South Western, the London, Chatham & Dover, and the South Eastern, their receipts for the period of the Great Exhibition, compared with the same period of the previous year, were increased by £821,964, or an average of some £92,000 each. But this traffic was not carried without additional expenditure on carriages and staff, and extra wear and tear on locomotives and rolling-stock, for which no figures are available.

As the Great Exhibition closed, *Herepath's Journal* questioned its benefits for the railway companies:

> EFFECTS OF THE EXHIBITION ON THE RAILWAYS. A notion is abroad with regard to the effects of the Exhibition on the railways, which it is necessary to correct. People believe that the exhibition has done wonders for the railways. That the railways have done wonders for the Exhibition no-one can dispute; for had it not been for the enormous powers the railways possess for transporting persons, of bringing them to the metropolis and taking them back, and the low fares they have charged, the Exhibition would have been a dead failure. That the railways have received from the Exhibition anything like an equivalent for the benefit they have conferred upon it is a mistake, as the dividends we have no doubt will at the end of the next half year show. The receipts have, as might have been expected, very much increased on the lines having a terminus in London, but what have been the expenses? We presume it is not supposed that all the extra income has been carried at no extra expense . . . On the whole railways of the United Kingdom the good the Exhibition has done is very trifling.[11]

One suggestion, understandably not adopted, probably came from a canny Scot:

> The experience of last summer has shown that the public will readily make use of facilities for travelling; and railway companies . . . have proved their willingness to accommodate pleasure seekers even it is feared, at the expense of their shareholders. But excursion trains are but a rude way of meeting the travelling propensity of the public and are open to objections . . . they are confined to certain days. The consequence is that when advertised they are frequently over-crowded, prove too heavy for the engines, delay the ordinary trains, and thus disorder the traffic of the line. Besides there is frequently such a scramble to secure places, that females are terrified, if not really injured, and can seldom be tempted to venture on a second excursion . . . I would suggest to the railway companies the issuing of tickets not from town to town but for a certain distance, say for 500 or 1,000 miles, such tickets to entitle the holder to be carried, in broken journeys . . . until the whole distance was travelled . . . 'North Briton'.[12]

As we have seen, aware of the disastrous effect of cut-throat competition in fares to the 1851 Exhibition, the London & North Western, Great Northern, Great Western and Manchester, Sheffield & Lincolnshire companies had entered into a mutual agreement on

Crowds of excursionists pour off the trains at Blackpool before the First World War. Did the railways benefit from this traffic as much as the Blackpool traders did? *(Lancashire Record Office)*

excursion fares to London, and this was also applied to the 1862 Exhibition.

> . . . Much diversity of view existed among Managers as to the advantages of encouraging Excursions, some considering they impaired the receipts from ordinary traffic, while others viewed them as furnishing entirely new revenue.[13]

There were also differences of attitude between managers, who considered it their responsibility to meet public demand, and the shareholders, whose primary interest was the rate of dividend on their investment. There were also differences of opinion over policy between the two main classes of shareholder, the permanent investors, and the temporary investors and speculators. In 1850 Dr Lardner wrote:

> . . . Now, the class of proprietors first mentioned have less regard to the amount of present dividends than to the payment value of the stock, and they chiefly expect from the directors of the railway a due regard to the efficient maintainence of the permanent way and the moveable stock out of revenue, before any surplus be appropriated to dividend. On the other hand, the latter class, and especially the speculators, care nothing for the permanent value of

the concern, and only look to the present amount of dividend.[14]

The importance of the two groups of shareholders fluctuated with the changing economic situation, but in a period when additional capital was difficult, or impossible, to raise in order to carry out improvements or expansions to the system, then the so-called permanent investors would favour funding these out of revenue, even though this meant lower dividends. An example of this concerning the Great Northern Railway is given by Grinling:

> . . . At the time of the financial panic in 1886 . . . in distributing expenses between revenue and capital it had continued to be the policy of the Board to err, if anything, on the side of overburdening the revenue. Thus the whole cost of renewing the line with 84 lb instead of 72 lb rails had been charged to revenue . . . More recently too we have seen an example of the same practice in the charging to revenue of the whole cost of the renewal of the Kings Cross roof.[15]

Now the significance of this in answering the question as to whether excursion traffic was profitable is that excursion traffic, even at low margins of profitability, increased total revenue whilst employing resources that might otherwise have stood idle.

It would be a mistake to assume that all excursion traffic was profitable, for some reports indicate that this was not the case. One observer at Rugby in 1851 reported:

> On Monday last a trip train on its way from Birmingham to London and back passed this station at 8.55, it consisted of 16 carriages and contained about 50 passengers. The fares for both ways were 5s second and 9s first class – 226 miles; it must have been anything but a profitable speculation.[16]

Not all the special provisions for race traffic were remunerative either, as Ackworth pointed out:

> Surprise is often expressed that railway companies are not ready to grant larger concessions from the ordinary fares to special traffic coming in large quantity such as that to race meetings. It would, however, be no paradox to maintain that a Company would often be better without such traffic altogether. It is true that for two or three days in the year it may be profitable, but the profit may only be earned at an expenditure of many thousands of pounds of capital, which, except on those two or three days, is absolutely unproductive. It would be difficult to find a better illustration of this than is afforded at Singleton Station, on the Chichester and Midhurst branch, a mile or two from the Goodwood race-course. What the ordinary takings at Singleton may be, I cannot say, but I should be much surprised if they amount to £20 a week, and that sum would certainly not do more than pay the wages of the station staff and interest at 5% on the cost of the station buildings. For the whole place – four wide and long platforms, with waiting rooms, refreshment rooms, telegraph offices, and so forth, in addition to water tanks, and cranes, and engine turntable – has had to be built on a lofty viaduct or else on an embankment. And all this, of course, is purely for the accommodation of the Goodwood traffic. A wooden platform and lean-to shed on it would be all to which the importance of the place would naturally entitle it.[17]

'Plenty of room up front!' – excursion crowds at Birmingham Snow Hill. Excursion fares were obviously attracting passengers, but were they covering the costs? (*Birmingham Post & Mail*)

Reduced excursion fares call for huge volumes of passengers if the concession is to be justified, as C. J. Allen explained when writing of the facilities provided by the Great Eastern Railway for the Newmarket race meetings. With an excursion fare of 6s 6d against the standard fare of 11s 9d from London, he suggested that

> . . . something approaching treble the present traffic will require to be conveyed before the railway company can recoup itself financially.[18]

Whether a treble increase was achieved is not stated, but on the next Cesarewitch Day

6,332 racegoers travelled by the specials to Newmarket's two stations.

Brighton's race meetings lost the support of Royalty and the aristocracy from the mid-19th century onwards, the Queen's Plate being withdrawn in 1849.[19] A new race committee was formed, and a new stand erected in 1851, when the London, Brighton & South Coast Railway gave £100 to the stand fund, and thereafter subscribed £200 annually to the race fund. At Stratford-on-Avon, the Stratford-upon-Avon & Midland Junction Railway provided stabling for 20 racehorses in the yard of the General Manager's house, at the same time responding to an appeal by donating £40 to the United Hunt Farmers' Steeplechases in 1921.[20]

These are but two examples of the railway companies' wish to foster a good relationship with the racing world, which generated considerable profitable traffic in the conveyance of horses and specials for the racing elite, as well as the racegoers' excursions.

Whilst available railway statistics do not reveal the profitability, or otherwise, of excursion traffic, there is plenty of evidence that many non-railway organisers of excursion trains failed to cover their costs. The Passenger Traffic Committee Minutes of the London & North Western Railway, for 17 June 1891, contain a long list of applications from such loss making charterers, among them:

> 74. On the 21st March last the 'Ardwick Football Club' consisting principally of members of the Manchester, Sheffield & Lincolnshire Company's staff arranged a Guaranteed Excursion to Preston where they were engaged in a match. A net guarantee of 300 passengers amounting to £29-7s-6d was given but the trip only realised £27-3s-4d, the loss being £2-4s-2d. The failure is attributed to the fact that the Lancashire & Yorkshire Company announced an Excursion to Deepdale (Preston) which is nearer to the football field than

With guaranteed excursions the railways had nothing to lose. Here a works outing heads for Euston past Ashton loops, near Northampton, in August 1937. LMSR 'Patriot' Class 4-6-0 No 5527 carries its special train number on the smokebox. (L. Hanson)

Preston station, the result being that many people took advantage of that route.

Application is made for the Company to accept the actual receipts in lieu of the guaranteed amount.

It was agreed to accede the application.

75. On 27th March (Easter) Lancashire & Yorkshire Company ran a guaranteed trip from Bacup to Windermere and Morecambe, Mr Shaw the promoter giving guarantee of 300 passengers (£54). Realized £19-2s-3d, leaving net loss of £34-17s-9d – failure due to bad weather. Allowed $^1/_2$ of LNWR proportion of loss in accordance with L&Y proposal.

171. 12th August. Loss application as follows. $^1/_2$ allowed on each
Adult Bible Class 19th May
    James Bridge to Blackpool   £18-5s-6d
Rev J. Binnie Parochial Trip 22nd June
    Kenilworth to Liverpool   £7-5s-6d
St Stephens Sunday School 22nd May
    Manchester to Keswick   £12-15s-6d
Oldham Brass Band 23rd May
    Oldham to Malvern   £5-1s-10d
Huddersfield Conservative Association 15th July
    Huddersfield to Leamington   £3-7s-6d
India and China Tea Company 18th May
    Abergavenny, Hereford, Leominster
    to Southport   £17-17s-0d
Windermere Primrose League 6th June
    Windermere to Southport   £8-16s-0d
All due to unfavourable weather and prevalence of illness.

In contrast, that pioneering excursion organiser, Thomas Cook, when celebrating his Tenth Excursion Season in 1850, considered that his success had demonstrated that: 'LOW FARES are the best for Railway Proprietors as well as the public'.[21]

Studying railway economics and policy decisions from about 1850 until the 1950s tempts one to conclude that the companies accepted a responsibility for providing a public service, which was increasingly opposed to their private enterprise, capitalist responsibility of maximising profits for their shareholders. Just as most branch lines were cross-subsidised from main-line receipts, perhaps too, excursion trains were partly, or wholly, cross-subsidised. Sir George Findlay, ex-General Manager of the London & North Western Railway, in 1899 expressed his company's policy in this manner:

. . . in order to bring holiday travelling for shorter periods within even the modest means of the toiling millions, excursion trains at extremely low fares, are run frequently during the summer, and at Easter and Whitsuntide, between all the large towns, and from large centres of population to the seaside resorts, and as these trains are for the most part run during the night, they enable the artisan who can, perhaps, only afford to lose a single day's wages, to spend the whole of that day at the seaside . . . It will afford some idea of the extent to which advantage is taken of these exceptional facilities, to mention the fact that during nine months of last year the LNW Company alone carried considerably more than 1,500,000 excursion passengers.[22]

THE WONDER OF 1851!

FROM YORK
TO LONDON AND BACK FOR A CROWN.

THE MIDLAND RAILWAY COMPANY
Will continue to run

TWO TRAINS DAILY
(Excepted Sunday, when only one Train is available)

FOR THE GREAT EXHIBITION,
UNTIL SATURDAY, OCTOBER 11.

Without any Advance of Payment

RETURN SPECIAL TRAINS leave the Euston Station on MONDAYS, TUESDAYS, THURSDA.S, & ATURDAYS at 11 a m., on WEDNESDAYS and FRIDAYS at 1 p.m., and EVERY NIGHT (Sundays excepted) at 9 p.m.

First and Second Class Tickets are available for returning any day (except Sunday) up to and including Monday, Oct. 20. Third Class Tickets issued before the 6th instant are available for 14 days, and all issued after the 6th are returnable any day up to Monday the 20th.

The Trains leave York at 9-40 a.m. every day except Sunday, and also every day, including Sunday, at 7-20 p.m.

Fares to London and Back :--

1st Class 15s. 2nd, 10s. 3rd, 5s.

The Midland is the only Company that runs Trains Daily at these Fares.
Ask for Midland Tickets!

Children above 3 and under 12 years of age, Half-price. Luggage allowed—112 lbs. to First Class, 100 lbs. to Second, and 56 lbs. to Third Class Passengers.

APPROVED LODGINGS, of all classes, are provided in London for Passengers by Midland Trains. The Agents will give Tickets of reference on application, without charge, and an Office is opened in London, at DONALD's WATERLOO DINING ROOMS, 14. Seymour-street, near Euston Station, where an agent is in regular attendance to conduct parties who go up unprepared with Lodgings.

The Managers have much pleasure in stating that the immense numbers who have travelled under their arrangements have been conducted in perfect safety—indeed in the history of the Midland Lines, no accident, attended with personal injury, has ever happened to an Excursion Train. In conducting the extraordinary traffic of this Great Occasion the first object is to ensure safety, and that object has hitherto been most happily achieved.

With the fullest confidence, inspired by past success, the Conductors have pleasure in urging those who have not yet visited the Exhibition, to avail themselves of the present facilities, and to improve the opportunity which will close on the 11th of October.

All communications respecting the Trains to be addressed to the Managers, for the Company,

John Cuttle & John Calverley, Wakefield;
Thomas Cook, Leicester.

October 2nd, 1851.

T. COOK, PRINTER, 28, GRANBY-STREET, LEICESTER.

'Low fares are best for the Railway Proprietors as well as the public.' *(Thomas Cook Archives)*

Lower rates of return, together with a large business, were policies which the LNWR General Manager, Mark Huish, had advocated in the 1850s and may well have gained support among the other railway managements.[23] Extensive excursion facilities at low fares would accord with such a policy.

When the Lancashire & Yorkshire Railway carried 100,000 in 135 special trains to the miners' demonstration at Blackpool in 1919, the receipts were said to have amounted to £30,000.[24] This works out at approximately £220 per train which, over comparatively short distances, may have been remunerative traffic. Many coal train locomotives, normally idle on Saturdays, would have been rostered for these special trains.

It has been suggested that some excursion trains were run as what the supermarkets term 'loss-leaders'. The train-loads of beer which issued from Burton-on-Trent breweries

Cleethorpes Pier in 1905, having been bought by the Great Central Railway in 1904.

daily throughout the year must have been very remunerative rail traffic, so that whether the annual Bass employees' outing was profitable for the Midland Railway Company or not, it was good customer relations.

A Great Western Railway excursion, running 137 miles non-stop from Paddington to Weston-super-Mare in 3 hours, and at a fare of only 4s 3d, less than 1 penny for 5 miles, in 1904, could have been such a loss-leader.[25] The company may have hoped that some of these day excursionists would be so impressed by Weston as to book their holiday there the following year, in which case they would travel by Great Western at ordinary fares.

Excursionists to Cleethorpes, conveyed at low fares, would, whilst in that resort, be patronising amenities provided by the Manchester, Sheffield & Lincolnshire Railway (later Great Central Railway), and the £100,000 which this company invested in developing Cleethorpes was considered to be one of its few profitable investments.[26] A case of 'What you lose on the excursion you gain on the pier'?

But what could have prompted the Great Central Railway to run a football excursion from Leicester to Birmingham (40 miles), via Woodford & Hinton and Banbury (80 miles), for 2s 3d return?[27] What induced the fans to make such a round-about journey? Did it pay the company?

From Poole to Burnham and back (138 miles) for 1s 6d cannot have been more than marginally profitable for the Somerset & Dorset Joint Railway, but at Burnham excursions linked with that company's steamers offering a return trip to Cardiff at 4s 6d fore-cabin, or 6 shillings aft-cabin.[28] The revenue from the steamers, including the catering takings, may well have made the combined venture worthwhile.

It is difficult to calculate the profitability of railway ancillary services from the published annual Railway Returns, but an example in 1903 for the Caledonian Railway's 'Steamboats, Canals and Harbours' suggests that Percentage Proportion of Expenditure to

The North Eastern Railway included motor charabancs in its facilities for excursionists. Three 'Saurer' Swiss-built chassis with York-built bodies stand at Scarborough station in about 1907.

Total Receipts was only 37 per cent, whereas for railway operation the figure was 56 per cent. This figure does not include profits from catering on the steamers.

A number of railway companies operated motor charabanc tours in connection with summer excursion traffic. The North Eastern Railway, for example, starting with three vehicles in Scarborough in 1905, expanded to some 20 vehicles in 1912, operating from centres at Bridlington, Harrogate and Whitby. Such expansion indicates the profitability of this combined rail-road excursion traffic.[29]

After all these factors have been taken into consideration, the question as to whether excursion trains were profitable to the railway companies remains a matter for speculation. No separate costings have survived, if they were ever made, nor was revenue from day excursion trains recorded separately from other passenger revenue.

Whilst it is true that coaching stock otherwise idle, and often well past its 'sell-by' date, was utilised for excursion trains, it is also the case that the GWR, LMSR and LNER introduced new, luxuriously appointed excursion trains during the 1930s.

An argument has been advanced that railway working costs, as a proportion of gross receipts, were increasing yearly from the 1870s onwards, yet passenger fares were not increased, as they could have been, since neither legislation nor competition prevented this until after the 1914-18 war.

> Quite the reverse: the years before 1914 saw the heyday of cut-rate excursion traffic. It is not surprising that those who still remember this pre-war period recall their train travelling with much obvious satisfaction and relish. But while these cheap, well-organised journeys, in general faster and more comfortable than ever before, may have benefited the travelling public, they did not help the railways to bring down their operating ratio from its new, higher level.[30]

The financial aspect of excursion traffic was considered by another economist in 1959:

In 1934 the LNER introduced the first of its special trains for excursions – 'Tourist Stock'. This publicity photo shows the wide windows giving every passenger a good view.

Excursion traffic can be likened to bargain sales – but bargain sales with a difference. Whereas a shop will accumulate unsold surplus stocks, a railway deals in <u>seat miles</u> which must be sold and consumed the moment they are produced or they are lost for ever.

So a shop can get rid of unsold stock at periodical sales, the railway must try to sell off its surplus at bargain prices at the <u>moment of production</u> and while selling a similar article at standard prices.

The railway, unlike most shops, controls its own production. It has the possibility of specially manufacturing a particular line solely with the object of offering it at a bargain price (though this is not unknown in other commercial undertakings) such is the case when special trains are run for excursion passengers.

It must be a matter of judgement as to where additional traffic is sought but now regard must be had to the cost of providing special trains.[31]

Regrettably, on British Rail in the 1990s the shortage of rolling-stock is such that not only are there no 'unsold surplus stocks' of seats; indeed, there are insufficient seats for passengers who are paying high standard fares.

Whilst some excursion trains may have been run as loss-leaders, at least one could be regarded as keeping on the right side of the law. A minute of the London & South Western Railway records: 'From the Mayor of Portsmouth requesting that 70 policemen may be conveyed on an excursion train from Portsmouth to Cosham and back without charge. Approved.'[32]

Chapter 15
BEHIND THE SCENES

'All arrived Burton safely, last special five minutes before time. Grateful thanks yourself and all concerned.'

Many accounts of excursion trains which have been quoted concluded with expressions of appreciation for the manner in which the railway staff had handled the large crowds, and that the day had passed off without a single accident. How many of those happy excursionists knew of the extensive planning involved in the organising of just one excursion train, not to mention the numbers descending on popular resorts such as Blackpool, Scarborough or Skegness?

Before 1923, when the GWR, LMSR, LNER and SR were formed, there were more than 120 separate railway companies, some very large, as the Great Western or the London & North Western, others quite small, as the Cambrian or the Midland & South Western, but all had daily services of both passenger and goods trains operating to a timetable, and into which excursion trains had to be slotted.

The illustration opposite shows how a timetable could be compiled. On a large train board, marked out in squares as on graph paper, the two verticle sides are marked off in miles with the station names between, in this case, Euston and Rugby. Across the top and bottom the board is divided into 24 hours and each hour sub-divided into minutes. Suppose a train departs Euston at midnight, then a pin is inserted on the top line at point 0. Suppose the train to be expected to average 40 mph, then a second pin may be inserted where the line descending from 1 am intersects the horizontal line coinciding with 40 miles. This procedure is repeated as far as Rugby, after which the pins are joined by a length of thread.

If all the trains traversing the down line throughout a day are indicated in this manner, it will be possible to identify just where faster will overtake slower trains, and, most important for excursion traffic, to identify what 'paths' are available for extra trains.

Whilst the organiser of a guaranteed excursion was responsible for advertising, selling tickets and shepherding his flock, the railway officials still had a great deal to do in arranging the satisfactory running of the train. An example might be a visit to Cadbury's chocolate factory and Garden Village at Bourneville, by some 350 members of women's organisations in the Newcastle area, in 1959.

First, a date for the visit had to be agreed with the special visits department at Cadbury's. Next, a general plan was given to the Newcastle District Passenger Superintendent's staff. Open vestibule coaches, requested by the organisers, were selected and registered with the Coaching Stock section at York, and the Restaurant Car Superintendent was asked to provide staff and facilities to serve morning coffee and biscuits, and lunch on the outward journey, with dinner on the return journey; also to suggest menus.

Arrangements had to be made for the passengers to join the special train at stations

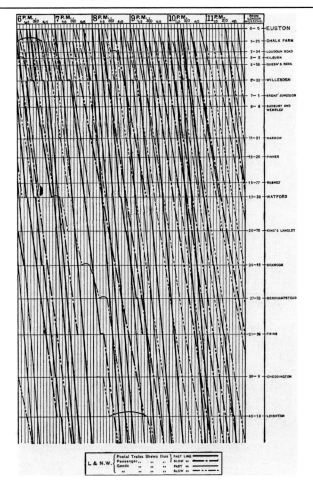

Part of a London & North Western Railway train diagram, leaving few spare paths for excursion trains.

along the route, and for others to travel by ordinary train to Newcastle to connect with the special.

Cadbury Bros required the party to arrive at Bourneville at 2 pm and to depart at 5.15 pm, so the Central Timing staff at York had to work out detailed timings to fit in with the firm's requirements. Since the train would originate in the North Eastern Region, and then traverse both the Eastern and the Midland Regions to reach Bourneville, those regions had also to be involved in deciding point-to-point timings. Regional timings were co-ordinated back at the York Central Timing office, with allowances being made for changing locomotive and train crews, accommodating any temporary speed restrictions, and for servicing the train at Kings Norton sidings whilst the party visited Bourneville.

Meanwhile, British Railway's commercial representative kept in touch with the party organisers, allocating places on the train for each group and making correctly numbered tickets available. To ensure that everyone concerned was properly instructed, final details of passenger numbers, marshalling and labelling of coaches, provision of meals and agreed

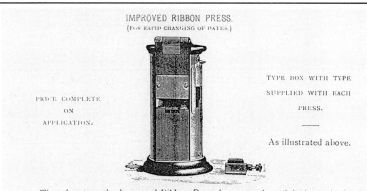

IMPROVED RIBBON PRESS.
(FOR RAPID CHANGING OF DATES.)

PRICE COMPLETE
ON
APPLICATION.

TYPE BOX WITH TYPE
SUPPLIED WITH EACH
PRESS.

As illustrated above.

The advantage the Improved Ribbon Press has over the original one is that it enables the operator to have several dates set up in holders as above, any of which can be used, and changed again in a very short space of time. This press is specially convenient at stations where large numbers of excursion tickets are issued, or where tickets are dated in advance of current date.

Messrs Edmondsons stress the advantages of their ticket dating machines – 'This press is specially convenient at stations where huge numbers of excursion tickets are issued . . .'

timings were supplied to the District Operating Superintendent, Stationmasters, commercial representatives, the Restaurant Car Superintendent and the Carriage Inspector at Newcastle.

On the day before the trip, the coaches were assembled in nearby sidings, cleaned and labelled, and kitchen cars victualled, whilst some catering staff worked overnight

Weekly Train Notices, kept near the 'booking desk' (left background), advised signalmen of excursion train workings, but specials run at short notice would be arranged by telegraph or, when installed, by telephone.

289. DAY EXCURSION.

Class					A	Class				A
					a.m.					p.m.
Neepsend					5†40	Boston				3 45
Sheffield Victoria					5†45					
,,					6 16	Lincoln Central				5A28
Darnall					6 23	Saxilby				5c45
Woodhouse					6 30	Sykes Junction				5 49
Kiveton Bridge					6 40	Torksey				5c54
Kiveton Park					6 44	Cottam				6c 0
Shireoaks					6 50	Clarborough Junction				6 6
Worksop					6c56	Retford				6 13
Retford					7 8	,,				6 17
,,					7 11	Worksop				6c32
Clarborough Junction					7 18	Shireoaks				6c38
Cottam					7 25	Kiveton Park				6c46
Torksey					7 30	Kiveton Bridge				6c51
Sykes Junction					7 37	Woodhouse East Junction				7* 0
Saxilby					7 41	,,				7F 6
Lincoln Central					7 51	Woodhouse				7c10
						Darnall				7c18
Boston					9 25	Sheffield Victoria				7 26
										E.C.S. to Neepsend.

A.—Follow 346 Down. 140 Down to arrive Lincoln Central 5.33 p.m.   F.—Follow 3.20 p.m. Marylebone to Manchester L. Road.

STOCK.—T.B.S.O., 8 T.S.O., T.B.S.O.

GUARD.—Stationmaster, Sheffield Victoria.

Weekly Train Notice for a day excursion from Sheffield to Boston on an October Saturday in the 1950s.

preparing food. This one excursion train involved two locomotives, a Class 'V2' 2-6-2 from Newcastle to Masborough and return, and a Class '6P5F' 2-6-0 between Masborough and Bourneville and return. Train crews from Newcastle, York, Masborough and Derby took part in the working. The Newcastle District Passenger Superintendent's representative travelled on the train to ensure the smooth working of the arrangements – they did, and the 350 members of the party had a most enjoyable day without knowing anything of what went on behind the scenes.[1]

Unlike road vehicle drivers who, in possession of a licence, may drive over any roads, no matter how unfamiliar, railway engine drivers may only drive over routes for which they have been passed by an Inspector. 'Learning the road' means knowing the position of every signal, every milepost, up and down grades, speed restrictions, acceptable train lengths, etc. If the driver rostered for an excursion does not 'know the road' throughout, then either the crew must be relieved or a pilotman (a driver with the necessary route knowledge) must be on the footplate or in the cab.

Of course, in the latter years of the 20th century, timetables are compiled on computers (not always without error), just as signalling of trains is mostly by power signalling centres covering many miles of line, instead of by manual signal boxes spaced along the line. Consequently, most of what follows is more relevant to the pre-1960s than the present day.

Stationmasters, signalmen, guards and drivers are familiar with the regular train workings which are, in any case, printed in the Working Timetable (WTT), but need to be appraised of special train workings. This is done by means of the Weekly Train Notice issued to all concerned, who are expected to make themselves familiar with its contents so far as it affects them.

All trains in the WTT have a unique Train Number, whilst special and excursion trains

A LMSR Class '4F' 0-6-0 goods engine hauls an 11-coach excursion over the Midland & Great Northern Joint line to Great Yarmouth. The fireman holds the single line tablet to hand to the signalman.

are given a Special Number, which in the past most companies carried on a disc on the front of the engine. Thus, a signalman advised of several excursion trains due during his shift was enabled to recognise just which of those trains was passing his box.

If an excursion train is to run over single line sections then the stations at which it will pass other trains must be indicated and, very important, the train must not be too long for the passing loops.

As the pleasure-seeking excursionists alight from the train at their destination, there still remains much for the railway staff to do before the return journey later in the day. The coaches have to be stabled (parked) out of the way of other traffic, water tanks and gas cylinders of carriages filled and compartments swept. The locomotive will need turning for the return journey, and to take on coal and water. In the afternoon, the driver and fireman might be seen sitting in deck-chairs taking a well-earned rest before resuming their duties. Such breaks in a shift lasting perhaps 12 or up to 16 hours, were termed 'short breaks' and, until later years, were not paid for.[2]

An 1860 'Working Timetable of Excursion and Special Trains', issued by the Manchester, Sheffield & Lincolnshire Railway for 23-24 September contains instructions for working an excursion from Doncaster to Ashburys, Manchester, the station for Belle Vue Pleasure Gardens:

> Empty Train to leave Sheffield at 3.0 am. No 1 Down Halifax Goods Train to carry the Train Staff, which must be transferred to the Empty Special Train at Penistone. Outwards, to be worked over Barnsley Branch with Train Staff. The 6.30 am Ordinary Train from Barnsley to Penistone to be worked with EXTRA (Green) TRAIN TICKET. Return, to be worked over Barnsley Branch with

EXTRA (Yellow) TRAIN TICKET. No 12 Down Barnsley Branch Night
Goods etc Train must reach Penistone not later than 11.30 pm (SPECIAL due
Penistone 11.45 pm). Sheffield to provide Power, Carriages and Guards.

Excursion trains and other specials were not always planned well in advance as, for
example, when the Epsom British Legion, in 1935, had booked 19 motor coaches to take
600 members to Bognor Regis for the day. The motor coaches failed to turn up. In
desperation, the organiser, at 8 am, contacted the Southern Railway's Stationmaster for
help and, 'always out to oblige and to meet emergencies', that official put the problem to
the Control Department. At 8.19 am a message came through that a ten-coach train would
pick up the party soon after 9.30 am. In fact, with 600 cheering passengers and one relieved
organiser on board, the train departed at 10.30 am, reaching Bognor at 11.47 am.[3]

Twenty excursionists from Sheffield stood on the platform at Wembley expecting to be
picked up by a special train returning from Marylebone. The driver forgot he had to stop
and sped through Wembley, much to the amazement of the unfortunate 20. The
Stationmaster contacted Control at Marylebone and was instructed to stop another
excursion train, which was heading towards Marylebone, and to put the unfortunate
travellers on board. Upon arrival at the terminus, they were relieved to discover that a
special train had been formed to take them in comfort, and at speed, to their homes.
Furthermore, their train called at several local stations in the Sheffield vicinity to set
down its passengers. 'The excursionists were loud in their praises of the consideration
shown by the LNER'.[4]

This is how excursion traffic was dealt with at Scarborough which, in addition to its
nine platforms at Central station, also had, from 1908, an excursion platform at
Londesborough Road, a few hundred yards before reaching Central station. Excursion
trains arriving at Londesborough Road deposited their passengers, then drew forwards on
to the Whitby branch, through the tunnel, and into 4 miles of sidings which had been
laid out for their reception. The incoming locomotive crew were immediately relieved
and booked off duty, whilst a local crew took the engine for turning and servicing.

Evening departures were from both the Central and Londesborough Road stations, but
a problem was that only Platform 1 at Central could accommodate a 13-coach train, and
only the through platform at Londesborough Road a 14-coach train. Empty coaching
stock was hauled from the sidings by a pilot engine into Londesborough Road and then
reversed into the platforms at Central, an operation calling for considerable skill on the
part of the station pilot drivers. A 13-coach train backed into a platform holding only
eight resulted in the 'fouling' of departure operations.[5]

At Llandudno, another seaside terminus, there were only four platforms, numbers eight
and 4 being used for ordinary traffic, and numbers 1 and 2 for excursion trains. At the
approach to the station were laid out ten sidings capable of holding long trains so that,
after an excursion had deposited its passengers, it was reversed into one of these sidings.

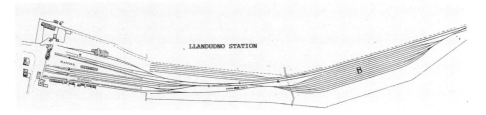

Plan of Llandudno station and carriage sidings.

There being no engine shed at Llandudno, the engine was released and then ran tender-first to Llandudno Junction for turning and preparation for the return trip. In the evening, the engine ran tender-first from the Junction to the carriage sidings, where it coupled to the front end of its train, which it then propelled into one of the platforms. Over two days of a typical August Bank Holiday, 182 trains composed of 1,822 vehicles were handled at this station.[6]

What to do with the empty coaches whilst the excursionists were enjoying themselves was a problem more difficult of solution at some of the smaller resorts than at, say, Blackpool. Hunstanton had only four platforms and three carriage sidings, so that on a Sunday, when as many as 14 excursion trains arrived, the empty stock was taken back to Heacham Junction and stabled on the Wells branch, which had no scheduled Sunday service. In the evening, engines of incoming empty stock were trapped at the Hunstanton buffer stops until the trains which they had brought in had departed.

At Skegness, in 1936, the LNER put in nine additional sidings to accommodate empty excursion trains. For the turning of engines a triangle was laid out and a pit 120 feet long installed for the cleaning out of fireboxes. As many as 126 trains could be expected to arrive in a day during August.[7]

When an International Aviation Week was held at Lanark in 1910, elaborate arrangements were outlined in a 32-page Supplement to the Working Timetable, to ensure the safety of excursionists and the smooth handling of trains over the Caledonian Railway's single-line branch from Lanark to Poneil Junction.

> The Electric Train Tablet Working between Lanark Race Course Junction Box and Sandilands will be suspended . . . Signal Boxes will be worked under the Regulations for Working Single Lines of Railway by Pilot Guard. The Pilot Guard may send forward Empty Carriage Trains into the section as far as the Line is clear, and he must inform the Engine driver when a Train or Trains are in front, and as two or more Trains (other than trains carrying Passengers) may be in the Section at the same time, Engine Drivers must keep a sharp look-out, and be prepared to stop short of any other Trains in front. The Pilot Guard will provide a Flagman, who must keep himself a sufficient distance in the rear of each train, as it arrives, to give the necessary protection. The Pilot Guard will be distinguished by a Red Cap and an Armlet bearing the words 'Pilot Guard', which latter will be worn on the left arm. During the hours Pilot Guard Working is in operation the Pilot Guard will hold in his possession the Tablet for the Section and Engine Drivers leaving the Race Course station for Sandilands in the one direction and leaving Sandilands for the Race Course station in the other direction, must not leave either of these stations until the Pilot Guard has verbally authorised them to do so, and, if the Pilot Guard is not accompanying the train, until the Engine Driver has received from the Guard of his Train the Pilot Guard's Ticket and the usual signal to start from the Guard of the Train. No Train carrying passengers must be allowed to pass through this section except when it is absolutely clear, and the Engine Driver of each train carrying Passengers will receive the Train Tablet for the Section from the Pilot Guard . . .

> STORING OF EMPTY CARRIAGE TRAINS AT PONFEIGH,
> DOUGLAS AND PONEIL JUNCTION
> The Engine arriving with the first Empty Carriage Train must be retained to assist with disposal of the following Train, the Engine of the next retained to

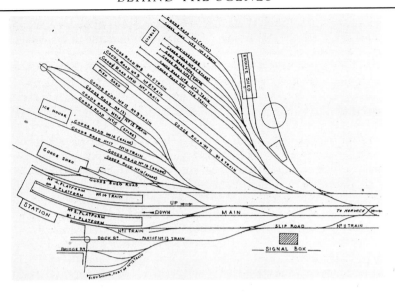

Diagram showing how Bass's 1913 excursion trains were stabled at Yarmouth Vauxhall Station.

assist with the third Special and so on. In the case of trains stored on the Douglas Colliery Branch, Guards must arrange for both Hand Brakes being firmly applied and the Brakes chained up and padlocked. The padlocks and chains will be supplied by the Stationmaster. . .Two sleepers must be placed on the rails in front of each Empty Carriage Train. The Engineering Department to provide sleepers and the necessary men to affix them to the rails. STEAM CRANE – A 20 Ton Steam Crane will be stationed at Carstairs during the period of the Meeting and it must be kept in steam ready for use in case of emergency.[8]

Great Yarmouth Vauxhall station, on the Great Eastern Railway, was the destination for the 1913 Bass Brewery employees' annual outing, when 14 special trains composed of 230 coaches were provided. The plan above shows how each siding was dedicated for the stabling of a particular train, the last to arrive being stored in Platform 4. As each train was unloaded, a station pilot engine hauled the empty stock out of the platform and then shunted it into its appropriate siding. It is reported that this operation took only 2 minutes, after which the train engine made its way to the turntable and servicing facilities. In the evening, train engines backed up to their trains, pulled on to the main line, and then reversed into their appointed platform ready for departure, and in the correct sequence. On the arrival of the last train at Burton, Bass's Traffic Manager sent this telegram to the GER's Superintendent of the Line: 'All arrived Burton safely, last special five minutes before time. Grateful thanks yourself and all concerned.'[9]

For the above-mentioned viewing of the eclipse of the sun in 1927, the LNER ran numerous excursion trains to Leyburn and Richmond in Yorkshire. The arrangements for such an event were most complex, but were all set out in 'Excursion and Special Train Arrangements, LNER (GN section)', which provided, inter alia, for breakdown vans and a steam crane to be held in readiness at Ardsley, and for pilot passenger engines to stand at King's Cross, Hitchin, Peterborough, Grantham and Doncaster during the times the special trains were passing.

... Should an engine fail at any intermediate station the station master must immediately telephone or wire to the station from which an emergency engine can be obtained.

Shunting engines were provided at Leyburn, Richmond and West Hartlepool, whilst ten signal boxes were kept open throughout the night to handle the eclipse traffic. To provide the refreshments

> ... a kitchen car and two open thirds will stand in the Horse Dock at Leyburn during the morning so that refreshments may be served to passengers. Two gas holders will supply the kitchen cars with gas. Table d'hote breakfast to cost 2s.6d. The district engineer will supply thirty flat fish boxes without lids to Leyburn and six to Redmire. One of these must be placed in the four-foot-way under each lavatory outlet of the two trains stabled at the East end of Leyburn station.

Some unfortunate railwayman would be detailed to remove them later!

Additional holiday and excursion traffic created operating problems for railway operators, not only at the resort, but also at busy junction stations along the line. Preston could be described as the 'Gateway to Blackpool', since every train to and from that resort must pass through Preston at least twice. Yes, some passed through twice on the way to Blackpool, and twice more on their return journey! Trains from Scotland passed through the station in a southerly direction, taking the line to Preston Junction, then via Lostock Hall to pass over the main line from Wigan, then taking the curve northwards via Farington West Junction, and once again through Preston station before branching off at Preston & Wyre Junction to gain the line to Blackpool and Fleetwood. This must have frequently caused consternation to excursionists, particularly on the return journey if they had spent too long in Yates Wine Lodge!

In the 1930s, some 200 passenger trains per day normally called at Preston in each direction, whilst a further 50 each way passed through without stopping; but on summer Saturdays, and at Bank Holiday times, as many as a hundred or more extra trains ran through in each direction. Easter Monday was a particularly busy day when, in addition to the extra through specials, several brought excursionists to Preston for 'egg rolling' in the Park, whilst at Whitsun crowds travelled in for Roman Catholic and Protestant processions.

The second week in August was Preston Wakes Week when many excursion trains originated from Preston, adding further to the vast volume of traffic through this station. Once every 20 years the Preston Merchant Guild week attracted even more special trains, and the congestion of the main platforms compelled many visiting excursion trains to be dealt with at neighbouring stations, even goods stations.

There were two categories of excursion train, one being trains run on the railway company's own initiative, and the other being guaranteed trains which the promoter hired at an agreed price, making a charge sufficient to cover his overheads, and to provide a margin of profit. Most famous of excursion organisers was, of course, Thomas Cook, but there were several others. Mr Marcus was very active in the North West and became Excursion Agent for the LNWR; Caygills operated in the Leeds area; Mr Henry Courtney in Birmingham; and Stanley's at Manchester. Mr F. J. Restall organised five trips to Brighton in 1894, and by 1910 this figure had risen to 408 to Brighton and other south coast resorts. Dean & Dawson, a travel firm, became the official agents for the Great Central Railway, whilst Easons of Grimsby ran regular excursion trains to London.

This song emphasised the advantages of travelling on an organised excursion:

FOLLOW THE MAN FROM COOK'S
Ladies and gentlemen leave it to me,
Follow the man from Cook's.
Nobody else is as clever as he,
Follow the man from Cook's.
And whether your stay be short or long,
He'll show you the sights. He can't go wrong.
It's twenty to one, you've plenty of fun,
So follow the man from Cook's.

Whereas the coaching stock requirements for a guaranteed excursion were known well in advance of its running, the position with a railway company's own speculative excursions was different, because total demand would not be known until shortly before the time of departure. This often resulted in one or more extra trains having to be hastily organised. It could also create problems at the destination station where the precise number of trains to be accommodated during the day would not be known until shortly before their arrival.

Excursionists were seldom aware of what was happening 'at the front end' of their train, as for instance on a Whit Monday in 1880, when a London, Brighton & South Coast excursion was advertised to run from Liverpool Street to Brighton. A train of eight suburban four-wheeler coaches behind a 'Terrier' 0-6-0T, No 61 *Sutton*, was to proceed from Liverpool Street over the East London Line as far as East Croydon, where it would be attached to a similar excursion from Addison Road for the onward journey to Brighton.

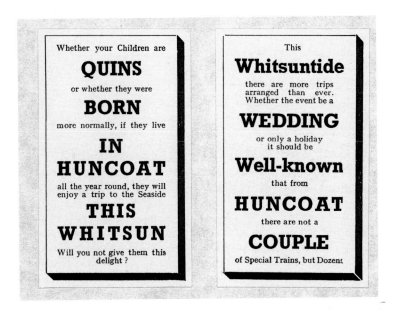

Examples of the artistry and enterprise of the LMSR Stationmaster at Huncoat, Lancashire, in 1936. Five such boards were displayed along the line facing the road used by workers at nearby factories.

After leaving Liverpool Street a stop was made at Wapping to pick up more passengers, but a dispute arose among them which resulted in delay to the train; consequently it lost its position in the procession of trains heading for East Croydon. On arrival at the latter station, the portion of the train from Addison Road had gone ahead to Brighton. The Stationmaster asked the driver of the diminutive tank locomotive if he was prepared to take his train on to Brighton, to which he agreed, but first more water had to be taken. Several excursionists took the opportunity to attend to 'personal needs' or to obtain refreshment, but they underestimated the speed with which a 'Terrier's' tanks could be filled, and so were left behind when their train departed.

However, the intrepid driver, and his courageous *Sutton*, proceeded on his way, narrowly running out of water before reaching Three Bridges, but at last Brighton hove into view. Astonished station staff rubbed their eyes as No 61, proudly displaying its 'East London Line Special' headboard, came to a stand in 'Old Ocean's Bauble, Glittering Brighton'.[10]

One facet of dealing with excursion traffic not always appreciated by the public was the manner in which railway staff handled the huge crowds. In the days before the Tannoy public address system, it was upon the lowly porter and other uniformed staff that this task fell.

Arriving crowds presented little problem since all were keen to leave the station and reach the sea or other attraction as quickly as possible. The very real problem came when the crowds returned to the station and had to be shepherded to their appropriate

Miners and their families arriving at Blackpool's Talbot Road station in 1919 were soon off the platform and out of the station. Handling such large crowds, before the introduction of 'Tannoy' systems, was much more of a problem for the railway staff. *(National Railway Museum, York)*

Blackpool Talbot Road excursion station with the latest Benn & Cronin 'All-weather Indicator', installed in 1922 to facilitate the direction of passengers to their correct platforms. (*Lancashire Record Office*)

platform, and admitted to their correct train. Anxious not to be left behind, huge numbers arrived back at the station long before the scheduled time of departure for their train, and in so doing jammed the station entrances, the concourse, the platforms, the refreshment rooms and the lavatories. Penny-in-the-slot chocolate machines were emptied and the pointers of 'Try Your Weight' machines were made dizzy as they oscillated between the extremes of avoirdupois which they were called upon to register.

Which railway ran the very first excursion train will continue to be disputed, but the Great Eastern Railway was in no doubt that it had the distinction of running the first excursion following the First World War, during which all such trains had been suspended. There can be no gainsaying the speed with which this company acted to resume excursion traffic. For immediately the word was given by the Railway Executive (the wartime committee controlling the railways) on 10 August 1920, the machinery for arranging times, rolling-stock and motive power was at once set in motion. Within a few hours public notices were exhibited at stations announcing day excursions to Clacton, Frinton, Walton-on-the-Naze and Southend-on-Sea. After six excursionless years, the public flocked to these trains and, within a few days, the facilities were extended to Great Yarmouth, Lowestoft and other East Anglian resorts.[11]

It will be apparent from this summary of the railway excursion over the past 150 and more years that, whereas an excursion once attracted considerable newspaper coverage, today

Going on an excursion appears to have been a serious matter! Excursion trains, suspended during the First World War, were not restored until 1920. These trippers at Liverpool Street station were for the first excursion to Southend-on-sea by the Great Eastern Railway. *(Newham Library)*

not only are railway excursions ignored by the media, there are, in fact, few excursion trains. This is largely, though not entirely, explained by the popularity of road travel, especially the private car. As recently as 1983, British Rail ran 1,268 excursion trains such as 'Merrymakers', 1,025 football specials and 1,227 chartered trains, but by the 1990s the total number of excursion trains amount to a few hundred, and these almost entirely chartered by commercial operators, by societies with a railway interest, or are BR steam-hauled trains for which high fares are charged. These are no longer cheap day excursions for families.

This falling off in excursion traffic is not so much due to absence of potential passengers as to political dogma which aims to impose 19th-century economic policies on a late-20th-century public transport system. Starved of investment capital, British Rail is desperately short of rolling-stock with which to meet the demands of its scheduled services, leaving none for excursion traffic. The few dedicated trains available for charter are priced beyond the reach of most organisations. This was considered by one correspondent to *Modern Railways* in December 1990, to be

> . . . due to InterCity's top brass deciding that only rich companies like Shell, BP, ICI etc would be able to afford charter trains in future.[12]

Will the concept of 'Away for the Day' by railway excursion ever again become popular? Just as there is a steady increase in the number of travellers opting to park their cars and travel by train to work or on business trips, so too may long tail-backs on the roads, increasing atmospheric pollution and greater concern about the quality of life cause more and more people to question whether there is not a better way of enjoying a day away. The man who wrote those lines:

> I took the train to Brighton
> I walked beside the sea,
> And thirty thousand Londoners
> Were there along with me.

was *there* – beside the sea – and not sweating it out with his family, cooped up in a metal box, inhaling traffic fumes instead of sea air, hearing on the car radio that 'there is a six mile tail-back on the A23. Drivers are asked to avoid Brighton if they can'.

A future British Rail advertisement could well be:

ENJOY YOUR DAY AWAY – BY RAIL!

REFERENCES

Chapter 1

1 *The Liverpool & Manchester Railway Project 1821-1831*, Carlson, R. E., 1969, p235
2 op cit, p237
3 *The 150th Anniversary of the Opening of The Canterbury & Whitstable Railway*, Ellis, P., 1980, p20
4 *A Regional History of Railways*, Vol 8, Joy, D., 1975, p35
5 *Railway Magazine*, May 1966, p299
6 *The Ways of Our Railways*, Grinling, C. H. 1905, p172
7 *Leicester Journal*, 28 Aug 1840
8 *Railway Magazine*, Nov 1939, p360
9 *North Eastern Railway*, Tomlinson, W., 1915, p372
10 *Liverpool & Manchester Railway Operations 1831-45*, Donaghy, T. J., 1972, p148
11 *Regional History of Railways*, Vol 10, Holt, G., 1978, p23
12 *Railway Lovers' Companion*, Morgan, B., 1963, p398
13 *History of the Midland Railway*, Stretton, C., 1901, p45
14 *London & South Western Railway*, Williams, R. A., p210
15 *Sheffield Mercury*, 5 June 1841
16 *Preston Pilot*, 17 Sep 1842
17 *A Regional History of Railways*, Vol 8, Joy, D., 1975, p39
18 *Liverpool Albion*, 28 Sep 1841
19 *Preston Pilot*, 17 June 1843
20 *Paisley Advertiser*, 28 Sep 1843
21 *Railway Chronicle*, 7 Sep 1844
22 ibid
23 *Great Central Railway Journal*, June 1906
24 *Norfolk Annals*, 1846, p456 (Norwich City Library)
25 op cit, p457
26 *Edinburgh Evening Courant*, 23 July 1846
27 *Glasgow Argus*, 12 March 1846
28 *North British Advertiser*, 26 June 1852
29 *Glasgow Argus*, 16 July 1846
30 op cit, 20 July 1846
31 *Railway Reminiscences*, Neele, G. P., 1904, p18
32 *Pictorial Times*, 4 July 1846
33 *Northern Daily Telegraph*, 18 Aug 1956
34 *Cambridge Chronicle*, 11 April 1846
35 *LNER Magazine*, April 1927, p227
36 *Railway Record*, 15 May 1852
37 *The Somerset & Dorset Rly*, Atthill, R., 1967, p176
38 *Great Central Railway*, Vol 1, Dow, G., 1959, p235
39 *Northern Daily Telegraph*, 18 Aug 1956
40 ibid
41 *Railway Magazine*, April 1902, p378
42 *Gloucester Chronicle*, 23 July 1853
43 *Herepath's Journal*, 25 Sep 1841
44 *British Railway History*, Vol 1, Hamilton Ellis, C., 1954, p91

45 *Preston Pilot*, 1 April 1843
46 *Observations on the Making of a Line of Railroad from York to Scarborough*, Knowles, G., 1841
47 *A Dissertation on Scarborough*, Dixon, P., 1965
48 op cit
49 *Scarborough – Romantic Queen of Watering Places*, Hopkins H.
50 *Scarborough Evening News*, 8 Feb 1944
51 *Railway Magazine*, June 1898, p568
52 *Beside the Seaside*, Walvin, J., p40
53 ibid
54 *Leisure in the Industrial Society*, Cunningham, H., 1980
55 ibid
56 *Railway Magazine*, Aug 1967, p470
57 *A Regional History of Railways*, Vol 8, Joy, D., 1975, p146

Chapter 2

1 *Beside the Seaside*, Walvin, J. 1978
2 *Memoirs of the Rev W. C. Burns MA*, 1870, p218
3 *The Newcastle & Carlisle Rly*, Whittle, G., 1979, p49
4 *Liverpool & Manchester Railway Operations 1831-45*, Donaghy, T. J. ,1972, p93
5 *Barnsley Chronicle*, 6 Aug 1859
6 RAIL 226/410, PRO Kew
7 *Rhymes of the Rail*, Skerrett, F. W., 1920
8 *Newcastle Daily Journal*, 17 March 1849
9 *LNWR Traffic Committee Minutes 2283*, 1894, PRO Kew
10 RAIL 256/73, PRO Kew
11 RAIL 236/12, PRO Kew
12 *Leisure Hour*, 1883, p660
13 RAIL 667/817, PRO Kew
14 *The Blackpool Story*, Turner & Palmer
15 ibid
16 *Beside the Seaside*, Walvin, J., 1978, p38
17 *Preston Pilot*, 1851
18 *Railway Magazine*, Dec 1913, p484
19 *The Manchester Critic*, 14 Sep 1872, p79
20 *Southport Visitor*, 7 June 1855
21 *Illustrated Historical Guide to Poole & Bournemouth*, Brannon, P., 1855
22 *South Western Magazine*, 7 July 1888
23 *Bournemouth Railway History*, Popplewell, L., p150
24 *Bournemouth Visitor's Directory*, 4 July 1888
25 *Bournemouth Observer*, 27 May 1885
26 *Leisure & Pleasure in the 19th Century*, Margetson, S., 1969
27 Carey's 'Itinerary', 1821
28 *Brighton, Old Ocean's Bauble*, Gilbert, E. W., 1954, p172
29 *Brighton As I Have Known It*, Sala, G. A., p16
30 *Hull & Barnsley Railway*, Hinchcliffe (Ed), 1980
31 *Great Central Railway Journal*, Feb 1906

32   Scottish Record Office, BR/CAL/7/1
33   *Birmingham Post*, 9 July 1925
34   *Birmingham Mail*, 21 July 1925
35   ibid
36   *The Skye Railway*, Thomas, J., 1977, p144
37   *History of the Southern Railway*, Dendy Marshall, C. F. & Kidner, R. W., 1963, p212

Chapter 3
1   Preston Record Office, DD PR 35/3
2   *Weston-super-Mare Gazette & General Advertiser*, 13 June 1846
3   *Railway Times*, 9 August 1851, p780
4   *Railways in Rutland*, Traylen, A. R., 1980, p8
5   *Hull News*, 31 Aug 1861
6   *Brighton: The Road, The Place, The People*, J. H. Thompson (Pub), 1862
7   *Memories of Old Poplar*, Blake, J.
8   *Hull News*, 6 July 1861
9   *The Cambrian*, 14 Sep 1866
10   *Diary of Rev Francis Kilvert*, 18 May 1870
11   *The Cambrian*, 14 Oct 1881
12   *Rock & Roll to Paradise*, Gittins, R., 1982, p46
13   *The Cambrian*, 6 Aug 1897
14   *Rock & Roll to Paradise*, Gittins, R., 1982, p50
15   *The Cambrian*, 8 June 1900
16   *The Story of the Cambrian*, Gasquoine, C. P., p95
17   *North British Railway*, Thomas, J., Vol I, 1969
18   *Neath Antiquarian Society Transactions*, 1978, p60
19   *Stratford Herald*, 28 July 1876
20   *Book of the Lincolnshire Seaside*, Robinson, D., 1981
21   op cit
22   op cit
23   *Railway Magazine*, June 1954, p429
24   *Lincolnshire Echo*, 28 July 1983
25   *Cleethorpes and the 'Meggies'*, Hart, M., Cleethorpes Library
26   *Birmingham Mail*, 3 Aug 1925
27   op cit, 5 Oct 1928
28   *Birmingham Post*, 9 Oct 1929
29   *Railway Magazine*, April 1968, p236

Chapter 4
1   *Norfolk Annals*, 1846, p456 (Norwich City Library)
2   *Deeside Railway Minutes*, 31 July 1860 (Scottish Record Office)
3   *Edinburgh Advertiser*, 4 Sep 1849
4   *Edinburgh Courant*, 6 July 1846
5   *Pearson's Weekly*, 6 Jan 1910
6   op cit, 24 June 1893, p784
7   op cit, 1 July 1892, p795
8   *Cambrian Daily Leader*, 11 July 1906
9   OURS, 1921, p93 (Hull Local History Library)
10   *The Cambrian*, 10 Aug 1900
11   *Bournemouth Visitor's Directory*, 17 July 1897
12   *Penwortham Parish Magazine*, Sept 1882
13   *Great Northern Railway*, Vol I, Wrottesley, J., 1979, p143
14   RAIL 410/2000, PRO Kew
15   *Progress*, July 1901, p261 (Port Sunlight Heritage Centre)
16   *Reading Mercury*, 8 Aug 1857
17   op cit, 1 Aug 1857
18   *Railway World*, July 1969
19   *Railway Review*, Sept 1969
20   *Railway Gazette*, 7 July 1911
21   *Carrow Works Magazine*, 1920 (Colman's Archives, Norwich)

22   *LNER Magazine*, Sept 1931, p458
23   *Aberdare Leader*, 30 July 1932
24   *LNER Magazine*, June 1938, p326
25   *GWR Magazine*, Sept 1939, p386
26   op cit, Jan 1935
27   op cit, Sept 1946
28   *Daily Telegraph*, 18 July 1983
29   op cit, 25 Aug 1984
30   *Railway Reminiscences*, Neele, G. P., 1904, p18

Chapter 5
1   *The Early Stuarts*, Davies G., 1959, p146
2   *Leisure and Society*, Walvin, J., 1978, p24
3   op cit, p25
4   *The Liverpool & Manchester Railway*, Thomas, R. H. G., 1980, p198
5   *The Railways of England*, Ackworth, W. M., 1889, p323
6   *History of the Great Western Railway*, Vol I, MacDermott E. T., 1964, p353
7   *Glasgow Argus*, 2 March 1846
8   *Carlisle Journal*, 4 July 1846
9   *The Later Stuarts*, Clark, Sir G., 1956, p408
10   *Horse Racing*, Herbert, I., 1980, p146
11   *Railway Magazine*, May 1913, p409
12   'As You Like It', Shakespeare, Act II
13   *Industry and Empire*, Hobsbawm, E. J., 1968, p154
14   *Doncaster Gazette*, 21 Sept 1888
15   *Railway Magazine*, Oct 1897, p314
16   *Doncaster Gazette*, 4 Sept 1840
17   *History of the Great Northern Railway*, Grinling, C. H., 1903, p79
18   *Railway & Canal Historical Society Journal*, Vol XXVII, No. 9, p267
19   *The Great Northern Railway*, Vol I, Wrottesley, J., 1979, p55
20   *History of the Great Northern Railway*, Grinling, C. H., 1903, p86
21   *Illustrated London News*, 17 Sept 1853, p240
22   *Our Home Railways*, Vol II, Gordon, W. J., 1910, p72
23   *Doncaster Gazette*, 13 Sept 1867
24   op cit, 9 Sept 1910
25   *Railways of England*, Ackworth, W. M., 1889, p224
26   *Doncaster Gazette*, 12 Sept 1929
27   *Reading Mercury*, 18 Aug 1857
28   *The Cambrian*, 21 April 1876
29   *The Buckingham Express*, 8 May 1886
30   *Railway Magazine*, Nov 1908, p373
31   *Horse Racing*, Herbert, I., 1980, p137
32   *Southern Railway Magazine*, July 1937, p245
33   *History of the Southern Railway*, Dendy Marshall, C. F. & Kidner, R. W., 1963, p44
34   *LMS Magazine*, May 1930, p145
35   op cit, March 1938, p146
36   *GWR Magazine*, Aug 1937, p371
37   *Railway Magazine*, Aug 1935, p122
38   *Southern Electric*, Moody, G. T., 1957, p122
39   *Railway Magazine*, May 1950, p351
40   op cit, Nov 1953, p783
41   *Great Eastern Railway Magazine*, Oct 1913, p332

Chapter 6
1   *The People's Game*, Walvin, J., 1975
2   *The Contemporary Review*, Jevons, W. S., 1878
3   *The Football Industry*, Hutchinson, J., 1982, p18
4   LNWR Passenger Traffic Committee Minute 656, 16/3/1892, PRO Kew
5   *Railway Magazine*, June 1904, p518

6 *Great Central Railway*, Vol III, Dow, G., 1971, p35
7 *The Bailie*, 7 April 1897
8 *Railway Magazine*, June 1923, p482
9 op cit, May 1923, p420
10 op cit, June 1923, p482
11 *LMS Magazine*, May 1931, p152
12 *Railways of Peterborough*, Dane, R., 1978, p40
13 *Railway World*, April 1921, p146
14 *Southern Railway Magazine*, Feb 1932
15 *Railway Magazine*, March 1934, p226
16 op cit, March 1973, p113
17 op cit, April 1973, p198
18 op cit, Oct 1937, p237
19 *Great Central Railway*, Vol II, Dow, G., 1971, p117
20 *LMS Magazine*, Feb 1936, p56
21 *Railway Magazine*, Nov 1986, p703
22 *Bodmin Guardian*, 17 April 1840
23 *Norfolk Annals*, 1846, p484, Norwich City Library
24 *Liverpool Courier*, 19 Sept 1849
25 *Staffordshire Advertiser*, 14 June 1856
26 *Doncaster Gazette*, 22 Oct 1909
27 *Railway Magazine*, Nov 1909, p435
28 *The Scotsman*, 6 & 10 Aug 1910
29 op cit, 19 Aug 1910
30 *Southern Railway Magazine*, May 1931, p335
31 *LNER Magazine*, July 1933, p357
32 *Southern Railway Magazine*, July 1938, p253
33 *Railway Magazine*, Sept 1981, p454
34 *Great Central Journal*, Nov 1905
35 *GWR Magazine*, 1927, p232
36 *Yorkshire Herald*, 29 June 1927
37 *GWR Magazine*, 1927, p314
38 *Hull Daily Mail*, 29 June 1927
39 *Railway Magazine*, April 1934, p306

Chapter 7
1 *Our Home Railways*, Vol I, Gordon, W. G., 1910, p257
2 *Beside the Seaside*, Walvin, J., 1978, p38
3 *Sir Titus Salt*, Balgarnie, R., 1877, p102
4 *Railway Times*, 2 Aug 1851, p756
5 *Hull News*, 8 Sep 1860
6 op cit, 7 Sep 1861
7 *Wimborne Journal*, 1 Aug 1873
8 *The Scotsman*, 11 July 1884
9 *Railway Magazine*, Aug 1950, p563
10 *Hull News*, 7 Aug 1897
11 *Bourneville Works Magazine*, 1902, p16 (Birmingham City Library)
12 op cit, 1903, p203
13 *Great Central Railway Journal*, Aug 1912
14 *Great Central Railway*, Vol III, Dow, G., 1971, p311
15 *Railway History of Lincoln*, Ruddock and Pearson, 1974, p215
16 *Press Cuttings of Col Williams*, 1900, p98 (Lincoln Reference Library)
17 *Great Western Railway Magazine*, 1912, p255
18 *The Springburn Story*, Thomas, J., 1974, p184
19 op cit, p190
20 *Railway Magazine*, March 1953, p205
21 RAIL/527/408, PRO Kew
22 *Reading Mercury*, 10 Oct 1857
23 *Quaker Enterprise in Biscuits: Huntley & Palmers of Reading, 1822-1872*, Corley, T. A. B., p102
24 *Port Sunlight Journal*, July 1897, p195 (Port Sunlight Heritage Centre)
25 *Progress*, 1900, p387 (Port Sunlight Heritage Centre)
26 op cit, Aug 1908, p98

27 op cit, Aug 190, p111
28 Excursion to Great Yarmouth 1893, Bass Museum
29 *LMS Magazine*, Nov 1929, p361
30 *Southern Railway Magazine*, Aug 1935
31 *Railway Magazine*, March 1936, p224
32 *Hull Daily Mail*, 13 June 1927
33 OURS, Vol 8, 1926-7 (Hull Reference Library)
34 op cit, Vol 15, 1933-4 (Hull Reference Library)
35 *Raligram*, Vol II, May 1949 (Nottingham Reference Library)
36 *Somerdale Magazine*, April 1970, p62 (Bristol City Library)
37 *Railway Magazine*, Aug 1932, p146
38 *Bourneville Works Magazine*, Aug 1906 (Birmingham City Library)
39 *Railway Magazine*, Jan 1932, p64
40 op cit, Dec 1927, p492
41 op cit, Nov 1953, p784
42 *A Family and a Railway*, C. & J. Clark Ltd
43 *Railway Magazine*, July 1963, p510

Chapter 8
1 *Victorian People*, Asa Briggs, 1985, p51
2 *The Railway Clearing House*, Bagwell, P., 1968, p56
3 RCH 1/70, Min 6, GM Conference, 2 May 1851, PRO Kew
4 RCH 1/70, Min 16, GM Conference, 22 May 1851, PRO Kew
5 RCH 1/70, GM Conference, 30 Apr 1851, PRO Kew
6 *Railway Times*, 7 June 1851, p572
7 RCH 1/70, Min 28, GM Conference, 10 June 1851, PRO Kew
8 *Railway Times*, 21 June 1851
9 *Chelmsford Chronicle*, 28 June 1851
10 *Wiltshire Independent*, 12 July 1851
11 *Railway Times*, 2 Aug 1851, p756
12 *Railway Magazine*, Jan 1960, p33
13 *History of the Great Northern Railway*, Grinling, C. H., 1903, p105
14 *Holidays*, Gordon, S., 1972, p61
15 *Victorian People*, Asa Briggs, 1985, p46
16 *Victorian Engineering*, Rolt, L. T. C., 1970, p156
17 *Cook's Exhibition Herald and Excursion Advertiser*, No 1, 31 May 1851 (Thomas Cook Archives)
18 *History of the Great Northern Railway*, Grinling, C. H., 1903, p105
19 *Illustrated London News*, July-Dec 1851, p102
20 *Northampton Mercury*, 11 Oct 1851
21 Letter in Colman's Works' Archives
22 *Glasgow Evening News*, 4 May 1888
23 *The Scotsman*, 9 May 1888
24 *Evening News*, 22 May 1888
25 Caledonian Railway Minutes, BR/CAL/4/57 (Scottish Record Office)
26 Caledonian Railway Minutes, 11/3/1901 (Scottish Record Office)
27 *Great Eastern Railway Magazine*, Dec 1921, p258
28 *Manchester Evening News*, 17 April 1946
29 *Great Central Railway*, Vol II, Dow, G., 1967, p282
30 *Railway Magazine*, Sept 1924, p413
31 op cit, Dec 1924, p495
32 *Scarborough Evening News*, 12 July 1924
33 *Carrow Works Magazine*, Vol XVII, No 4, Supplement (Colman's Works' Archives)
34 op cit, Vol XVIII, No 1, p2
35 *Port Sunlight News*, July 1924, p127 (Port Sunlight Heritage Centre)
36 op cit, Aug 1938, p311

37   *Leicester Co-operative Magazine*, Aug 1938, p16
38   *Railway Magazine*, Dec 1928, p495

Chapter 9
1   *Liverpool & Manchester Railway*, Thomas, R. H. G., 1980, p195
2   *Great Eastern Railway Magazine*, 1912, p312
3   *Stamford Mercury*, 7 Aug 1863
4   *Buckingham Express*, 23 April 1887
5   *Railway Magazine*, March 1935, p222
6   Booklet in Thomas Cook Archives, London
7   *Nottingham Mercury*, 9 Oct 1850
8   *Glasgow Evening Argus*, 17 July 1845
9   op cit, 4 Aug 1845
10   *Hull News*,4 Aug 1860
11   *Edinburgh Evening Courant*, 27 July 1846
12   *Berkshire Chronicle*, 27 Aug 1859
13   *Stratford Herald*, 22 Aug 1873
14   op cit, 6 Nov 1874
15   *Liverpool & Manchester Railway*, Thomas, R. H. G., 1980, p195
16   *Sydenham Times*, 19 April 1864
17   *Coventry Independent Journal*, 22 Aug 1883
18   *Stratford Herald*, 19 Aug 1887
19   *Crewe Chronicle*, 4 June 1887
20   ibid
21   *Stratford Herald*, 25 June 1880
22   RAIL 267/184, PRO Kew
23   *Blackpool Herald & Fylde Advertiser*, 24 June 1919
24   *Railway Magazine*, Dec 1950, p854
25   *Great Eastern Railway Magazine*, Sep 1920, p176

Chapter 10
1   *Railway Magazine*, July 1937, p3
2   op cit, July 1969, p427
3   *Southern Railway Magazine*, July 1932, p251
4   *LNER Magazine*, April 1934, p202
5   *Southern Railway Magazine*, Nov 1935, p405
6   *Railway Magazine*, June 1981, p289
7   *Preston Guardian*, 1845
8   *Glasgow Herald*, 27 July 1846
9   *Barnsley Chronicle*, 30 July 1859
10   op cit, 27 Aug 1859
11   op cit, 17 Aug 1889
12   ibid
13   op cit, 24 Aug 1889
14   op cit, 26 Aug 1889
15   *LMS Magazine*, Aug 1939, p365
16   *Railway Magazine*, April 1972, p192
17   GCR handbill, RAIL/226/95, PRO Kew
18   *The Stratford-upon-Avon and Midland Junction Railway*, Jordan, A., 1982, p86
19   *Nottingham Mercury and General Avertiser*, 2 Oct 1850
20   *Historic Fairground Scenes*, Ware, E. W., 1977, p6
21   Report in Hull Local History Library
22   *Amusements*, 1905 (Hull Local History Library)
23   Letter by W. E. Leffler (Hull Local History Library)
24   *Edinburgh Evening Courant*, 18 July 1846
25   *Leeds Mercury*, 4 Sep 1802
26   *Preston Pilot*, 3 Sep 1842
27   op cit, 30 Aug 1862
28   *Preston Guardian*, 2 Sep 1882
29   op cit, 9 Sep 1882
30   op cit, 2 Aug 1952
31   *Kettering Guardian*, 23 May 1902
32   *Coventry Independant Journal*, 8 Aug 1883
33   op cit, 8 Aug 1883

34   ibid

Chapter 11
1   *Railway Magazine*, Feb 1937, p154
2   op cit, Dec 1928, p502
3   *Railway Wonders of the World*, Part 24, p767
4   *LMS Magazine*, July 1934, p251
5   *Railway Magazine*, Sept 1936, p231
6   op cit, Aug 1935, p142
7   *LNER Magazine*, June 1933, p296
8   op cit, June 1936, p330
9   op cit, Aug 1934, p454
10   *Railway Magazine*, Nov 1951, p782
11   *Railway World*, April 1970, p156
12   *Railway Magazine*, March 1974, p119
13   op cit, April 1980, p177
14   op cit, March 1980, p149
15   *Southern Railway Magazine*, 1927, p262
16   op cit, June 1936, p201
17   op cit, April 1936
18   *LMS Magazine*, May 1931, p178
19   *Birmingham & Derby Junction Railway*, Clinker, C. R., 1982, p16
20   *The Book of Boston*, Wright, N. R., 1986, p117
21   *Lincoln, Rutland & Stamford Mercury*, 29 April 1859
22   op cit, 22 July 1859
23   *Railway Magazine*, July 1925, p358
24   *LMS Magazine*, Nov 1932, p373
25   *Southern Railway Magazine*, July 1936, p246
26   *Railway Magazine*, June 1936, p456
27   *Stratford Herald*, 29 April 1932
28   *Railway Magazine*, June 1937, p456
29   *The West Highland Railway*, Thomas, J., 1970, p137
30   *Railway Gazette*, Oct 1958
31   *Railway World*, Sept 1970, p417
32   *Railway Magazine*, July 1929, p71
33   op cit, April 1972, p211
34   op cit, Jan 1973, p42
35   *Western Daily Press*, 9 March 1970
36   *Modern Railways*, April 1980, p182
37   *Railway Magazine*, Dec 1930, p434
38   *LNER Magazine*, Oct 1937, p582
39   op cit, July 1934, p375
40   *Railway Magazine*, Dec 1936, p465
41   op cit, Oct 1955, p728
42   op cit, July 1957, p511
43   op cit, Aug 1964, p661
44   *LNER Magazine*, Sept 1928, p182
45   op cit, June 1929, p305
46   *Railway Magazine*, May 1956, p364
47   op cit, Aug 1958, p514
48   op cit, Nov 1978, p527
49   op cit, June 1939, p423
50   *Lincoln Echo*, 3 March 1984
51   *Railway Magazine*, June 1934, p463

Chapter 12
1   *Railway Magazine*, Oct 1938, p267
2   *LNER Magazine*, Nov 1938, p604
3   *Railway Magazine*, June 1904, p502
4   *Railway World*, May 1972, p198
5   *Modern Railways*, April 1967, p221
6   *Railway Magazine*, May 1967, p287
7   *Railway World*, Oct 1968, p465
8   *Railway Magazine*, Dec 1971, p636
9   op cit, Dec 1978, p598
10   op cit, June 1929, p268
11   op cit, Nov 1987, p730

12   *Lincolnshire Standard*, 9 Oct 1970
13   *Railway Magazine*, June 1972, p330
14   *Rail Enthusiast*, Dec/Jan 1982, p25

Chapter 13

1   *Railway Times*, 28 Aug 1852
2   RAIL 667/1221, PRO Kew
3   *The Cambrian*, 14 Sep 1866
4   *The Railwaymen*, Bagwell, P. S., 1963, p47
5   *The Leisure Hour*, 1883, p658
6   Scottish Record Office, RAIL/527/1260
7   *The Scarborough Gazette*, 9 Aug 1850
8   *The Cambrian*, 18 Aug 1876
9   *Red for Danger*, Rolt, L. T. C., 1959, p149
10   *Railway Chronicle*, 21 Sep 1844, p568
11   *Edinburgh Evening Courant*, 6 Aug 1844
12   *The Cambrian*, 14 Sep 1866
13   op cit, 28 Sep 1866
14   *Railways in Rutland*, Traylen, A. R., 1980, p10
15   *Brighton Herald*, 31 Aug 1861
16   *Brighton*, Gilbert, E. W., 1954, p141
17   *Historic Railway Disasters*, Nock, O. S., 1966, p24
18   *Railway Magazine*, Oct 1924, p324
19   op cit, Dec 1924, p484
20   *Liverpool Courier*, 26 July 1924
21   *Great Central Railway*, Vol II, Dow, G., 1967, p56
22   *The Somerset & Dorset Railway*, Atthill, R., 1967, p122
23   *Hull News*, 2 June 1860
24   *British Railway History*, Vol I, Hamilton Ellis, 1954, p219
25   *Red for Danger*, Rolt, L. T. C., 1955, p151
26   *Hull News*, 8 Sep 1860
27   *Grimsby Herald*, 7 Aug 1863
28   *Norwich Argus*, 15 Aug 1863
29   *Railway Times*, 1851 p697
30   *Northampton Mercury*, 13 Sep 1851
31   *Reading Mercury*, 1 Aug 1857
32   LNWR minutes, Oct 1860, PRO Kew
33   *Northampton Mercury*, 10 May 1851
34   *Historic Railway Disasters*, Nock, O. S., 1966, p58
35   *Illustrated Midland News*, 16 Oct 1869
36   *Railway Magazine*, July 1897, p93
37   *Railway Times*, 21 Aug 1897
38   *Railway Magazine*, Aug 1900, p127
39   *Kettering Leader & Guardian*, 21 Aug 1903
40   *Railway Magazine*, Dec 1906, p511
41   op cit, March 1968, p143
42   op cit, May 1973, p265
43   LNWR Northern Sub Committee Minute 1454, 1861 PRO Kew
44   *The Cambrian*, 1851
45   *Reading Mercury*, 15 Aug 1857
46   *Railway Reminiscences*, Neele, G. P., 1904, p395
47   *Red for Danger*, Rolt, L. T. C., 1955, p204
48   *Railway Magazine*, Dec 1928, p490
49   op cit, May 1974, p262
50   op cit, Jan 1956, p65
51   op cit, Aug 1972, p423
52   op cit, Nov 1987, p690

Chapter 14

1   *North Eastern Railway*, Tomlinson, W., 1915, p373
2   *Government & the Railways in Nineteenth Century Britain*, Parris H., 1965, p141
3   RAIL 631/29, PRO Kew
4   *Herepath's Journal*, 7 June 1851, p616
5   *Railway Times*, 24 May 1851, p526
6   op cit, 26 July 1861, p742
7   *The Midland Railway*, Williams, F. S., 1875, p131
8   *History of the Great Northern Railway*, Grinling, C. H., 1903, p115
9   ibid
10   LNWR Road and Traffic Cttee Minutes, 10 Feb 1852, LNW1/140, PRO Kew
11   *Herepath's Journal*, 25 Oct 1851
12   op cit, 1 Nov 1851
13   *Railway Reminiscences*, Neele, G. P., 1904, p94
14   quoted in *Railways in the Victorian Economy*, Reed, M. C., 1969, p160
15   *History of the Great Northern Railway*, Grinling, C. H., 1903, p261
16   *Northampton Mercury*, 26 April 1851
17   *The Railways of England*, Ackworth, W. M., 1889, p351
18   *Railway Magazine*, 1908, p373
19   *Brighton – Old Ocean's Bauble*, Gilbert, E. W., 1954, p194
20   *Stratford-upon-Avon and Midland Junction Railway*, Jordan A., 1982, p98
21   *Nottingham Mercury*, 9 Oct 1880
22   *The Working & Management of an English Railway*, Findlay, Sir G., 1899, p399
23   *Mark Huish & the LNWR*, Gourvish, T. R., 1972, p244
24   *Blackpool Herald and Fylde Advertiser*, 24 June 1919
25   *Railway Magazine*, Sept 1904, p261
26   *Great Central Railway*, Vol II, Dow, G., 1967, p172
27   *Railway & Travel Monthly*, No 15, 1917, p235
28   *Somerset & Dorset Railway*, Atthill, R., 1967, pp74 & 176
29   *Railway Motor Bus Services in the British Isles*, Cummings, J., 1978, p42
30   *An Economic History of Transport in Britain*, Baker, T. C. & Savage, C. I., 1959, p113
31   *British Transport Review*, Vol 5, Coulson, B. A., 1959
32   LSWR Minute 1115, 1858 PRO Kew

Chapter 15

1   *Railway Magazine*, Feb 1960, p90
2   *The Railway Workers, 1840-1970*, McKenna, F., 1980, p219
3   *Southern Railway Magazine*, Sept 1935
4   *Railway Magazine*, Feb 1937, p155
5   *Regional History of Railways*, Vol 4, Hoole, K., 1974, p80
6   *The Working and Management of an English Railway*, Findlay, Sir G., 1899, p357
7   *Railway Magazine*, Feb 1936, p153
8   BR/CAL/4/184 (Scottish Record Office)
9   *Great Eastern Railway Magazine*, 1913, p336
10   *Railway Magazine*, May 1951, p346
11   *Great Eastern Railway Magazine*, 1912, p73
12   *Modern Railways*, Dec 1990, p663

INDEX